# Busy Ant Maths

# Assessment Guide 4

Series editor: Peter Clarke

William Collins' dream of knowledge for all began with the publication of his first book in 1819.
A self-educated mill worker, he not only enriched millions of lives, but also founded a flourishing publishing house. Today, staying true to this spirit, Collins books are packed with inspiration, innovation and practical expertise. They place you at the centre of a world of possibility and give you exactly what you need to explore it.

Collins. Freedom to teach.

Published by Collins

An imprint of HarperCollins Publishers
1 London Bridge Street
London
SE1 9GF

Browse the complete Collins catalogue at
**www.collins.co.uk**

© HarperCollins*Publishers* Limited 2015

10 9 8 7 6 5 4 3 2 1

ISBN 978-0-00-756234-3

Peter Clarke and Steven Matchett assert their moral rights to be identified as the authors of this work.

British Library Cataloguing in Publication Data
A Catalogue record for this publication is available from the British Library.

Commissioned by Fiona McGlade
Managing editor Caroline Green
Project editor Amanda Redstone
Edited by Tanya Solomons and Marie Taylor
Proofread by Laura Booth
Cover design and artwork by Amparo Barrera
Internal design and typesetting by Ken Vail Graphic Design
Illustrations by Ken Vail Graphic Design, Louise Forshaw and Eva Sassin
Production by Robin Forrester

Printed and bound by Martins the Printer, Berwick upon Tweed

# Contents

## End-of-unit Tests

## Pupil Self-assessments

## Record-keeping formats

## Resources to accompany the Assessment Tasks

## Tracking back and forward through the Mathematics National Curriculum attainment targets – Year 4

# Introduction
## Assessment Tasks and Exercises

| Domain | | National Curriculum attainment target | Assessment Task(s)/Exercise(s) |
|---|---|---|---|
| Number – Number and place value | | Count in multiples of 6, 7, 9, 25 and 1000 | 1 |
| | | Find 1000 more or less than a given number | 2 |
| | | Count backwards through zero to include negative numbers | 3 |
| | | Recognise the place value of each digit in a four-digit number (thousands, hundreds, tens, and ones) | 4 |
| | | Order and compare numbers beyond 1000 | 5 |
| | | Identify, represent and estimate numbers using different representations | 6 |
| | | Round any number to the nearest 10, 100 or 1000 | 7 |
| | | Solve number and practical problems that involve all of the above and with increasingly large positive numbers | 8 |
| | | Read Roman numerals to 100 (I to C) and know that over time, the numeral system changed to include the concept of zero and place value | 9 |
| Number – Addition and subtraction | | Add and subtract numbers with up to 4 digits using the formal written methods of columnar addition and subtraction where appropriate | 10 and 11 |
| | | Estimate and use inverse operations to check answers to a calculation | |
| | | Solve addition and subtraction two-step problems in contexts, deciding which operations and methods to use and why | Tasks: 12 and 17 Exercise: 12 |
| Number – Multiplication and division | | Recall multiplication and division facts for multiplication tables up to 12 × 12 | 13 |
| | | Use place value, known and derived facts to multiply and divide mentally, including: multiplying by 0 and 1; dividing by 1; multiplying together three numbers | 14 |
| | | Recognise and use factor pairs and commutativity in mental calculations | 15 |
| | | Multiply two-digit and three-digit numbers by a one-digit number using formal written layout | 16 |
| | | Solve problems involving multiplying and adding, including using the distributive law to multiply two digit numbers by one digit, integer scaling problems and harder correspondence problems such as n objects are connected to m objects | Tasks: 12 and 17 Exercise: 17 |
| Number – Fractions (including decimals) | | Recognise and show, using diagrams, families of common equivalent fractions | 18 |
| | | Count up and down in hundredths; recognise that hundredths arise when dividing an object by 100 and dividing tenths by 10 | 19 |
| | | Solve problems involving increasingly harder fractions to calculate quantities, and fractions to divide quantities, including non-unit fractions where the answer is a whole number | 20 |
| | | Add and subtract fractions with the same denominator | 21 |
| | | Recognise and write decimal equivalents of any number of tenths or hundredths | 22 |

Introduction

| Domain | | National Curriculum attainment target | Assessment Task(s)/Exercise(s) |
|---|---|---|---|
| Number – | Fractions (including decimals) | Recognise and write decimal equivalents to $\frac{1}{4}$, $\frac{1}{2}$, $\frac{3}{4}$ | 23 |
| | | Find the effect of dividing a one- or two-digit number by 10 and 100, identifying the value of the digits in the answer as ones, tenths and hundredths | 24 |
| | | Round decimals with one decimal place to the nearest whole number | 25 |
| | | Compare numbers with the same number of decimal places up to two decimal places | 26 |
| | | Solve simple measure and money problems involving fractions and decimals to two decimal places | 27 |
| | Measurement | Convert between different units of measure [for example, kilometre to metre; hour to minute] | 28 |
| | | Measure and calculate the perimeter of a rectilinear figure (including squares) in centimetres and metres | 29 |
| | | Find the area of rectilinear shapes by counting squares | 30 |
| | | Estimate, compare and calculate different measures, including money in pounds and pence | 31 |
| | | Read, write and convert time between analogue and digital 12- and 24-hour clocks | 32 |
| | | Solve problems involving converting from hours to minutes; minutes to seconds; years to months; weeks to days | 33 |
| Geometry – | Properties of shapes | Compare and classify geometric shapes, including quadrilaterals and triangles, based on their properties and sizes | 34 |
| | | Identify acute and obtuse angles and compare and order angles up to two right angles by size | 35 |
| | | Identify lines of symmetry in 2-D shapes presented in different orientations | 36 |
| | | Complete a simple symmetric figure with respect to a specific line of symmetry | 37 |
| Geometry – | Position and direction | Describe positions on a 2-D grid as coordinates in the first quadrant | 38 |
| | | Describe movements between positions as translations of a given unit to the left/right and up/down | 39 |
| | | Plot specified points and draw sides to complete a given polygon | 40 |
| | Statistics | Interpret and present discrete and continuous data using appropriate graphical methods, including bar charts and time graphs | 41 |
| | | Solve comparison, sum and difference problems using information presented in bar charts, pictograms, tables and other graphs | 42 |

6

# Key Principles of Busy Ant Maths Assessment

Busy Ant Maths identifies two main purposes of assessment:

- assessment *for* learning (ongoing formative assessment)

- assessment *of* learning (summative assessment).

Assessment *for* learning involves both pupils and teachers finding out about the specific strengths and weaknesses of individual pupils, and the class as a whole, and using this to inform future teaching and learning.

Assessment *for* learning:

- – is part of the planning process
- – is informed by learning objectives
- – engages pupils in the assessment process
- – recognises the achievements of *all* pupils
- – takes account of how pupils learn
- – motivates learners.

Assessment *of* learning is any assessment that summarises at what level individual pupils, and the class as a whole, are working at a given point in time. It provides a snapshot of what has been learned.

The Busy Ant Maths Assessment Guides provide guidance in both assessment *for* learning and assessment *of* learning.

The Busy Ant Maths Assessment Guides consist of seven key components:

- Assessment Tasks

- Assessment Exercises

- End-of-unit Tests

- Pupil Self-assessments

- Record-keeping formats

- Resources to accompany the Assessment Tasks

- Tracking back and forward through the Mathematics National Curriculum attainment targets – Year 4.

The contents of the Assessment Guide is available in Word and PDF formats on our online learning platform, Collins Connect. Collins Connect also contains a powerful record-keeping tool that can be used to record results and teacher judgements, as well as track the progress and attainment of pupils throughout a year, between year groups and across a Key Stage. Assessment data can be stored online and presented digitally for class and whole-school analysis.

# Introduction

Assessment, record-keeping and reporting continue the teaching and learning cycle and are used to form the basis of adjustments to the teaching programme.

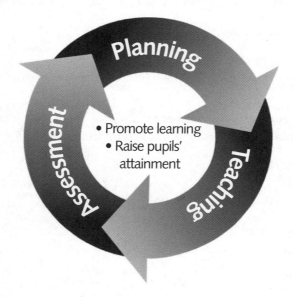

Busy Ant Maths offers manageable and meaningful assessment on four levels:

- **Diagnostic assessment**

    The Assessment Tasks are designed to assist teachers in determining pupils' readiness for a particular Busy Ant Maths unit of work. They are designed to yield information that will directly support individual pupils and whole-class teaching.

- **Short-term 'ongoing' assessment**

    Progress Check Questions ▶ are an important feature of every Busy Ant Maths lesson and are linked to specific learning objectives. They are designed to provide immediate feedback to pupils and to gauge pupil progress in order to adapt teaching.

    Shared Success criteria are also provided in each lesson to assist pupils in identifying the steps required to achieve mastery of the learning objective.

- **Medium-term 'formative' assessment**

    As well as being used for diagnostic assessment, the Assessment Tasks, along with the Assessment Exercises, can be used to review and record the progress of both individual pupils and the class as a whole, in relation to the National Curriculum attainment targets.

    An End-of-unit Test is provided for each of the 12 Busy Ant Maths units. Each test is designed to assess the mathematics covered during the three-week unit.

    The formative Assessment Tasks, Exercises and Tests provide individual and/or group opportunities to identify those pupils who have Not yet achieved (NYA), or who have Achieved and exceeded (A&E) national expectations. They can also be used to set individual targets for pupils.

- **Long-term 'summative' assessment**

    The various record-keeping formats found in this Assessment Guide and on Collins Connect are designed to show individual pupils' level of mastery against national standards. They draw on the data gathered throughout the year, including results from Assessment Tasks, Exercises and Tests, performance in whole-class discussions, participation in group work, written evidence and any other supplementary notes. It is these documents that form the basis for reporting to parents and guardians and informing the next year's teacher. Importantly, they also help to identify whether pupils are on track to meet end of key stage expectations.

# Assessment Tasks

## Purposes

- To assess individual pupils' level of mastery in a specific National Curriculum attainment target (NC AT).
- To identify individual pupils' strengths and weaknesses in a specific NC AT.
- To provide guidance about what to do for those pupils who are achieving *above* or *below* expectations.
- To inform future planning and teaching of individual pupils and the class as a whole.

## When to use the Assessment Tasks

When teachers are uncertain about a pupil's, or group of pupils', level of mastery in a specific NC AT, the Assessment Tasks can be used as diagnostic tools either:

- at the start of a new unit, or
- at any other time throughout the year.

## How to use the Assessment Tasks

- An Assessment Task is used in conjunction with the *Assessment Task Record* (see page 11). There are two versions of the *Assessment Task Record*: a paper version (see page 124) and an electronic, pre-populated version found on Collins Connect and accessed via computer or tablet.
- If using the paper version of the *Assessment Task Record*:
  - Photocopy page 124 and complete the top section.
  - Write the names of the pupils you are assessing (there is sufficient space for up to four pupils).
  - Copy the Success criteria from the relevant Assessment Task (there is sufficient space for up to eleven criteria (A–K)). Only complete the number of rows required for the particular task you are undertaking.
- If using the electronic version of the *Assessment Task Record* on Collins Connect:
  - Locate the relevant *Assessment Task Record*.
  - Complete the top section.
  - Add the names of the pupils you are assessing.
- Use the *Assessment Task Record* to record each pupil's performance during the task, indicating how competent a pupil is in each of the Success criteria, commenting on particular strengths and weaknesses. If necessary, make a note of any additional considerations observed. Once the pupils have completed the task, make a judgement of each pupil's mastery of the NC AT by highlighting whether the pupil has 'Not yet achieved' (NYA), 'Achieved' (A) or 'Achieved and exceeded' (A&E). Also make a note of any future action that may be considered appropriate. Refer to page 11 for a more detailed explanation of how to use the *Assessment Task Record*.

# Introduction

- If using the paper version, transfer the information collected on the *Assessment Task Record* onto the *Whole-class National Curriculum attainment targets* record (see pages 18 and 19) and the pupil's *Individual Pupil National Curriculum attainment targets and Domains* record (see page 22).

- If using the electronic version of the *Assessment Task Record,* you can populate the data in the record-keeping tool. This data can be presented digitally as per the *Whole-class National Curriculum attainment targets* record (see pages 18 and 19) and the pupil's *Individual Pupil National Curriculum attainment targets and Domains* record (see page 22).

**❶ Assessment Task number**
In most cases the numbering of the Assessment Tasks corresponds with the numbering of the Assessment Exercises.

**❷ National Curriculum Programme of Study Domain**

**❸ National Curriculum attainment target (NC AT)**

**❹ Prerequisite checklist**
List of the prerequisite knowledge, skills and understanding pupils need to have in order to achieve mastery of the NC AT.

**❺ Success criteria**
A list of the Success criteria that pupils need to know, understand and do in order to demonstrate that they have achieved mastery of the NC AT.

**❻ Resources**
List of resources required to undertake the task, including reference to any resource sheets.

**❼ Assessment Task**
Description of the task, including 'What to do', 'What to say' and 'What to look out for'.

**❽ What to do for those pupils** working *below* or ***above*** **expectations**
If a pupil has Not yet achieved (NYA) mastery or has Achieved and exceeded (A&E) mastery, the ❾ 'Tracking back and forward through the Mathematics National Curriculum attainment targets' charts on pages 310–320 will help to determine at what year group the pupil is currently working. Related Assessment Tasks and Assessment Exercises can then be located in the corresponding Busy Ant Maths Assessment Guide. Related teaching and learning opportunities can be found in the corresponding Busy Ant Maths Teacher's Guide.

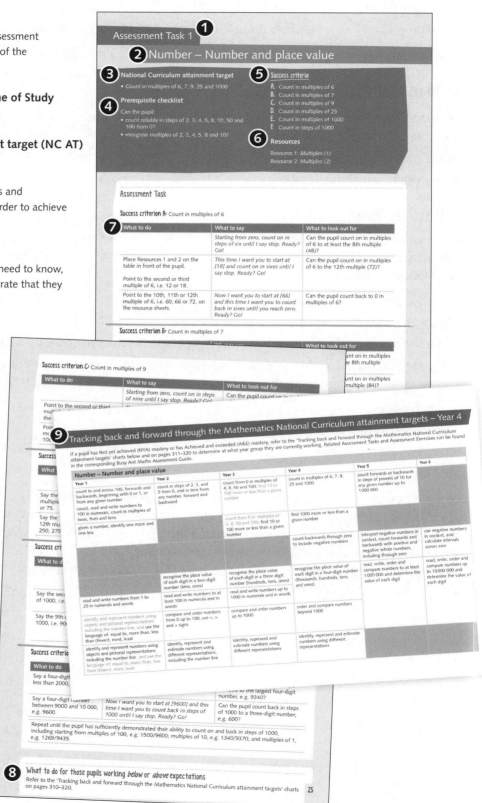

# Assessment Task Record

The Assessment Task Record is used in conjunction with the Assessment Tasks (see pages 9 and 10).

**❶ National Curriculum Programme of Study Domain**
Copy this information from the relevant Assessment Task.

**❷ National Curriculum attainment target (NC AT)**
Copy this information from the relevant Assessment Task.

**❸ Teacher, class and date reference**

**❹ Pupils' names**
Write the names of the pupils you are assessing (there is sufficient space for up to four pupils).

**❺ Success criteria**
The Success criteria for the relevant task are written in the spaces provided. There is sufficient space for up to eleven criteria (A–K). Only complete the number of rows required for the particular task you are undertaking. As you assess each pupil against the different Success criteria, either make a written comment on their level of mastery or use the following abbreviations: NYA (Not yet achieved), A (Achieved) or A&E (Achieved and exceeded).

**❻ Other observations**
For commenting on particular strengths or weaknesses or any other relevant observations made while undertaking the task with the pupil.

**❼ Level of mastery of NC AT**
The degree to which a pupil has mastered the specific NC AT is shown by ticking one of the following boxes:
NYA – Not yet achieved
A – Achieved
A&E – Achieved and exceeded

**❽ Future action**
Notes on any future action that may be considered appropriate.

---

BUSY ANT MATHS | Assessment Guide 4 | Assessment Task Record

**❶** Domain: _____

**❷** National Curriculum attainment target (NC AT): _____
_____

**❸** Teacher: _____ Class: _____ Date: _____

| **❺** Success criteria | **❹** Name | | | |
|---|---|---|---|---|
| A | | | | |
| B | | | | |
| C | | | | |
| D | | | | |
| E | | | | |
| F | | | | |
| G | | | | |
| H | | | | |
| I | | | | |
| J | | | | |
| K | | | | |
| **❻** Other observations | | | | |
| **❼** Level of mastery of NC AT* | NYA  A  A&E | NYA  A  A&E | NYA  A  A&E | NYA  A  A&E |
| **❽** Future action | | | | |

124        Level of mastery key: NYA – Not yet achieved | A – Achieved | A&E – Achieved and exceeded

## Assessment Exercises

### Purposes

- To assess individual pupils' level of mastery in a specific National Curriculum attainment target (NC AT).

- To identify individual pupils' strengths and weaknesses in a specific NC AT.

- To identify those pupils who are achieving *above* or *below* expectations.

- To inform future planning and teaching of individual pupils and the class as a whole.

### When to use the Assessment Exercises

- Any time throughout the year when teachers are uncertain about a pupil's, or group of pupils', level of mastery in a specific NC AT.

- When requiring written evidence of a pupil's level of mastery in a specific NC AT.

- Assessment Exercises differ from the End-of-unit Tests (see pages 14 and 15) in that an Assessment Exercise is designed to assess mastery in a specific NC AT, i.e. the *end-of-year level of expectation*, whereas an End-of-unit Test assesses all of the NC ATs taught in a particular Busy Ant Maths unit. It is designed to assess the exact mathematical content that has been taught during the unit and therefore will not always assess *the end-of-year level of expectation*.

### How to use the Assessment Exercises

- This section provides a photocopiable pupil Assessment Exercise and accompanying teacher's notes with answers and marking commentary for each of the NC ATs.

- The way in which the Assessment Exercises are administered is entirely up to the discretion of the individual teacher.

- It is advised that before pupils begin an exercise, you read through and explain the exercise to the pupils to ensure that they understand each of the questions. Also ensure that pupils have any necessary resources.

- After marking the Assessment Exercise, you then decide, based on the results of the exercise, the level of mastery achieved by the pupil for that specific NC AT, i.e. 'Not yet achieved' (NYA), 'Achieved' (A) or 'Achieved and exceeded' (A&E).

- The data collected can then be used to update either the paper or electronic versions of the *Whole-class National Curriculum attainment targets* record (see pages 18 and 19) and the pupil's *Individual Pupil National Curriculum attainment targets and Domains* record (see page 22).

**❶ Assessment Exercise number**

In most cases the numbering of the Assessment Exercises corresponds with the numbering of the Assessment Tasks.

**❷ National Curriculum Programme of Study Domain**

**❸ National Curriculum attainment target (NC AT)**

**❹ Marking scheme**

**❺ Results panel**

This includes the pupil's score and the level of mastery achieved.

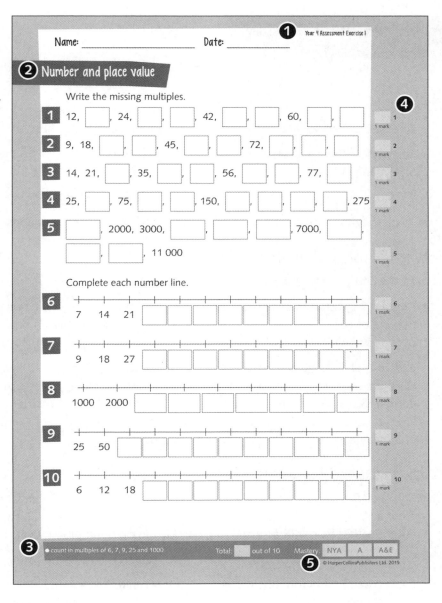

**❻ Answers**

**❼ Marking commentary**

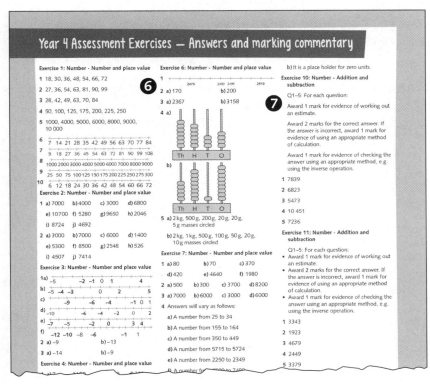

# End-of-unit Tests

## Purposes

- To assess understanding of the concepts taught in a Busy Ant Maths unit.

- To assist teachers in assessing individual pupils' level of mastery in a particular National Curriculum Programme of Study Domain.

- To inform future planning and teaching of individual pupils and the class as a whole.

- To identify those pupils who are achieving *above* or *below* expectations.

## When to use the End-of-unit Tests

- At the end of a three-week Busy Ant Maths unit.

- Alternatively, as each End-of-unit Test consists of three pages – one page per week, a page (test) could be used at the end of each week. However, this use of the End-of-unit Tests is not recommended as it could result in Friday becoming 'maths test day'.

- End-of-unit Tests differ from the Assessment Exercises (see pages 12 and 13) in that an End-of-unit Test assesses all of the National Curriculum attainment targets (NC ATs) taught in a particular Busy Ant Maths unit. They are designed to assess the exact mathematical content that has been taught during the unit and therefore will not always assess *the end-of-year level of expectation*. An Assessment Exercise, however, is designed to assess mastery in a specific NC AT, i.e. the *end-of-year level of expectation*.

## How to use the End-of-unit Tests

- This section provides a three-page photocopiable test, and accompanying teacher's notes with answers and marking commentary, for each of the 12 Busy Ant Maths units. End-of-unit Tests consist of one page of questions per week taught within that unit, assessing the NC ATs taught during that week.

- The way that the End-of-unit Tests are administered is entirely up to the discretion of the individual teacher.

- It is advised that before pupils begin a test, you read through and explain the test to the pupils to ensure that they understand each of the questions. Also ensure that pupils have any necessary resources.

- After marking each page of an End-of-unit Test, you then decide, based on the results of the page, the level of mastery achieved by the pupil for that particular Domain, i.e. 'Not yet achieved' (NYA), 'Achieved' (A) or 'Achieved and exceeded' (A&E).

- The data collected can then be used to update either the paper or electronic version of the *Whole-class National Curriculum attainment targets* record (see pages 18 and 19), the *Whole-class Domains* record (see pages 20 and 21) and the pupil's *Individual Pupil National Curriculum attainment targets and Domains* record (see page 22).

**❶ Marking scheme**

**❷ Teacher reference and results panel**
This includes year group, Busy Ant Maths unit number and week, National Curriculum Programme of Study Domain and the pupil's score and level of mastery achieved.

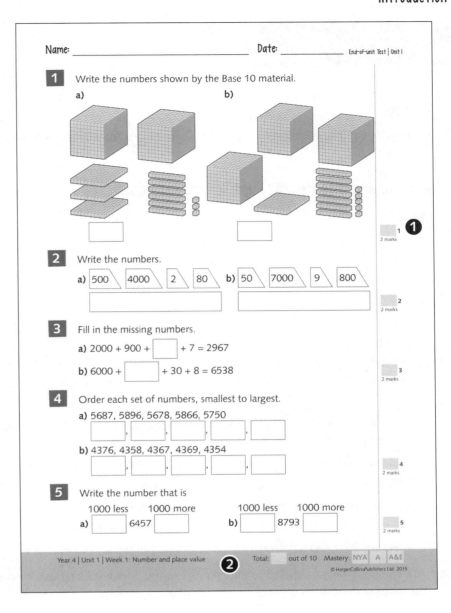

**❸ Answers**

**❹ Marking commentary**

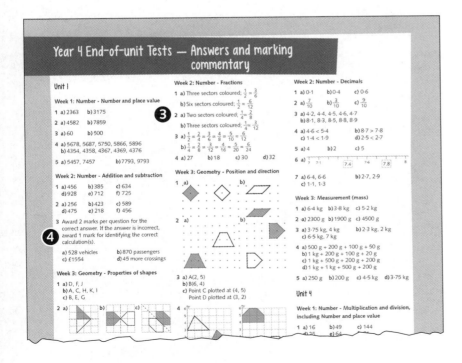

## Pupil Self-assessments

### Purpose
- To provide pupils with the opportunity to undertake some form of self-assessment at the end of a Busy Ant Maths unit.

### When and how to use the Pupil Self-assessments

**Either:**

1. Distribute the relevant Pupil Self-assessment at the *start of each week*. Pupils make a judgement about their current level of understanding for each of the 'I can' statements for the week. At the end of each week pupils revisit the booklet to re-assess their level of understanding.

   or

2. Distribute the relevant Pupil Self-assessment at the *end of the unit*. Pupils think back to the start of the unit and make a judgement about their level of understanding for each of the 'I can' statements for each week. At the same time they also make a judgement about their current level of understanding now that the unit has been taught.

- The empty box at the bottom of each page is designed to be used by pupils to record anything special that you may like them to have a record of, for example:
  - a relevant piece of work, drawing, calculation, statement or other piece of written evidence
  - anything the pupil feels they need more practice on
  - what the pupil thinks they should or could learn next
  - any special equipment that the pupil used to help them during the unit
  - anything the pupil particularly liked or disliked that they did during the unit.

- After pupils have completed a page (or the entire booklet) as a class, discuss specific statements, asking individual pupils to comment on what they have written.

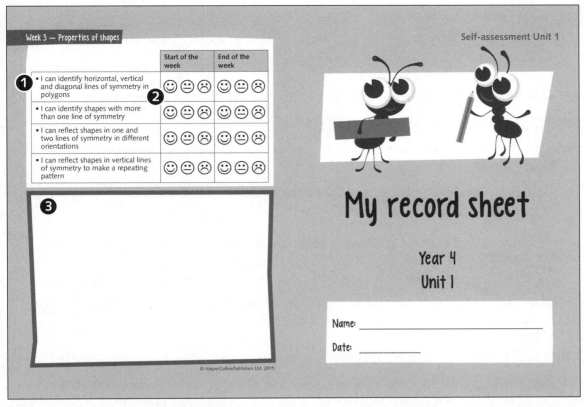

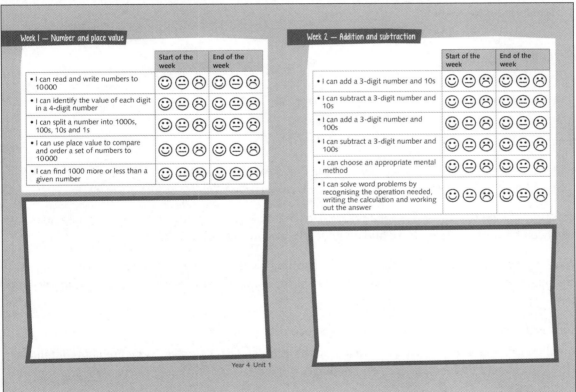

**1** List of assessment criteria in pupil-friendly language

**2** Icons for the pupil's self-assessment, both at the start and end of each week

**3** Box for the pupil to record something the teacher wants them to have a record of

# Record-keeping formats

There are three different types of record-keeping format in each of the Busy Ant Maths Assessment Guides:

- *Whole-class National Curriculum attainment targets* (see pages 240–247)

- *Whole-class Domains* (two versions: Views 1 and 2 – schools should choose their preferred version) (see pages 248 and 249)

- *Individual Pupil National Curriculum attainment targets and Domains* (see pages 250–252).

 Each of these formats is available as a paper version to photocopy and complete, and in electronic format on Collins Connect.

To ensure that pupils' attainment within a year group, and progression across the year groups, is easy to track, the same formats have been used throughout the entire Busy Ant Maths course.

## Whole-class National Curriculum attainment targets

This record-keeping format is designed to record the level of mastery that all the pupils in the class have achieved in each of the National Curriculum attainment targets (NC ATs). Decisions as to an individual pupil's level of mastery in each of the NC ATs should take into account:

- performance in whole-class discussions

- participation in group work

- work presented in exercise books

- observations made during Assessment Tasks

- performance in the Assessment Exercises or End-of-unit Tests

- any other evidence.

As a result of the evidence collected for each NC AT, you can then make a judgement regarding the overall level of mastery in each of the National Curriculum Programme of Study Domains.

This record-keeping format is intended to be a working document that teachers start to complete at the beginning of the academic year that can be continually updated and amended throughout the course of the year.

At the end of the year, this document will help teachers when reporting to parents. It will also help senior managers with data analysis and assist in informing the next year's teacher of those pupils who are working *above* and *below* national expectations in each of the NC ATs and Domains.

Using the *Whole-class National Curriculum attainment targets* record-keeping format:

- When a judgement concerning a specific NC AT is made on the *Whole-class National Curriculum attainment targets* record, this data should then be updated on the pupil's *Individual Pupil National Curriculum attainment targets and Domains* record.

- When a judgement concerning the overall level of mastery in a particular Domain is made on the *Whole-class National Curriculum attainment targets* record, this data should then be updated on the pupil's *Individual Pupil National Curriculum attainment targets and Domains* record and either version of the *Whole-class Domains* record.

**❶ Year group**

**❷ Class and academic year reference**

**❸ National Curriculum Programme of Study Domain**

**❹ Pupils' names**

**❺ National Curriculum attainment targets (NC ATs)**

**❻ Level of mastery in each NC AT**

The degree to which a pupil has mastered a NC AT is shown by writing one of the following initials or sets of initials in the appropriate column:

NYA – Not yet achieved

A – Achieved

A&E – Achieved and exceeded

**❼ Overall level of mastery for this National Curriculum Programme of Study Domain**

The degree to which a pupil has mastered the Domain is shown by writing one of the following initials or sets of initials in the appropriate column:

NYA – Not yet achieved

A – Achieved

A&E – Achieved and exceeded

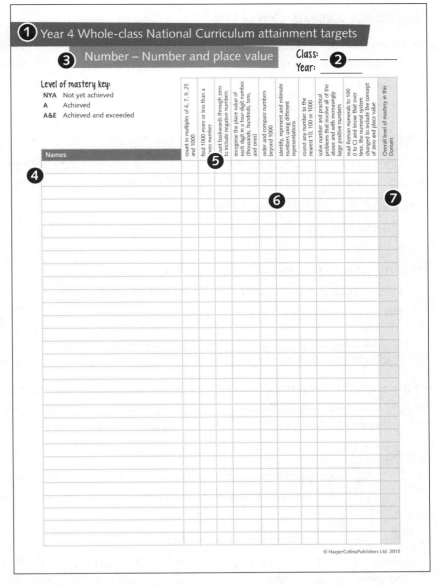

❶ Year 4 Whole-class National Curriculum attainment targets

❸ Number – Number and place value     Class: ❷ _____
Year: _____

Level of mastery key:

NYA  Not yet achieved
A    Achieved
A&E  Achieved and exceeded

Names ❹

Column headers: count in multiples of 6, 7, 9, 25 and 1000 · find 1000 more or less than a given number · count backwards through zero to include negative numbers · recognise the place value of each digit in a four-digit number (thousands, hundreds, tens, and ones) · order and compare numbers beyond 1000 · identify, represent and estimate numbers using different representations · round any number to the nearest 10, 100 or 1000 · solve number and practical problems that involve all of the above and with increasingly large positive numbers · read Roman numerals to 100 (I to C) and know that over time, the numeral system changed to include the concept of zero and place value · Overall level of mastery in this Domain

❺ ❻ ❼

© HarperCollins*Publishers* Ltd. 2015

## Whole-class Domains Views 1 and 2

There are two record-keeping formats designed to record the level of mastery that all the pupils in the class have achieved in each of the National Curriculum Programme of Study Domains. These are:

– *Whole-class Domains* (View 1)

– *Whole-class Domains* (View 2).

Schools should decide which version they prefer and just use *one* of these record-keeping formats.

Decisions as to an individual pupil's level of mastery in each of the National Curriculum Programme of Study Domains should be based on each of the Domain's attainment targets and take into account:

– performance in whole-class discussions

– participation in group work

– work presented in exercise books

– observations made during Assessment Tasks

– performance in the Assessment Exercises or End-of-unit Tests

– any other evidence.

This record-keeping format is intended to be a working document that teachers start to complete at the beginning of the academic year that can be continually updated and amended throughout the course of the year.

At the end of the year, this document will help teachers when reporting to parents. It will also help senior managers with data analysis and assist in informing the next year's teacher of those pupils who are working *above* and *below* national expectations in each of the National Curriculum Programme of Study Domains.

As with the other record-keeping formats, this format is available as a paper version to photocopy and complete, as well as in electronic format on Collins Connect.

Using the *Whole-class Domains* record-keeping format:

– When a judgement concerning the overall level of mastery in a particular Domain is made on either version of the *Whole-class Domains* records, this data should then be updated on a pupil's *Individual Pupil attainment targets and Domains* record and in the Domain column of the *Whole-class National Curriculum attainment targets* record.

# Whole-class Domains (View 1)

**❶ Year group**

**❷ Class and academic year reference**

**❸ National Curriculum Programme of Study Domains**

**❹ Pupils' names**

**❺ Overall level of mastery in the National Curriculum Programme of Study Domain**

The degree of mastery achieved by a pupil in each Domain is shown by writing one of the following initials or sets of initials in the appropriate column:

NYA – Not yet achieved

A – Achieved

A&E – Achieved and exceeded

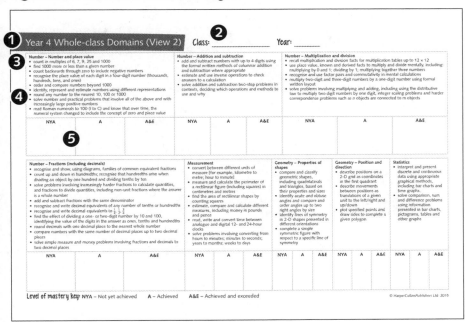

# Whole-class Domains (View 2)

**❶ Year group**

**❷ Class and academic year reference**

**❸ National Curriculum Programme of Study Domains**

**❹ National Curriculum attainment targets**

**❺ Overall level of mastery in the National Curriculum Programme of Study Domain**

The degree of mastery achieved by a pupil in each Domain is shown by writing the pupil's name in the appropriate column:

NYA – Not yet achieved

A – Achieved

A&E – Achieved and exceeded

# Individual Pupil National Curriculum attainment targets and Domains

This record-keeping format is designed to record individual pupils' level of mastery in each of the National Curriculum attainment targets (NC ATs) and in each of the Programme of Study Domains, taking into account the following:

– performance in whole-class discussions

– participation in group work

– work presented in exercise books

– observations made during Assessment Tasks

– performance in the Assessment Exercises or End-of-unit Tests

– any other evidence.

This record-keeping format is intended to be a working document that teachers start to complete at the beginning of the academic year that can be continually updated and amended throughout the course of the year.

At the end of the year, this document will help teachers when reporting to parents. It will also help senior managers with data analysis and assist in informing the next year's teacher of those pupils who are working *above* and *below* national expectations in each of the NC ATs and Domains.

 As with the other record-keeping formats, this format is available as a paper version to photocopy and complete, as well as in electronic format on Collins Connect.

Using the *Individual Pupil National Curriculum attainment targets and Domains* record-keeping format:

– When a judgement about a pupil's level of mastery in a specific NC AT is made on the *Individual Pupil National Curriculum attainment targets and Domains* record, this data should then be updated on the *Whole-class National Curriculum attainment targets* record.

– When a judgement concerning a pupil's overall level of mastery in a particular Domain is made on the *Individual Pupil National Curriculum attainment targets and Domains* record, this data should then be updated on the *Whole-class National Curriculum attainment targets* record and either version of the *Whole-class Domains* record.

**❶ Pupil's name**

**❷ Class and academic year reference**

**❸ National Curriculum Programme of Study Domain**

**❹ National Curriculum attainment target (NC AT)**

**❺ Level of mastery in each of the NC ATs**
The level of mastered achieved for each of the NC ATs is shown by ticking the appropriate column.

**❻ Overall level of mastery in each of the National Curriculum Programme of Study Domains**
The level of mastered achieved in each of the Domains is shown by ticking the appropriate column.

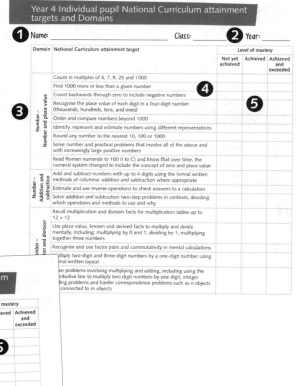

# Resources to accompany the Assessment Tasks

This section includes all of the photocopiable resources that are required to administer each of the Assessment Tasks.

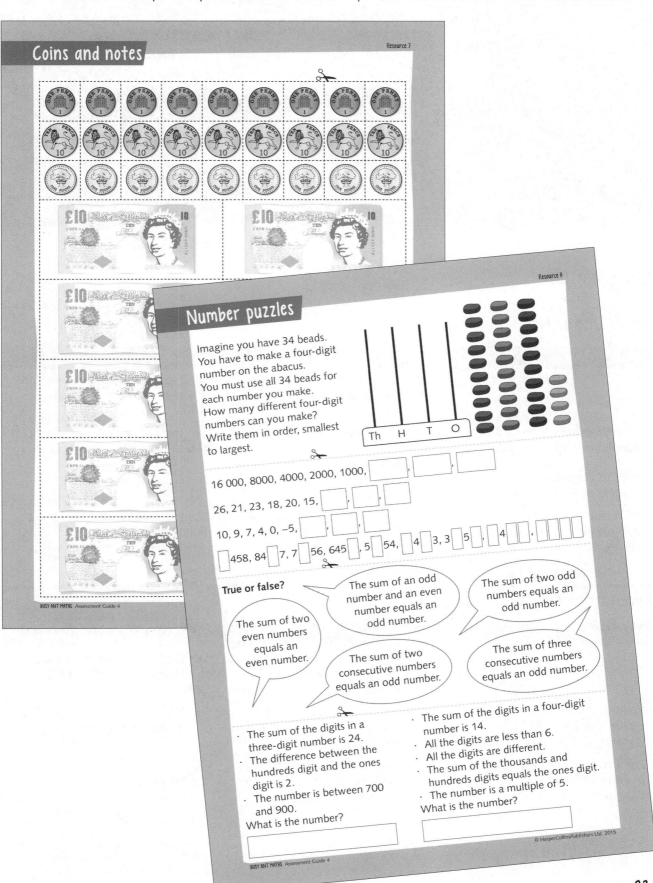

# Number – Number and place value

## National Curriculum attainment target

- Count in multiples of 6, 7, 9, 25 and 1000

## Prerequisite checklist

Can the pupil:
- count reliably in steps of 2, 3, 4, 5, 8, 10, 50 and 100 from 0?
- recognise multiples of 2, 3, 4, 5, 8 and 10?

## Success criteria

A. Count in multiples of 6
B. Count in multiples of 7
C. Count in multiples of 9
D. Count in multiples of 25
E. Count in multiples of 1000
F. Count in steps of 1000

## Resources

Resource 1: Multiples (1)
Resource 2: Multiples (2)

## Assessment Task

### Success criterion A: Count in multiples of 6

| What to do | What to say | What to look out for |
|---|---|---|
| | *Starting from zero, count on in steps of six until I say stop. Ready? Go!* | Can the pupil count on in multiples of 6 to at least the 8th multiple (48)? |
| Place Resources 1 and 2 on the table in front of the pupil.<br><br>Point to the second or third multiple of 6, i.e. 12 or 18. | *This time I want you to start at [18] and count on in sixes until I say stop. Ready? Go!* | Can the pupil count on in multiples of 6 to the 12th multiple (72)? |
| Point to the 10th, 11th or 12th multiple of 6, i.e. 60, 66 or 72, on the resource sheets. | *Now I want you to start at [66] and this time I want you to count back in sixes until you reach zero. Ready? Go!* | Can the pupil count back to 0 in multiples of 6? |

### Success criterion B: Count in multiples of 7

| What to do | What to say | What to look out for |
|---|---|---|
| | *Starting from zero, count on in steps of seven until I say stop. Ready? Go!* | Can the pupil count on in multiples of 7 to at least the 8th multiple (56)? |
| Point to the second or third multiple of 7, i.e. 14 or 21, on the resource sheets. | *This time I want you to start at [14] and count on in sevens until I say stop. Ready? Go!* | Can the pupil count on in multiples of 7 to the 12th multiple (84)? |
| Point to the 10th, 11th or 12th multiple of 7, i.e. 70, 77 or 84, on the resource sheets. | *Now I want you to start at [84] and this time I want you to count back in sevens until you reach zero. Ready? Go!* | Can the pupil count back to 0 in multiples of 7? |

## Success criterion C: Count in multiples of 9

| What to do | What to say | What to look out for |
|---|---|---|
| | *Starting from zero, count on in steps of nine until I say stop. Ready? Go!* | Can the pupil count on in multiples of 9 to at least the 8th multiple (72)? |
| Point to the second or third multiple of 9, i.e. 18 or 27, on the resource sheets. | *This time I want you to start at [18] and count on in nines until I say stop. Ready? Go!* | Can the pupil count on in multiples of 9 to the 12th multiple (108)? |
| Point to the 10th, 11th or 12th multiple of 9, i.e. 90, 99 or 108, on the resource sheets. | *Now I want you to start at [90] and this time I want you to count back in nines until you reach zero. Ready? Go!* | Can the pupil count back to 0 in multiples of 9? |

## Success criterion D: Count in multiples of 25

| What to do | What to say | What to look out for |
|---|---|---|
| | *Starting from zero, count on in [multiples] of 25 until I say stop. Ready? Go!* | Can the pupil count on in multiples of 25 to at least the 8th multiple (200)? |
| Say the second or third multiple of 25, i.e. 50 or 75. | *This time I want you to start at [75] and count on in [multiples] of 25 until I say stop. Ready? Go!* | Can the pupil count on in multiples of 25 to the 12th multiple (300)? |
| Say the 10th, 11th or 12th multiple of 25, i.e. 250, 275 or 300. | *Now I want you to start at [275] and this time I want you to count back in [multiples] of 25 until you reach zero. Ready? Go!* | Can the pupil count back to 0 in multiples of 25? |

## Success criterion E: Count in multiples of 1000

| What to do | What to say | What to look out for |
|---|---|---|
| | *Starting from zero, count on in multiples of 1000 until I say stop. Ready? Go!* | Can the pupil count on in multiples of 1000 to at least the 8th multiple (8000)? |
| Say the second or third multiple of 1000, i.e. 2000 or 3000. | *This time I want you to start at [3000] and count on in multiples of 1000 until I say stop. Ready? Go!* | Can the pupil count on in multiples of 1000 to the 10th multiple (10 000)? |
| Say the 9th or 10th multiple of 1000, i.e. 9000 or 10 000. | *Now I want you to start at [9000] and this time I want you to count back in multiples of 1000 until you reach zero. Ready? Go!* | Can the pupil count back to 0 in multiples of 1000? |

## Success criterion F: Count in steps of 1000

| What to do | What to say | What to look out for |
|---|---|---|
| Say a four-digit number less than 2000, e.g. 1340. | *Starting from [1340], count on in steps of 1000 until I say stop. Ready? Go!* | Can the pupil count on in steps of 1000 to the largest four-digit number, e.g. 9340? |
| Say a four-digit number between 9000 and 10 000, e.g. 9600. | *Now I want you to start at [9600] and this time I want you to count back in steps of 1000 until I say stop. Ready? Go!* | Can the pupil count back in steps of 1000 to a three-digit number, e.g. 600? |

Repeat until the pupil has sufficiently demonstrated their ability to count on and back in steps of 1000, including starting from multiples of 100, e.g. 1500/9600; multiples of 10, e.g. 1340/9370; and multiples of 1, e.g. 1269/9435.

## What to do for those pupils working *below* or *above* expectations

Refer to the 'Tracking back and forward through the Mathematics National Curriculum attainment targets' charts on pages 310–320.

# Number – Number and place value

## National Curriculum attainment target

• Find 1000 more or less than a given number

## Prerequisite checklist

Can the pupil:
• find 1 more or less than a given number?
• find 10 more or less than a given number?
• find 100 more or less than a given number?

## Success criteria

**A.** Find 1000 more than a given number
**B.** Find 1000 less than a given number

## Resources

Resource 3: Numbers to 10 000

---

**NOTE**

• This Assessment Task focuses on the National Curriculum attainment target 'Find 1000 more or less than a given number'. If appropriate, also ask the pupil to find 1, 10 or 100 more or less than a given number.

---

## Assessment Task

### Success criterion A: Find 1000 more than a given number

| What to do | What to say | What to look out for |
|---|---|---|
| Display Resource 3 and point to a number (not 9413). | *What is 1000 more than this number?* | Can the pupil say the number that is 1000 more than a:<br>– one-digit number?<br>– two-digit number?<br>– three-digit number?<br>– four-digit number? |
| Repeat several times pointing to different one-, two-, three- and four-digit numbers. | | |
| If appropriate, point to other numbers on the sheet and ask the pupil to say the number that is 1, 10 or 100 more than the number.<br><br>Ask questions similar to the ones shown here: | *What is one more than this number?*<br><br>*Tell me the number that is ten more than this number.*<br><br>*What number is 100 more than […]?* | Can the pupil say the number that is:<br>– 1 more than a given number?<br>– 10 more than a given number?<br>– 100 more than a given number? |

Repeat until the pupil has sufficiently demonstrated their ability to say the number that is 1000 (and 1, 10 or 100) more than a given number.

## Success criterion B: Find 1000 less than a given number

| What to do | What to say | What to look out for |
|---|---|---|
| Point to one of the four-digit numbers on the sheet, e.g. 5106. | *What is 1000 less than this number?* | Can the pupil say the number that is 1000 less than a four-digit number? |
| Repeat, pointing to the other four-digit numbers on the sheet. | | |
| If appropriate, point to other numbers on the sheet and ask the pupil to say the number that is 1, 10 or 100 less than the number (positive number answers only).<br><br>Ask questions similar to the ones shown here: | *What is one less than [2358/702/39/2]?*<br><br>*Tell me the number that is ten less than [7031/236/14].*<br><br>*What number is 100 less than [6249/827]?* | Can the pupil say the number that is:<br>– 1 less than a one-, two-, three- or four-digit number?<br>– 10 less than a two-, three- or four-digit number?<br>– 100 less than a three- or four-digit number? |

Repeat until the pupil has sufficiently demonstrated their ability to say the number that is 1000 (and 1, 10 or 100) less than a given number.

## What to do for those pupils working *below* or *above* expectations

Refer to the 'Tracking back and forward through the Mathematics National Curriculum attainment targets' charts on pages 310–320.

# Number – Number and place value

## National Curriculum attainment target

• Count backwards through zero to include negative numbers

## Prerequisite checklist

Does the pupil:
• have an understanding of negative numbers?
Can the pupil:
• count on and back in steps of a constant size?

## Success criteria

A. Count backwards in steps of 1, extending the count beyond zero
B. Count backwards in steps of a constant size, extending the count beyond zero

## Assessment Task

**Success criterion A:** Count backwards in steps of 1, extending the count beyond zero

| What to do | What to say | What to look out for |
| --- | --- | --- |
| Tell the pupil a one-digit number and ask them to count back in steps in 1, extending the count beyond 0. | *Starting from [six], count back in steps of one until I say stop. Ready? Go!* | Can the pupil count back in steps of 1 to at least −10? |
| Repeat for other one-digit and 'teen' numbers. | | |

**Success criterion B:** Count backwards in steps of a constant size, extending the count beyond zero

| What to do | What to say | What to look out for |
| --- | --- | --- |
| Tell the pupil an even 'teen' number, e.g. 16, and ask them to count back in steps in 2, extending the count beyond 0. | *Starting at [16], count back in steps of two until I say stop. Ready? Go!* | Can the pupil count back in steps of 2 to at least −10? |
| Repeat, starting the count from other even 'teen' numbers. | | |
| Repeat, starting the count from 5, 10, 15 or 20, asking the pupil to count back in steps of 5. | *Starting at [ten], count back in steps of five until I say stop. Ready? Go!* | Can the pupil count back in steps of 5 to at least −10? |
| Repeat, starting the count from 20 or 30, asking the pupil to count back in steps of 10. | *Starting from [30], count back in steps of ten until I say stop. Ready? Go!* | Can the pupil count back in steps of 10 to at least −20? |
| If appropriate, ask the pupil to count back beyond 0:<br>– starting the count from 9, 12 or 15 and counting back in steps of 3; | *Starting from [15], count back in steps of three until I say stop. Ready? Go!* | Can the pupil count back in steps of 3 to at least −9? |
| – starting the count from 12, 16 or 20 and counting back in steps of 4. | *Starting from [12], count back in steps of four until I say stop. Ready? Go!* | Can the pupil count back in steps of 4 to at least −12? |

## What to do for those pupils working *below* or *above* expectations

Refer to the 'Tracking back and forward through the Mathematics National Curriculum attainment targets' charts on pages 310–320.

# Number – Number and place value

## National Curriculum attainment target

- Recognise the place value of each digit in a four-digit number (thousands, hundreds, tens, and ones)

## Prerequisite checklist

Can the pupil:

- recognise the place value of each digit in a two-digit number (tens, ones)?
- partition a two-digit number into multiples of 10 and 1?
- recognise the place value of each digit in a three-digit number (hundreds, tens, ones)?
- partition a three-digit number into multiples of 100, 10 and 1?

## Success criteria

**A.** Know what each digit represents in a four-digit number

**B.** Partition four-digit numbers into multiples of 1000, 100, 10 and 1

**C.** Partition four-digit numbers in different ways

## Resources

Resource 4: Four-digit numbers

pencil and paper (per pupil)

## Assessment Task

**Success criterion A:** Know what each digit represents in a four-digit number

| What to do | What to say | What to look out for |
|---|---|---|
| Display Resource 4 and point to a specific digit in one of the four-digit numbers. | *What is the value of this digit?* | Can the pupil identify the value of a digit in a four-digit number? |
| Repeat several times pointing to different place values in other four-digit numbers. | | |
| Point to a different four-digit number. | *Point to the digit that shows how many tens are in the number.* | Can the pupil identify the tens digit in a four-digit number? |
| Repeat for the ones, hundreds and thousands digits in other four-digit numbers. | *Point to the digit that shows how many [ones/hundreds/thousands] are in the number.* | Can the pupil identify the ones digit in a four-digit number? |
| | | Can the pupil identify the hundreds digit in a four-digit number? |
| | | Can the pupil identify the thousands digit in a four-digit number? |
| | *Point to a number that has three tens.* | Can the pupil identify a specific four-digit number based on the value of one of its digits? |
| | *Point to a number that has seven hundreds.* | |
| | *Point to a number that has five thousands.* | |
| | *Point to a number that has two ones.* | |
| Repeat for other four-digit numbers. | | |

**Success criterion B:** Partition four-digit numbers into multiples of 1000, 100, 10 and 1

| What to do | What to say | What to look out for |
|---|---|---|
| On the sheet of paper write a four-digit number in expanded notation, e.g. 2000 + 500 + 70 + 4. | *What is this number? Write it for me as a four-digit number.* | Can the pupil identify a four-digit number when written in expanded notation? |
| Display Resource 4 and point to a number. | *Look at this number. Write it for me in the same way that I did, showing how many thousands, hundreds, tens and ones there are in the number.* | Can the pupil partition a four-digit number into multiples of 1000, 100, 10 and 1? |

Repeat for other four-digit numbers.

**Success criterion C:** Partition four-digit numbers in different ways

| What to do | What to say | What to look out for |
|---|---|---|
| Refer back to the number you had previously partitioned into multiples of 1000, 100, 10 and 1, i.e. 2574. | *I can partition this number into multiples of 100, 10 and 1 in different ways.* | |
| On the sheet of paper write 2574 = 1000 + 1500 + 70 + 4. | *I can partition the number 2574 into 1000 add 1500 add 70 add 4.* | |
| Refer back to the number you asked the pupil to partition into multiples of 1000, 100, 10 and 1. | *I want you to partition this number in a different way.*<br><br>*Can you partition this number in yet another way?* | Can the pupil partition a four-digit number in at least two different ways? |

Repeat until the pupil has sufficiently demonstrated their ability to partition four-digit numbers into multiples of 1000, 100, 10 and 1 in different ways.

## What to do for those pupils working *below* or *above* expectations

Refer to the 'Tracking back and forward through the Mathematics National Curriculum attainment targets' charts on pages 310–320.

# Number – Number and place value

## National Curriculum attainment target

• Order and compare numbers beyond 1000

## Prerequisite checklist

Can the pupil:

• compare two, two-, three- or four-digit numbers, using language such as 'larger', 'greater', 'more', 'smaller' and 'less'?

• order sets of two- and/or three-digit numbers?

• order sets of consecutive four-digit numbers, e.g. 5746, 5748, 5745, 5749, 5747?

## Success criteria

A. Compare two four-digit numbers

B. Use the < and > symbols to compare two four-digit numbers

C. Order numbers beyond 1000

## Resources

Resource 3: Numbers to 10 000 (made into number cards)

Resource 4: Four-digit numbers (made into number cards)

Resource 5: Symbol cards

## NOTE

• Prior to the task, cut out the number cards from Resource 3 and arrange them into four separate piles: one-digit numbers, two-digit numbers, three-digit numbers and four-digit numbers. To the pile of four-digit number cards add the cards from Resource 4.

## Assessment Task

### Success criterion A: Compare two four-digit numbers

| What to do | What to say | What to look out for |
|---|---|---|
| Lay two four-digit cards face up in front of the pupil. | *Point to the larger number.* | Can the pupil identify the larger number? |

Repeat for other pairs of four-digit numbers, asking the pupil to identify the number that is smaller/less/bigger/more. Include pairs of numbers with:
– different thousands digits, e.g. 6104 and 2810
– the same thousands digits, e.g. 2483 and 2358
– the same thousands and hundreds digits, e.g. 7052 and 7031.

**Success criterion B:** Use the < and > symbols to compare two four-digit numbers

| What to do | What to say | What to look out for |
|---|---|---|
| Provide the pupil with a 'greater than/less than' card from Resource 5. Ensure that the pupil realises that the 'greater than/less than' card can be used to represent either symbol by turning the card upside down.<br><br>Choose two four-digit number cards and place them in front of the pupil, leaving a space between the two cards,<br><br>e.g. 4598  6104 . | Look at the two number cards in front of you. I want you to place your symbol card between these two cards so that it makes a correct statement. | Can the pupil correctly identify the greater than and less than symbols?<br><br>Can the pupil correctly use the greater than and less than symbols to compare two numbers? |
| When the pupil has done this, ask them to say their statement. | Can you read this statement to me? | |

Repeat above several times.

| What to do | What to say | What to look out for |
|---|---|---|
| Choose a four-digit number card and a symbol card and place them in front of the pupil, e.g. 5327  < .<br><br>Randomly spread a selection of the other four-digit number cards face up on the table. | Look at the two cards in front of you. Choose a number card from the table to put after the symbol card so that the statement is correct. | Can the pupil correctly identify the greater than and less than symbols?<br><br>Can the pupil identify a number that correctly completes the statement? |
| When the pupil has done this, ask them to say their statement. | Read me your statement. | |
| Remove the number card the pupil has used to complete the statement and place it with the other four-digit number cards. | Can you choose another number card so that the statement is still correct? | |

Repeat above several times, alternating the symbol card between < and > .

**Success criterion C:** Order numbers beyond 1000

| What to do | What to say | What to look out for |
|---|---|---|
| Lay five cards from Resources 3 and 4 face up in front of the pupil. | Look at the numbers in front of you. I want you to place these cards in order, smallest to largest. | Can the pupil order the numbers? |
| Give the pupil another number card. | Look at the cards you have just put in order. Where would you put this number so that the order is still correct? | |
| Referring to the set of six ordered number cards, point to two consecutive numbers. | Tell me a number that lies between these two numbers. | Can the pupil identify a number that lies between two other numbers? |

Repeat until the pupil has sufficiently demonstrated their ability to order numbers to 1000. Include sets of cards with:
- a mixture of one-, two-, three- and four-digit numbers, e.g. 3725, 8, 3169, 93, 236
- different thousands digits, e.g. 7052, 6104 , 1735, 2810, 5327
- several numbers with the same thousands digits, e.g. 3169, 2483, 3725, 3601, 2810.

## What to do for those pupils working *below* or *above* expectations
Refer to the 'Tracking back and forward through the Mathematics National Curriculum attainment targets' charts on pages 310–320.

# Number – Number and place value

## National Curriculum attainment target

- Identify, represent and estimate numbers using different representations

## Prerequisite checklist

Can the pupil:
- read, write, order and compare numbers to at least 1000 and recognise the value of each digit?

## Success criteria

A. Identify numbers to 10000 using different representations
B. Represent numbers to 10000 using different representations
C. Estimate numbers to 10000 using different representations

## Resources

Resource 6: Gattegno place value chart

Base 10 material: thousands 'blocks', hundreds 'flats', tens 'rods', ones

several £10 notes, £1 coins, 10p and 1p coins (alternatively, use several copies of Resource 7: Coins and notes)

place value cards: thousands, hundreds, tens and ones, i.e.

pencil and paper (per pupil)

container holding at least 100 of the same counting object, e.g. buttons

---

**NOTES**
- It is recommended that, if possible, real coins (and notes) are used for this Assessment Task. If this is not possible, then use realistic plastic coins and notes. Only as a final alternative use the coins and notes provided on Resource 7.
- Prior to the Assessment Task, place all the resources on the table and provide the pupil(s) with pencil and paper.

---

## Assessment Task

**Success criterion A:** Identify numbers to 10 000 using different representations

| What to do | What to say | What to look out for |
|---|---|---|
| Referring to each resource in turn, create (or in the case of the Gattegno place value chart, point to) different two-, three- and four-digit numbers.<br><br>Ask questions similar to the ones shown here that require the pupil to identify the number. | *Look as I point to numbers on this place value chart. What number is this?*<br><br>*What number have I created using the Base 10 material?*<br><br>*How much money is here? What is this in pounds and pence? What is this in pence only?*<br><br>*What number do these place value cards make?* | Can the pupil identify numbers to 10000 using the different representations? |

Continue until the pupil has sufficiently demonstrated their ability to identify numbers to 10 000 using different representations.

## Success criterion B: Represent numbers to 10 000 using different representations

| What to do | What to say | What to look out for |
| --- | --- | --- |
| Say, or write on the sheet of paper, a two-, three- or four-digit number, and ask the pupil to represent the number using one of the resources, e.g. Base 10 material. | *What is this number?*<br><br>*Can you show me this number using the Base 10 material?* | Can the pupil represent numbers to 10 000 using the different representations? |
| Repeat for other two-, three- or four-digit numbers, asking the pupil to use a particular resource to represent the number.<br><br>Ask questions similar to the ones shown here that require the pupil to represent the number. | *Point to the number 4539 on this place value chart.*<br><br>*Show me this number using the coins and notes. What is this number in pence only? What is this number in pounds and pence?*<br><br>*Use the place value cards to make this number.* | |

Continue until the pupil has sufficiently demonstrated their ability to represent numbers to 10 000 using different representations.

## Success criterion C: Estimate numbers to 10 000 using different representations

| What to do | What to say | What to look out for |
| --- | --- | --- |
| Referring to the container holding at least 100 of the same counting object, e.g. buttons, place a handful of the counting objects in front of the pupil and ask them to estimate how many there are. | *Without counting them, how many [buttons] do you think there are here?* | Can the pupil offer a reasonable estimate of the number of objects? |
| Repeat several times. | | |
| Using the Base 10 material, place a number of thousands 'blocks', hundreds 'flats', tens 'rods' and ones in front of the pupil. | *Without counting all of the Base 10 material, what number do these Base 10 materials make?* | Can the pupil offer a reasonable estimate of the number represented by the Base 10 material? |
| Repeat several times. | | |

## What to do for those pupils working *below* or *above* expectations

Refer to the 'Tracking back and forward through the Mathematics National Curriculum attainment targets' charts on pages 310–320.

# Number – Number and place value

## National Curriculum attainment target

• Round any number to the nearest 10, 100 or 1000

## Prerequisite checklist

Can the pupil:

• read, write, order and compare numbers to 10 000 and recognise the value of each digit?

## Success criteria

**A.** Round two-digit numbers to the nearest 10

**B.** Round three-digit numbers to the nearest 100 and 10

**C.** Round four-digit numbers to the nearest 1000, 100 and 10

## Resources

Resource 3: Numbers to 10 000

---

## Assessment Task

### Success criterion A: Round two-digit numbers to the nearest 10

| What to do | What to say | What to look out for |
|---|---|---|
| Place Resource 3 on the table in front of the pupil.<br><br>Point to each of the two-digit numbers in turn, asking questions similar to the ones shown here that require the pupil to round the number to the nearest multiple of 10. | *What is [14] rounded to the nearest multiple of ten?*<br><br>*Round [39] to the nearest multiple of ten.*<br><br>*What do you look for when you round a two-digit number to the nearest ten?* | Can the pupil round a two-digit number to the nearest multiple of 10?<br><br>Can the pupil explain how to round a two-digit number to the nearest 10? |

### Success criterion B: Round three-digit numbers to the nearest 100 and 10

| What to do | What to say | What to look out for |
|---|---|---|
| Point to each of the three-digit numbers in turn, asking questions similar to the ones shown here that require the pupil to round the number to the nearest multiple of 100. | *What is [236] rounded to the nearest multiple of 100?*<br><br>*Round [418] to the nearest 100.*<br><br>*Which digit is important when you round a three-digit number to the nearest 100?* | Can the pupil round a three-digit number to the nearest multiple of 100?<br><br>Can the pupil explain how to round a three-digit number to the nearest 100? |
| Once again, point to each of the three-digit numbers in turn, asking questions similar to the ones shown here that require the pupil to round the number to the nearest multiple of 10. | *What is [236] rounded to the nearest multiple of ten?*<br><br>*Round [418] to the nearest ten.*<br><br>*What do you have to do when you round a three-digit number to the nearest ten?* | Can the pupil round a three-digit number to the nearest multiple of 10?<br><br>Can the pupil explain how to round a three-digit number to the nearest 10? |

**Success criterion C:** Round four-digit numbers to the nearest 1000, 100 and 10

| What to do | What to say | What to look out for |
|---|---|---|
| Point to several of the four-digit numbers in turn, asking questions similar to the ones shown here that require the pupil to round the number to the nearest multiple of 1000. | *What is [3725] rounded to the nearest multiple of 1000?*<br><br>*Round [2358] to the nearest 1000.*<br><br>*Which digit is important when you round a four-digit number to the nearest multiple of 1000?* | Can the pupil round a four-digit number to the nearest multiple of 1000?<br><br>Can the pupil explain how to round a four-digit number to the nearest 1000? |
| Once again, point to several of the four-digit numbers in turn, asking questions similar to the ones shown here that require the pupil to round the number to the nearest multiple of 100. | *What is [9413] rounded to the nearest multiple of 100?*<br><br>*Round [1584] to the nearest 100.*<br><br>*What do you have to do when you round a four-digit number to the nearest 100?* | Can the pupil round a four-digit number to the nearest multiple of 100?<br><br>Can the pupil explain how to round a four-digit number to the nearest 100? |
| Once more, point to several of the four-digit numbers in turn, asking questions similar to the ones shown here that require the pupil to round the number to the nearest multiple of 10. | *What is [1584] rounded to the nearest multiple of ten?*<br><br>*Round [6249] to the nearest ten.*<br><br>*Which digit is important when you round a four-digit number to the nearest multiple of ten?* | Can the pupil round a four-digit number to the nearest multiple of 10?<br><br>Can the pupil explain how to round a four-digit number to the nearest 10? |

## What to do for those pupils working *below* or *above* expectations

Refer to the 'Tracking back and forward through the Mathematics National Curriculum attainment targets' charts on pages 310–320.

# Number – Number and place value

## National Curriculum attainment target

- Solve number and practical problems that involve all of the above and with increasingly large positive numbers

## Prerequisite checklist

Can the pupil:

- describe patterns and relationships involving numbers?
- describe ways of solving problems and puzzles?
- present solutions to problems and puzzles in an organised way?
- explain choices and decisions, orally or using pictures?

## Success criteria

A. Identify patterns, properties and relationships involving numbers

B. Represent the information in a problem or puzzle

C. Use these to find a solution and present it in context

D. Explain reasoning and methods

## Resources

1–9 digit cards

Resource 8: Number puzzles

pencil and paper (per pupil)

### NOTES

- Provide the pupil(s) with pencil and paper.
- Choose one of the following problems and present it to the pupil(s).
- The same Success criteria, as identified above, apply to each of the following four number problems.
- Choose other problems until the pupil has sufficiently demonstrated their ability to solve number problems and practical problems involving number and place value.

## Assessment Task

### Number Problem 1:

- Recognise multiples of 2, 3, 4, 5, 6, 7, 8, 9, 10, 25, 50 and 100
- Find 10, 100 or 1000 more or less than a given number
- Count backwards through zero to include negative numbers
- Recognise the place value of each digit in a number with up to four digits
- Order and compare numbers to 10 000
- Round any number to the nearest 10, 100 or 1000

#### What to do

Choose four digit cards and place them face up in front of the pupil, e.g. | 7 | | 5 | | 2 | | 1 |

Ask questions similar to the ones on page 38 that require the pupil to demonstrate their understanding of number and place value.

- *Choose three cards to make a three-digit number that is an even number.*
- *Choose two cards to make a two-digit number that is a multiple of [9/3/4/7/25].*
- *Choose two cards to make a two-digit number that is a square number.*
- *Choose two cards to make a two-digit number that is a factor of [96/100/63].*
- *Choose three cards to make a three-digit number that rounds to [530] when rounded to the nearest multiple of ten.*
- *Choose three cards to make a three-digit number that rounds to [200] when rounded to the nearest multiple of 100.*
- *Arrange these four cards to make a four-digit number that rounds to [6000] when rounded to the nearest multiple of 1000.*
- *Arrange these four cards to make a four-digit number that is between [4800] and [6800].*
- *Look at the four-digit number you have just made. What is [10 more/100 more/1000 more/10 less/100 less/1000 less] than this number?*
- *Choose any digit card. Count back in ones from this number until I say stop.*
- *Choose a different digit card. This time count back in twos from this number until I say stop.*

## What to look out for

Can the pupil use the digit cards to solve number problems involving place value and counting, reading, comparing, ordering and rounding whole numbers to 10 000 and beyond?

Repeat, choosing another set of four (or five) digit cards, asking similar questions to those above.

## Number Problem 2:

- Recognise the place value of each digit in a number with up to four digits
- Identify, represent and estimate numbers using different representations
- Order and compare numbers to 10 000

| What to do | What to say | What to look out for |
|---|---|---|
| Show the pupil the abacus problem on Resource 8. | *Look at this problem.*<br><br>*How might you begin working out the solution?* | Does the pupil know how to begin to solve the problem?<br><br>Does the pupil work in a systematic way? |
| Allow the pupil sufficient time to work on the problem. If necessary, ask appropriate questions to encourage the pupil as they progress through the problem. | *What other numbers can you make using these beads that have the same number of [thousands/hundreds/tens/ones]?*<br><br>*What are all the different possibilities? How can you be sure that you have accounted for them all?* | Does the pupil record the numbers in a systematic way?<br><br>Can the pupil identify all ten numbers?<br><br>Can the pupil order the numbers, smallest to largest? |

**Answers**

7999, 8899, 8989, 8998, 9799, 9889, 9898, 9979, 9988 and 9997

## Number Problem 3:

• Count on or back in steps of a constant size

| What to do | What to say | What to look out for |
|---|---|---|
| Show the pupil the four number sequences on Resource 8.<br><br>Referring to each sequence in turn, ask questions similar to the ones shown here.<br><br>If necessary, tell the pupil that:<br>  – the second sequence has two different alternating rules<br>  – the third sequence has a constant changing rule<br>  – in the fourth sequence they need to identify the rule and the missing digit(s) in each number in the sequence.<br><br>If further help is necessary, assist the pupil in identifying the rule(s). | *Look at this number sequence.*<br><br>*What do you notice about it?*<br><br>*Can you see any patterns?*<br><br>*What are the rules for this pattern?*<br><br>*What do you think will be the next number in this pattern?*<br><br>*How do you know that that is the next number in the sequence?* | Does the pupil recognise the pattern(s)/rule(s) in the number sequence?<br><br>Can the pupil write the next three numbers/identify the missing digits in the number sequence? |

**Answers**

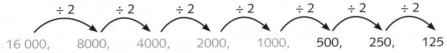

16 000,   8000,   4000,   2000,   1000,   500,   250,   125

Rule: Divide by 2 each time.

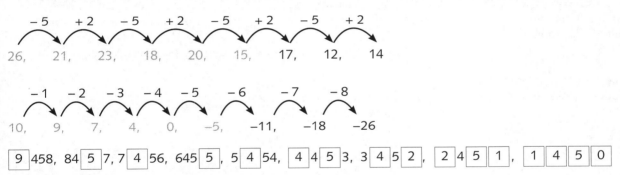

26,   21,   23,   18,   20,   15,   17,   12,   14

10,   9,   7,   4,   0,   −5,   −11,   −18   −26

9 | 458, 84| 5 |7, 7| 4 |56, 645| 5 |, 5| 4 |54, | 4 | 4 | 5 |3, 3| 4 | 5 |2, | 2 | 4 | 5 | 1, | 1 | 4 | 5 | 0

Rule: The thousands and the ones digits decrease by 1 each time.

## Number Problem 4:

• Investigate a statement involving numbers and test it with examples

| What to do | What to say | What to look out for |
|---|---|---|
| Show the pupil the five 'True or false?' statements on Resource 8. | *What are your first thoughts about this statement?* | Can the pupil explain their reasoning? |
| Referring to each of the first four statements in turn, ask questions similar to the ones show here: | *Is it true or false?*<br><br>*Why do you think that?* | Can the pupil justify their decision by providing suitable examples? |
| Extend the investigation further by referring to the final statement: *'The sum of three consecutive numbers equals an odd number.'* | *Can you give me some examples to justify your decision?* | Does the pupil recognise that the statement is both true and false depending on the three consecutive numbers? |

**Answers**

The sum of two consecutive numbers equals an odd number. **True**

The sum of two even numbers equals an even number. **True**

The sum of two odd numbers equals an odd number. **False**

The sum of an odd number and an even number equals an odd number. **True**

The sum of three consecutive numbers equals an odd number. E + O + E = O (**True**) / O + E + O = E (**False**)

## Number Problem 5:

• Recognise multiples of 5
• Recognise the place value of each digit in a number with up to four digits
• Order and compare numbers to 10 000

| What to do | What to say | What to look out for |
|---|---|---|
| Show the pupil the two 'What is the number?' problems on Resource 8.<br><br>Referring to each problem in turn, ask questions similar to the ones shown here: | *What might the number be?*<br><br>*Does it fulfil all of the conditions given?*<br><br>*Explain to me why you are certain that this is the number.* | Can the pupil identify the number?<br><br>Can the pupil justify their decision? |

**Answers**

789

2345 or 3245

## What to do for those pupils working *below* or *above* expectations

Refer to the 'Tracking back and forward through the Mathematics National Curriculum attainment targets' charts on pages 310–320.

# Number – Number and place value

## National Curriculum attainment target

- Read Roman numerals to 100 (I to C) and know that over time, the numeral system changed to include the concept of zero and place value

## Prerequisite checklist

Can the pupil:

- read, write, order and compare numbers to 10 000 and recognise the value of each digit?

## Success criteria

**A.** Read Roman numerals to 100 (I to C)
**B.** Write Roman numerals to 100 (I to C)
**C.** Understand the concept of zero, including as a placeholder

## Resources

Resource 3: Numbers to 10 000
Resource 9: Roman numerals
pencil and paper (per pupil)

## Assessment Task

**Success criterion A:** Read Roman numerals to 100 (I to C)

| What to do | What to say | What to look out for |
|---|---|---|
| Place Resource 9 on the table in front of the pupil.<br><br>Discuss the sheet with the pupil. | *What can you see on this sheet?*<br><br>*What can you tell me about these numbers?* | Can the pupil recognise numbers written in Roman numerals? |
| Point to the numbers in turn, asking the pupil to read the number. | *What is this number?*<br><br>*What does this number read?* | Can the pupil read numbers written in Roman numerals? |

Continue until the pupil has sufficiently demonstrated their ability to read Roman numerals to 100 (I to C).

**Answers**

## Success criterion B: Write Roman numerals to 100 (I to C)

| What to do | What to say | What to look out for |
|---|---|---|
| Place Resource 3 on the table in front of the pupil and provide the pupil with pencil and paper.<br><br>Point to each of the one- and two-digit numbers in turn, asking the pupil to write the number using Roman numerals. | *Write this number in Roman numerals.*<br><br>*How would you write this number using Roman numerals?* | Can the pupil write numbers in Roman numerals? |

Continue until the pupil has sufficiently demonstrated their ability to write Roman numerals to 100 (I to C).

### Answers

| 2 = II | 5 = V | 7 = VII | 8 = VIII |
|---|---|---|---|
| 14 = XIV | 39 = XXXIX | 65 = LXV | 93 = XCIII |

## Success criterion C: Understand the concept of zero, including as a placeholder

| What to do | What to say | What to look out for |
|---|---|---|
|  | *What does 'zero' mean?*<br><br>*Why is zero so important to our number system?*<br><br>*What is the purpose of the zero?*<br><br>*Does it serve any other purposes?* | Can the pupil demonstrate an understanding of the concept of zero, including as a way of representing nought or nothing, and as a placeholder in place value? |
| Referring to Resource 3, point to the numbers 702, 5106 and 7031 in turn, asking the pupil to explain the significance of the zero.<br><br>Ask questions similar to the ones shown here: | *What can you tell me about the zero in this number?*<br><br>*What would happen if zero wasn't one of the digits in this number?*<br><br>*Why is zero such an important digit on this number?* | Can the pupil explain the significance of zero as a placeholder?<br><br>Does the pupil realise that without the zero the value of all of the other digits in the number changes? |

## What to do for those pupils working *below* or *above* expectations

Refer to the 'Tracking back and forward through the Mathematics National Curriculum attainment targets' charts on pages 310–320.

# Number – Addition and subtraction

## NOTE

- The two National Curriculum attainment targets below have been combined into one Assessment Task, as the skills of estimating, calculating and checking answers to written calculations should be seen as a process and therefore need to be assessed simultaneously.

## National Curriculum attainment targets

- Add and subtract numbers with up to 4 digits using the formal written methods of columnar addition and subtraction where appropriate
- Estimate and use inverse operations to check answers to a calculation

## Prerequisite checklist

Can the pupil:

- read, write, order and compare numbers to at least 10 000 and determine the value of each digit?
- recall and use addition and subtraction facts to 20 and 100, including those involving multiples of 10, 100 and 1000?
- add and subtract numbers with up to three digits, using formal written methods of columnar addition and subtraction?

## Success criteria

A. Estimate the answer to an addition calculation
B. Add numbers with up to four digits using the formal written method of columnar addition
C. Check the answer to an addition calculation
D. Estimate the answer to a subtraction calculation
E. Subtract numbers with up to four digits using the formal written method of columnar subtraction
F. Check the answer to a subtraction calculation

## Resources

pencil and paper or Resource 10: Estimate, calculate and check (per pupil)

## Assessment Task

**Success criterion A:** Estimate the answer to an addition calculation

| What to do | What to say | What to look out for |
|---|---|---|
| On a sheet of paper or on Resource 10, write an addition calculation in the form: ThHTO + HTO, e.g. 4756 + 387 or ThHTO + ThHTO, e.g. 6574 + 2465. | *What is the approximate answer to this calculation?* | Can the pupil offer an approximation of the answer – verbally or written? |

**Success criterion B:** Add numbers with up to four digits using the formal written method of columnar addition

| What to do | What to say | What to look out for |
|---|---|---|
| | *Use a written method to find the answer to this calculation.* | Does the pupil have a thorough understanding of place value and how to apply this knowledge when calculating? |
| | | Does the pupil have instant recall of the addition number facts to 20 and the related facts involving multiples of 10, 100 and 1000? |
| | | Does the pupil use an effective and efficient written method? |
| | *As you work out the answer, can you explain to me what you're doing?* | Is the pupil able to explain their method? |

43

## Success criterion C: Check the answer to an addition calculation

| What to do | What to say | What to look out for |
|---|---|---|
| | *Now check your answer to make sure that it is correct.* | How does the pupil check their answer? |

Repeat until the pupil has sufficiently demonstrated their ability to estimate, calculate and check the answer to calculations in the form ThHTO + HTO and ThHTO + ThHTO.

## Success criterion D: Estimate the answer to a subtraction calculation

| What to do | What to say | What to look out for |
|---|---|---|
| On a sheet of paper or on Resource 10, write a subtraction calculation in the form: ThHTO – HTO, e.g. 8562 – 673 or ThHTO – ThHTO, e.g. 5462 – 1864. | *What is the approximate answer to this calculation?* | Can the pupil offer an approximation of the answer – verbally or written? |

## Success criterion E: Subtract numbers with up to four digits using the formal written method of columnar subtraction

| What to do | What to say | What to look out for |
|---|---|---|
| | *Use a written method to find the answer to this calculation.* | Does the pupil have a thorough understanding of place value and how to apply this knowledge when calculating? |
| | | Does the pupil have instant recall of the subtraction number facts to 20 and the related facts involving multiples of 10, 100 and 1000? |
| | | Does the pupil use an effective and efficient written method? |
| | *As you work out the answer, can you explain to me what you're doing?* | Is the pupil able to explain their method? |

## Success criterion F: Check the answer to a subtraction calculation

| What to do | What to say | What to look out for |
|---|---|---|
| | *Now check your answer to make sure that it is correct.* | How does the pupil check their answer? |

Repeat until the pupil has sufficiently demonstrated their ability to estimate, calculate and check the answer to calculations in the form ThHTO – HTO and ThHTO – ThHTO.

### What to do for those pupils working *below* or *above* expectations

Refer to the 'Tracking back and forward through the Mathematics National Curriculum attainment targets' charts on pages 310–320.

# Number – Addition and subtraction
# Number – Multiplication and division

## NOTES

- The two National Curriculum attainment targets below have been combined into one Assessment Task, as Success criterion B requires the pupil to be able to 'correctly identify which operation(s) to use' when solving word problems. Therefore the pupil needs to be presented with a range of problems that involve all four operations.

- These Assessment Tasks, Assessment Task 27 and Assessment Task 33 all have the same four Success criteria. The difference between these Assessment Tasks is as follows:
  - Assessment Tasks 12 and 17: Solve problems involving all four operations
  - Assessment Task 27: Solve measure and money problems involving fractions and decimals to two decimal places
  - Assessment Task 33: Solve problems involving time.

## National Curriculum attainment targets

- Solve addition and subtraction two-step problems in contexts, deciding which operations and methods to use and why
- Solve problems involving multiplying and adding, including using the distributive law to multiply two digit numbers by one digit, integer scaling problems and harder correspondence problems such as n objects are connected to m objects

## Prerequisite checklist

Can the pupil:

- calculate mentally with increasingly large numbers?
- add, subtract, multiply and divide using a written method?
- solve problems involving addition, subtraction, multiplication or division in contexts of numbers or measures?

- identify and record the information or calculation needed to solve a problem?
- carry out the steps or calculations and check the solution in the context of the problem?
- present solutions to problems in an organised way, explaining decisions, methods and results?

## Success criteria

A. Read and understand the problem
B. Correctly identify which operation(s) to use
C. Carry out the calculation(s) to obtain the correct answer using an appropriate method
D. Check the answer using an effective method

## Resources

Resource 11: Word problems
pencil and paper (per pupil)

## Assessment Task

**Success criterion A:** Read and understand the problem

| What to do | What to say | What to look out for |
|---|---|---|
| Provide the pupil with pencil and paper and one of the word problem cards from Resource 11. | *Read the problem on your card.*<br><br>*What is your problem about?*<br><br>*What do you have to find out?* | Can the pupil read and understand the problem? |

## Success criterion B: Correctly identify which operation(s) to use

| What to do | What to say | What to look out for |
|---|---|---|
| Ask the pupil to suggest which operation(s) they need to use to work out the answer to the word problem. | *Which operation(s) do you need to use to work out the answer to your problem?* | Can the pupil correctly identify which operation(s) to use? |
| Ask the pupil to explain how they know which operation to use. | *How do you know you need to [add/subtract/multiply/divide]? What clues are there in the problem?* | |

## Success criterion C: Carry out the calculation(s) to obtain the correct answer using an appropriate method

| What to do | What to say | What to look out for |
|---|---|---|
| Ask the pupil to write down the calculation(s) needed to solve the problem and work out the answer. | *On your sheet of paper I want you to write down the calculation(s) needed to solve your problem and then I want you to work out the answer.* | Can the pupil write the correct calculation(s)? Does the pupil obtain the correct answer to the calculation(s)? Does the pupil use an appropriate calculation method? Does the pupil obtain the correct answer to the problem? |
| Encourage the pupil to talk about the method they used to obtain their answer. | *Explain to me how you worked out the answer to this problem.* | Can the pupil explain their method of working out the answer to the problem? |

## Success criterion D: Check the answer using an effective method

| What to do | What to say | What to look out for |
|---|---|---|
| Ask the pupil to check the answer to their problem. | *Are you sure that the answer to this problem is right?* *How can you be so sure?* | Can the pupil check their answer using an effective method? |

Repeat Success criteria A–D until the pupil has sufficiently demonstrated their ability to solve word problems.

## What to do for those pupils working *below* or *above* expectations

Refer to the 'Tracking back and forward through the Mathematics National Curriculum attainment targets' charts on pages 310–320.

**Answers**

Resource 11: Word problems

| Question | Problem involving | Number of steps required/ Operation(s) required | Answer |
|---|---|---|---|
| 1 | Time | 3 steps: addition, subtraction and subtraction | 1 hr 35 min |
| 2 | Money | 2 steps: addition or multiplication, and subtraction | £3.78 |
| 3 | Real life | 1 step: division (fractions) | 6450 |
| 4 | Capacity | 2 steps: multiplication and subtraction | 30 litres |
| 5 | Real life | 2 steps: addition and subtraction | 44 |
| 6 | Money | 1 step: division | £8.50 |
| 7 | Real life | 1 step: geometry – position and direction | West |
| 8 | Length | 1 step: multiplication | 368 km |
| 9 | Length | 1 step: division | 35 cm |
| 10 | Temperature | 1 step: subtraction | −2°C |
| 11 | Length | 1 step: multiplication | 450 |
| 12 | Money | 1 step: multiplication | £2912 |
| 13 | Money | 2 steps: addition and subtraction | £19 |
| 14 | Mass | 2 steps: addition and division | 1 kg 750 g |
| 15 | Money | 2 steps: addition and subtraction | £867 |
| 16 | Real life | 3 steps: multiplication, division (fractions) and subtraction | 33 |
| 17 | Money | 1 step: division | £2.60 |
| 18 | Real life | 2 steps: multiplication and multiplication | 1152 |
| 19 | Money | 1 step: addition | £3.88 |
| 20 | Real life | 2 steps: addition and division | 15 |

# Number – Multiplication and division

## National Curriculum attainment target

- Recall multiplication and division facts for multiplication tables up to 12 × 12

## Prerequisite checklist

Can the pupil:
- recall and use multiplication and division facts for the 2, 3, 4, 5, 8 and 10 multiplication tables?
- recognise multiples of 2, 3, 4, 5, 8 and 10?

## Success criteria

A. Recognise multiples of numbers to 12 up to the 12th multiple

B. Recall multiplication facts for the 2, 5 and 10 multiplication tables

C. Recall multiplication facts for the 3, 4 and 8 multiplication tables

D. Recall multiplication facts for the 6, 7, 9, 11 and 12 multiplication tables

E. Recall division facts for the 2, 5 and 10 multiplication tables

F. Recall division facts for the 3, 4 and 8 multiplication tables

G. Recall division facts for the 6, 7, 9, 11 and 12 multiplication tables

## Resources

Resource 12: Multiples (3)

Resource 13: Multiplication and division facts (per pupil)

pencil (per pupil)

## Assessment Task

**Success criterion A:** Recognise multiples of numbers to 12 up to the 12th multiple

| What to do | What to say | What to look out for |
|---|---|---|
| Display Resource 12 and point to a number that is a multiple of 7. | *Is this number a multiple of seven?*<br><br>*Now point to another multiple of seven.*<br><br>*Can you point to some other multiples of seven?* | Can the pupil identify a multiple of 7? |
| Only if considered appropriate, ask the pupil to explain how they know that the number is a multiple of 7. | *How do you know that this number is a multiple of seven?* | Can the pupil explain why a number is a multiple of 7? |
| Point to a number, e.g. 16. | *Sixteen is a multiple of what number?*<br><br>*What other number is 16 a multiple of?*<br><br>*Are there any other numbers that 16 is a multiple of?* | Can the pupil identify all the factors of 16? |

Repeat for multiples of each number to 12, up to the 12th multiple, until the pupil has sufficiently demonstrated their ability to recognise multiples of numbers to 12 up to the 12th multiple.

**Success criterion B:** Recall multiplication facts for the 2, 5 and 10 multiplication tables

| What to do | What to say | What to look out for |
|---|---|---|
| Provide the pupil with a copy of Resource 13 and a pencil.<br><br>Draw the pupil's attention to the first pentagon in the top row of pentagons. | *Look at the first pentagon on your sheet. I'm going to call out a number. I then want you to multiply this number by two and write the answer in the top right-hand section of the pentagon. I'm then going to call out another number and I want you to multiply this number by two and, working clockwise, write the answer in the next section of the pentagon. Altogether I'm going to call out five numbers and I want you to multiply each of these numbers by two. Got the idea? Let's begin.* | |
| In turn, call out the following numbers, quickening the pace as the pupil becomes more confident with the task. | *2*<br>*8*<br>*5*<br>*3*<br>*7* | Does the pupil have instant recall of the multiplication facts for the 2 multiplication table? |
| Draw the pupil's attention to the second pentagon in the top row. | *Now look at the second pentagon. This time when I say a number I want you to multiply that number by five. Ready?* | |
| In turn, call out the following numbers. | *8*<br>*11*<br>*5*<br>*4*<br>*6* | Does the pupil have instant recall of the multiplication facts for the 5 multiplication table? |
| Next, draw the pupil's attention to the third pentagon in the top row. | *Now look at the third pentagon. This time when I say a number I want you to multiply that number by ten. Ready?* | |
| In turn, call out the following numbers. | *4*<br>*9*<br>*6*<br>*3*<br>*7* | Does the pupil have instant recall of the multiplication facts for the 10 multiplication table? |

**Success criterion C:** Recall multiplication facts for the 3, 4 and 8 multiplication tables

Repeat as above for the 3 multiplication table, referring to the first pentagon in the second row and asking the pupil to multiply each of the following numbers by 3: 9, 7, 3, 4 and 12.

Repeat as above for the 4 multiplication table, referring to the second pentagon in the second row and asking the pupil to multiply each of the following numbers by 4: 6, 2, 9, 4 and 8.

Repeat as above for the 8 multiplication table, referring to the third pentagon in the second row and asking the pupil to multiply each of the following numbers by 8: 7, 12, 3, 8 and 6.

**Success criterion D:** Recall multiplication facts for the 6, 7, 9, 11 and 12 multiplication tables

Repeat as above for the 6 multiplication table, referring to the first pentagon in the third row and asking the pupil to multiply each of the following numbers by 6: 9, 3, 7, 11 and 2.

Repeat as above for the 7 multiplication table, referring to the second pentagon in the third row and asking the pupil to multiply each of the following numbers by 7: 4, 12, 5, 7 and 11.

Repeat as above for the 9 multiplication table, referring to the third pentagon in the third row and asking the pupil to multiply each of the following numbers by 9: 7, 2, 8, 12 and 5.

Repeat as above for the 11 multiplication table, referring to the fourth pentagon in the third row and asking the pupil to multiply each of the following numbers by 11: 8, 4, 9, 10 and 12.

Repeat as above for the 12 multiplication table, referring to the fifth pentagon in the third row and asking the pupil to multiply each of the following numbers by 12: 6, 3, 7, 12 and 4.

**Success criterion E:** Recall division facts for the 2, 5 and 10 multiplication tables

| What to do | What to say | What to look out for |
|---|---|---|
| Draw the pupil's attention to the first pentagon in the fourth row of pentagons. | *Look at the first pentagon in the fourth row. I'm going to call out a number. I then want you to divide this number by two and write the answer in the top right-hand section of the pentagon. I'm then going to call out another number and I want you to divide this number by two and, working clockwise, write the answer in the next section of the pentagon. Altogether I'm going to call out five numbers and I want you to divide each of these numbers by two. Got the idea? Let's begin.* | |
| In turn, call out the following numbers, quickening the pace as the pupil becomes more confident with the task. | *22*<br>*8*<br>*12*<br>*18*<br>*24* | Does the pupil have instant recall of the division facts for the 2 multiplication table? |
| Draw the pupil's attention to the second pentagon in the fourth row. | *Now look at the second pentagon. This time when I say a number I want you to divide that number by five. Ready?* | |
| In turn, call out the following numbers. | *15*<br>*45*<br>*35*<br>*60*<br>*50* | Does the pupil have instant recall of the division facts for the 5 multiplication table? |
| Next, draw the pupil's attention to the third pentagon in the fourth row. | *Now look at the third pentagon. This time when I say a number I want you to divide that number by ten. Ready?* | |
| In turn, call out the following numbers. | *80*<br>*110*<br>*50*<br>*100*<br>*120* | Does the pupil have instant recall of the division facts for the 10 multiplication table? |

**Success criterion F:** Recall division facts for the 3, 4 and 8 multiplication tables

Repeat as above for the 3 multiplication table, referring to the first pentagon in the fifth row and asking the pupil to divide each of the following numbers by 3: 30, 18, 6, 33 and 24.

Repeat as above for the 4 multiplication table, referring to the second pentagon in the fifth row and asking the pupil to divide each of the following numbers by 4: 44, 28, 12, 48 and 20.

Repeat as above for the 8 multiplication table, referring to the third pentagon in the fifth row and asking the pupil to divide each of the following numbers by 8: 80, 16, 40, 32 and 72.

**Success criterion 6:** Recall division facts for the 6, 7, 9, 11 and 12 multiplication tables

Repeat as above for the 6 multiplication table, referring to the first pentagon in the sixth row and asking the pupil to divide each of the following numbers by 6: 36, 72, 30, 48 and 24.

Repeat as above for the 7 multiplication table, referring to the second pentagon in the sixth row and asking the pupil to divide each of the following numbers by 7: 21, 56, 14, 42 and 63.

Repeat as above for the 9 multiplication table, referring to the third pentagon in the sixth row and asking the pupil to divide each of the following numbers by 9: 81, 27, 54, 36 and 99.

Repeat as above for the 11 multiplication table, referring to the fourth pentagon in the sixth row and asking the pupil to divide each of the following numbers by 11: 55, 22, 121, 66 and 110.

Repeat as above for the 12 multiplication table, referring to the fifth pentagon in the sixth row and asking the pupil to divide each of the following numbers by 12: 96, 132, 24, 50 and 108.

## What to do for those pupils working *below* or *above* expectations

Refer to the 'Tracking back and forward through the Mathematics National Curriculum attainment targets' charts on pages 310–320.

# Number – Multiplication and division

**NOTE**

- Both this Assessment Task and Assessment Task 15: *Recognise and use factor pairs and commutativity in mental calculations* include a Success criterion that involves pupils multiplying together three numbers. If appropriate, only assess the pupil using the Success criterion from one of these two Assessment Tasks.

## National Curriculum attainment target

- Use place value, known and derived facts to multiply and divide mentally, including: multiplying by 0 and 1; dividing by 1; multiplying together three numbers

## Prerequisite checklist

Does the pupil:

- have an understanding of the commutative law and how it applies to multiplication?

Can the pupil:

- recall multiplication and division facts for multiplication tables up to 12 × 12?
- multiply a one- or two-digit number by 10 or 100?

## Success criteria

**A.** Use place value and known multiplication facts to derive related facts involving multiples of 10 and 100, e.g. 60 × 8, 800 × 7 and 30 × 90

**B.** Use place value and known division facts to derive related facts involving multiples of 10, e.g. 420 ÷ 7

**C.** Understand the effect of multiplying a number by 0 and 1 and dividing a number by 1

**D.** Use commutativity to multiply together three numbers

## Resources

Resource 14: Multiplying multiples of 10 and 100 (enlarged to A3)

two small counters

Resource 15: Dividing multiples of 10 (enlarged to A3)

Resource 16: Multiplying together three numbers (per pupil)

pencil (per pupil)

Resource 3: Numbers to 10 000 (optional)

## Assessment Task

**Success criterion A:** Use place value and known multiplication facts to derive related facts involving multiples of 10 and 100, e.g. 60 × 8, 800 × 7 and 30 × 90

| What to do | What to say | What to look out for |
|---|---|---|
| Place Resource 14 on the table in front of the pupil. | *I'm going to put these counters on two numbers and I want you to multiply the numbers together as quickly as you can. Ready? Let's go!* | |
| Place a counter on a one-digit number and a multiple of 10, e.g. 8 and 60. Occasionally ask questions similar to the ones shown here: | *Multiply these two numbers together.*<br><br>*What is [60 multiplied by eight]?* | Is the pupil able to use their understanding of place value and known multiplication facts to multiply a multiple of 10 by a one-digit number? |
| Occasionally ask the pupil to explain how they worked out the answer to the calculation. | *How did you work that out?* | |
| Repeat several times until the pupil has sufficiently demonstrated their ability to multiply a multiple of 10 by a one-digit number. | | |

| What to do | What to say | What to look out for |
|---|---|---|
| Place a counter on a one-digit number and a multiple of 100, e.g. 7 and 800. Occasionally ask questions similar to the ones shown here: | *What is the product of these two numbers?*<br><br>*Multiply these two numbers together.* | Is the pupil able to use their understanding of place value and known multiplication facts to multiply a multiple of 100 by a one-digit number? |
| Occasionally ask the pupil to explain how they worked out the answer to the calculation. | *How do you know this is the answer?* | |
| Repeat several times until the pupil has sufficiently demonstrated their ability to multiply a multiple of 100 by a one-digit number. | | |
| If appropriate, extend the task by placing a counter on two multiples of 10, e.g. 30 and 90. Occasionally ask questions similar to the ones shown here: | *Multiply these two multiples of ten together.*<br><br>*What is [30 times 90]?* | Is the pupil able to use their understanding of place value and known multiplication facts to multiply two multiples of 10? |
| Occasionally ask the pupil to explain how they worked out the answer to the calculation. | *What multiplication fact did you use to help you work out the answer to this?* | |
| Repeat several times until the pupil has sufficiently demonstrated their ability to multiply two multiples of 10. | | |

**Success criterion B:** Use place value and known division facts to derive related facts involving multiples of 10, e.g. 420 ÷ 7

| What to do | What to say | What to look out for |
|---|---|---|
| Place Resource 15 on the table in front of the pupil.<br><br>Referring to the first star, point to one of the multiples of 10 on the star, e.g. 160. | *What is [160 divided by 2]?* | Is the pupil able to use their understanding of place value and known division facts to divide a multiple of 10 by a one-digit number? |
| Repeat, pointing to other multiples of 10 on the different stars. | | |
| Occasionally ask the pupil to explain how they worked out the answer to the calculation. | *How did you work that out?*<br><br>*What division fact did you know that helped you work out the answer?* | |

Repeat several times until the pupil has sufficiently demonstrated their ability to use place value and known division facts to derive related facts involving multiples of 10.

**Success criterion C:** Understand the effect of multiplying a number by 0 and 1 and dividing a number by 1

| What to do | What to say | What to look out for |
|---|---|---|
| Place Resource 14 on the table in front of the pupil.<br><br>Place one counter on 1 and the other counter on any one of the numbers 2 to 12, e.g. 8. | *What is [eight] multiplied by one?* | Does the pupil recognise that if a number is multiplied by 1, the answer is always that same number? |
| Keep the counter on 1 and move the other counter to another number from 2 to 12, e.g. 11. | *What is [11] times one?* | |
| Repeat above, keeping the counter on 1 and moving the other counter to other numbers on the sheet, e.g. 60 and 500. | | |
| If necessary, place Resource 3 on the table in front of the pupil and, pointing to different numbers in turn, ask the pupil to multiply the number by 1. | *What is [65/702/6249] multiplied by one?* | |
| Next, place one counter on 0 on Resource 14 and the other counter on any one of the numbers 2 to 12, e.g. 5. | *What is [five] multiplied by zero?* | Does the pupil recognise that if a number is multiplied by zero, the answer is always zero? |
| Keep the counter on 0 and move the other counter to another number from 2 to 12, e.g. 10. | *What is [ten] times zero?* | |
| Repeat above, keeping the counter on 0 and moving the other counter to other numbers on the sheet, e.g. 40 and 900. | | |
| If necessary, point to numbers on Resource 3 and ask the pupil to multiply each number by 0. | *What is [39/236/8697] multiplied by zero?* | |
| Finally, place one counter back on 1 on Resource 14 and the other counter on any one of the numbers 2 to 12, e.g. 4. | *What is [four] divided by one?* | Does the pupil recognise that if a number is divided by 1, the answer is always that same number? |
| Keep the counter on 0 and move the other counter to another number from 2 to 12, e.g. 7. | *What is [seven] divided by one?* | |
| Repeat above, keeping the counter on 0 and moving the other counter to other numbers on the sheet, e.g. 80 and 300. | | |
| If necessary, point to numbers on Resource 3 and ask the pupil to divide each number by 1. | *What is [93/827/2358] divided by one?* | |

**Success criterion D:** Use commutativity to multiply together three numbers

| What to do | What to say | What to look out for |
|---|---|---|
| Place Resource 16 on the table in front of the pupil and provide them with a pencil.<br><br>**NOTE**<br>For each of the calculations on the sheet, if the pupil is able to work out the answer entirely mentally, there is no need for the pupil to make any recordings on the sheet.<br><br>Draw the pupil's attention to the first calculation, i.e. 3 × 9 × 2 =. | *What is the answer to this calculation?*<br><br>*How did you work that out?*<br><br>*What could you do to make this calculation easier to work out?* | Does the pupil use the commutative law to change the order of the three numbers to make the calculation more effective and efficient, e.g. 3 × 9 × 2 = 3 × 2 × 9? |

Repeat for other calculations on the sheet until the pupil has sufficiently demonstrated their ability to multiply together three numbers.

## What to do for those pupils working *below* or *above* expectations

Refer to the 'Tracking back and forward through the Mathematics National Curriculum attainment targets' charts on pages 310–320.

# Number – Multiplication and division

## NOTE

- Both this Assessment Task and Assessment Task 14: *Use place value, known and derived facts to multiply and divide mentally, including: multiplying by 0 and 1, dividing by 1; multiplying together three numbers* include a Success criterion that involves pupils multiplying together three numbers. If appropriate, only assess the pupil using the Success criterion from one of these two Assessment Tasks.

## National Curriculum attainment target

- Recognise and use factor pairs and commutativity in mental calculations

## Prerequisite checklist

Does the pupil:

- have an understanding of the commutative law and how it applies to multiplication?

Can the pupil:

- recall multiplication facts for multiplication tables up to 12 × 12?
- use place value and known multiplication facts to multiply mentally?

## Success criteria

A. Recognise pairs of factors in two-digit numbers
B. Use commutativity to multiply together three numbers
C. Use factor pairs and commutativity to multiply a two-digit number by a one-digit number

## Resources

Resource 17: Two-digit numbers (made into number cards)
Resource 16: Multiplying together three numbers (per pupil)
Resource 18: Mental multiplication (per pupil)
pencil and paper (per pupil)

## Assessment Task

### Success criterion A: Recognise pairs of factors in two-digit numbers

| What to do | What to say | What to look out for |
|---|---|---|
| | *What is a factor?* | Does the pupil describe a factor as a whole number that will divide exactly into another whole number? |
| Provide the pupil with pencil and paper. | *I'm going to give you a two-digit number card and I want you to write down all the pairs of factors for that number.* | |
| Place a two-digit number card on the table in front of the pupil, e.g. 40. | *Is two a factor of this number?*<br><br>*How do you know?*<br><br>*What about five?*<br><br>*What are the other factors of [40]?*<br><br>*How many factors does your number have?* | Does the pupil work systematically in order to identify pairs of factors?<br><br>Can the pupil recognise all the pairs of factors of the two-digit number? |

Repeat above, giving the pupil other number cards until they have sufficiently demonstrated their ability to identify pairs of factors of two-digit numbers.

**Success criterion B:** Use commutativity to multiply together three numbers

| What to do | What to say | What to look out for |
|---|---|---|
| Place Resource 16 on the table in front of the pupil and provide them with a pencil.<br><br>**NOTE**<br>For each of the calculations on the sheet, if the pupil is able to work out the answer entirely mentally, there is no need for the pupil to make any recordings on the sheet.<br><br>Draw the pupil's attention to the first calculation, i.e. $3 \times 9 \times 2 =$. | *What is the answer to this calculation?*<br><br>*How did you work that out?*<br><br>*What could you do to make this calculation easier to work out?* | Does the pupil use the commutative law to change the order of the three numbers to make the calculation more effective and efficient, e.g. $3 \times 9 \times 2 = 3 \times 2 \times 9$? |

Repeat for other calculations on the sheet until the pupil has sufficiently demonstrated their ability to multiply together three numbers.

**Success criterion C:** Use factor pairs and commutativity to multiply a two-digit number by a one-digit number

| What to do | What to say | What to look out for |
|---|---|---|
| Place Resource 18 on the table in front of the pupil and provide them with a pencil.<br><br>**NOTE**<br>For each of the calculations on the sheet, the pupil should be encouraged to work out the answer mentally, using and applying their knowledge of factor pairs and applying the associative and commutative laws, making appropriate jottings.<br><br>Draw the pupil's attention to the first calculation, i.e. $18 \times 9 =$. | *What is the answer to this calculation?*<br><br>*How might you work it out mentally?*<br><br>*Think about using factor pairs and applying what you know about being able to multiply numbers in any order.* | Does the pupil immediately realise that the calculation can be worked out using factor pairs of 18 and applying the associative and commutative laws, i.e.<br>$18 \times 9 = 2 \times 9 \times 9$<br>$\qquad = 2 \times 81$<br>$\qquad = 162$ |
| If necessary, prompt the pupil to use their knowledge of factor pairs and the associative and commutative laws to work out the answer. | *What are all the factors of 18?*<br>(1, 2, 3, 6, 9 and 18)<br><br>*The factors 2 and 9 would be a good pair to use because multiplying by two, or doubling, is easy.*<br><br>*So, how could rewrite the calculation $18 \times 9$ using the factors 2 and 9? ($2 \times 9 \times 9$)*<br><br>*Remember that multiplication can be done in any order. So, what two numbers would you multiply together first? ($9 \times 9$)*<br><br>*What is nine times nine? (81)*<br><br>*And 81 [multiplied by two/doubled] is? (162)*<br><br>*So what is the answer to 18 multiplied by nine? (162)* | With prompting, is the pupil able to use and apply their knowledge of factor pairs and the associative and commutative laws to work out the answer? |

Repeat for other calculations on the sheet until the pupil has sufficiently demonstrated their ability to use factor pairs and commutativity to multiply a two-digit number by a one-digit number.

## What to do for those pupils working *below* or *above* expectations

Refer to the 'Tracking back and forward through the Mathematics National Curriculum attainment targets' charts on pages 310–320.

# Number – Multiplication and division

## National Curriculum attainment target

- Multiply two-digit and three-digit numbers by a one-digit number using formal written layout

## Prerequisite checklist

Can the pupil:

- recall and use multiplication facts for the multiplication tables up to 10 × 10?
- multiply a one- or two-digit number by 10 or 100?
- recall and use addition and subtraction facts to 20 fluently?
- add a one-digit number to a two-digit number?
- recognise the place value of each digit in a two- and three-digit number?

## Success criteria

**A.** Multiply a two-digit number by a one-digit number
**B.** Multiply a three-digit number by a one-digit number

## Resources

Resource 19: Multiplying two-digit and three-digit numbers (made into cards)

pencil and paper (per pupil)

**NOTE**

- This National Curriculum attainment target requires the pupil to use the formal written method of short multiplication as shown below on the left. If, however, a pupil is not yet able to confidently use this method, then still assess their ability to use one of the other three methods shown below.

Formal written method

$$
\begin{array}{r}
3\ 5\ 6 \\
\times\ _3\ _4\ 7 \\
\hline
2\ 4\ 9\ 2 \\
\hline
\end{array}
$$

Expanded written method

$$
\begin{array}{r}
3\ 5\ 6 \\
\times\qquad 7 \\
\hline
4\ 2\quad (\ 6 \times 7) \\
3\ 5\ 0\quad (\ 50 \times 7) \\
2\ 1\ 0\ 0\quad (300 \times 7) \\
\hline
2\ 4\ 9\ 2 \\
\hline
\end{array}
$$

Grid method

| ×  | 300  | 50  | 6  |        |
|----|------|-----|----|--------|
| 7  | 2100 | 350 | 42 | = 2492 |

Partitioning

$356 \times 7 = (300 \times 7) + (50 \times 7) + (6 \times 7)$
$\qquad\qquad = 2100 + 350 + 42$
$\qquad\qquad = 2492$

## Assessment Task

**Success criterion A:** Multiply a two-digit number by a one-digit number

| What to do | What to say | What to look out for |
|---|---|---|
| Provide the pupil with pencil and paper.<br><br>Place the first calculation from Resource 19 on the table in front of the pupil, i.e. 76 × 8 =. | *What do you think is the approximate answer to this calculation?*<br><br>*How would you work out the exact answer to 76 multiplied by 8?*<br><br>*How will you record your working out?*<br><br>*As you work out the answer, explain to me what you're doing.* | Is the pupil able to offer a reasonable estimate of the answer?<br><br>Does the pupil use an effective and efficient written method?<br><br>Which method does the pupil automatically use:<br>– the formal written method<br>– the expanded written method<br>– the grid method<br>– partitioning?<br><br>Does the pupil have a thorough understanding of place value and how to apply this knowledge when calculating?<br><br>Does the pupil have instant recall of the multiplication facts up to 10 × 10?<br><br>Is the pupil able to multiply a two-digit multiple of 10 by a one-digit number (e.g. 70 × 8)?<br><br>For Success criterion B only:<br>Is the pupil able to multiply a three-digit multiple of 100 by a one-digit number (e.g. 600 x 6)?<br><br>Is the pupil able to succinctly explain their method? |
| Once the pupil has worked out the answer to the calculation, ask them to check their answer. | *Are you certain that your answer is correct? Can you check it for me?* | Is the pupil able to check their answer using an appropriate method? |

If necessary, repeat above for the second and/or third calculation(s) on Resource 19, until the pupil has sufficiently demonstrated their ability to multiply a two-digit number by a one-digit number.

**Success criterion B:** Multiply a three-digit number by a one-digit number

Repeat as above for multiplying a three-digit number by a one-digit number, using the fourth and, if necessary, fifth and/or sixth calculation(s) on Resource 19.

## What to do for those pupils working *below* or *above* expectations

Refer to the 'Tracking back and forward through the Mathematics National Curriculum attainment targets' charts on pages 310–320.

# Number – Fractions (including decimals)

## National Curriculum attainment target

- Recognise and show, using diagrams, families of common equivalent fractions

## Prerequisite checklist

Can the pupil:

- recognise equivalent fractions with small denominators?
- use and apply their knowledge of multiplication and division facts to recognise and show equivalent fractions?

## Success criteria

A. Recognise, using shapes, common equivalent fractions

B. Show, using shapes, common equivalent fractions

C. Use a fraction wall to establish families of common equivalent fractions

## Resources

Resource 20: Equivalent fractions (1)

Resource 21: Equivalent fractions (2) (per pupil)

Resource 22: Fractions wall

Resource 23: Equivalent fractions (3) (per pupil)

coloured pencil (per pupil)

pencil (per pupil)

## NOTE

- Prior to the Assessment Task, cut out the 16 cards from Resource 20. Place the eight cards from the top half of the sheet in one pile and the eight cards from the bottom half of the sheet in a separate pile.

## Assessment Task

### Success criterion A: Recognise, using shapes, common equivalent fractions

| What to do | What to say | What to look out for |
|---|---|---|
| Lay the eight cards from the bottom half of Resource 20 in a random order face up on the table. | | |
| Take one of the eight cards from the top half of Resource 20 and place it in front of the pupil, e.g. | What fraction of this shape is shaded? | Does the pupil recognise the fraction represented on the card? |
| | There is another shape among these eight cards that also has two-thirds shaded. Can you point to that shape? | Does the pupil recognise the equivalent fraction? |
| | How would you describe this fraction? | Is the pupil able to describe the equivalent fraction, i.e. eight twelfths? |

Continue until all eight pairs of equivalent fractions are matched or until the pupil has sufficiently demonstrated their ability to recognise, using shapes, common equivalent fractions.

**Success criterion B:** Show, using shapes, common equivalent fractions

| What to do | What to say | What to look out for |
|---|---|---|
| Lay the eight cards from the top half of Resource 20 in a random order face up on the table.<br><br>Provide the pupil with a copy of Resource 21 and a coloured pencil. | | |
| Take one of the cards and lay it in front of the pupil, e.g. | *What fraction of this shape is shaded?* | Does the pupil recognise the fraction represented on the card? |
| | *Look at all the shapes on your sheet. Can you find a shape where it is possible to shade the shape to show a fraction that is equivalent to [three quarters]?* | Can the pupil identify a shape where it is possible to show an equivalent fraction? |
| | *Can you colour this shape so that it shows a fraction that is equivalent to [three quarters]?* | Can the pupil show the equivalent fraction? |
| | *How would you describe this fraction?* | Is the pupil able to describe the equivalent fraction, e.g. six eighths? |
| If appropriate, ask the pupil to find another equivalent fraction. | *Can you find another shape on your sheet where it is possible to shade the shape to show a fraction that is equivalent to [three quarters]?* | Can the pupil identify another shape where it is possible to show an equivalent fraction? |
| | *Colour this shape so that it shows a fraction that is equivalent to [three quarters].* | Can the pupil show the equivalent fraction? |
| | *How would you describe this fraction?* | Is the pupil able to describe the equivalent fraction, e.g. nine twelfths/twelve sixteenths. |

Continue until the pupil has sufficiently demonstrated their ability to show, using shapes, common equivalent fractions.

**Success criterion C:** Use a fraction wall to establish families of common equivalent fractions

| What to do | What to say | What to look out for |
|---|---|---|
| Place Resource 22 on the table in front of the pupil.<br><br>Ensure that the pupil is familiar with a fraction wall and how it can be used to show families of equivalent fractions. | *This diagram is called a fraction wall. It can be used to help describe and compare fractions, and to find equivalent fractions.*<br><br>*The top row of this fraction wall represents one whole.* | |
| Draw the pupil's attention to the second row on the fraction wall, i.e. $\frac{1}{2}$. | *This row of the fraction wall represents a half.*<br><br>*Using this fraction wall, can you find me another fraction that is equivalent to a half?* | Can the pupil identify a fraction that is equivalent to a half, e.g. $\frac{2}{4}$? |
| Provide the pupil with a copy of Resource 23 and a pencil.<br><br>Ask the pupil to write the fraction they have identified as being equivalent to a half in the '$\frac{1}{2}$' section on the sheet. | *How would you describe this fraction?*<br><br>*Can you write this fraction in the 'half' section of your sheet?* | Is the pupil able to describe the equivalent fraction?<br><br>Is the pupil able to write the equivalent fraction? |
| Repeat several times, asking the pupil to use the fraction wall to identify fractions equivalent to a half and to write the equivalent fraction in the '$\frac{1}{2}$' section on the sheet. | *What other fractions can you find using this wall that are equivalent to a half?*<br><br>*Write this fraction in the 'half' section of your sheet.* | Can the pupil use the fraction wall to identify other fractions that are equivalent to a half, i.e. $\frac{2}{4}, \frac{3}{6}, \frac{4}{8}, \frac{5}{10}$ and $\frac{6}{12}$?<br><br>Is the pupil able to write the equivalent fractions? |
| If appropriate, ask the pupil to suggest other fractions, not represented on the fraction wall, that are equivalent to a half, e.g. $\frac{10}{20}$. | *Can you tell me another fraction that is equivalent to a half that is not on the fraction wall?*<br><br>*Add this to your list of fractions that are equivalent to a half.* | Can the pupil suggest other fractions, not represented on the fraction wall, that are equivalent to a half, e.g. $\frac{10}{20}$? |

Repeat above for the following fractions, asking the pupil to identify the equivalent fractions represented on the fraction wall and writing the fraction in the appropriate section on their sheet. If appropriate, ask the pupil to suggest other equivalent fractions not represented on the fraction wall.

| | Equivalent fractions represented on the fraction wall | Equivalent fractions not represented on the fraction wall |
|---|---|---|
| $\frac{1}{3}$ | $= \frac{2}{6} = \frac{3}{9} = \frac{4}{12}$ | $= \frac{5}{15} = \frac{6}{18}\ \cdots$ |
| $\frac{2}{3}$ | $= \frac{4}{6} = \frac{6}{9} = \frac{8}{12}$ | $= \frac{10}{15} = \frac{12}{18}\ \cdots$ |
| $\frac{1}{4}$ | $= \frac{2}{8} = \frac{3}{12}$ | $= \frac{4}{16} = \frac{5}{20}\ \cdots$ |
| $\frac{3}{4}$ | $= \frac{6}{8} = \frac{9}{12}$ | $= \frac{12}{16} = \frac{15}{20}\ \cdots$ |
| $\frac{1}{5}$ | $= \frac{2}{10}$ | $= \frac{3}{15} = \frac{4}{20}\ \cdots$ |
| $\frac{2}{5}$ | $= \frac{4}{10}$ | $= \frac{6}{15} = \frac{8}{20}\ \cdots$ |
| $\frac{3}{5}$ | $= \frac{6}{10}$ | $= \frac{9}{15} = \frac{12}{20}\ \cdots$ |

## What to do for those pupils working *below* or *above* expectations

Refer to the 'Tracking back and forward through the Mathematics National Curriculum attainment targets' charts on pages 310–320.

# Number – Fractions (including decimals)

## National Curriculum attainment target

- Count up and down in hundredths; recognise that hundredths arise when dividing an object by one hundred and dividing tenths by ten

## Prerequisite checklist

Can the pupil:

- count on from and back to zero in single-digit steps or multiples of 10?
- count up and down in tenths?
- recognise and use fractions as numbers: unit fractions and non-unit fractions with small denominators?
- divide a number by 10 and 100 and understand the effect?

Does the pupil:

- recognise that tenths arise from dividing an object into 10 equal parts?
- recognise that tenths arise from dividing one-digit numbers or quantities by 10?

## Success criteria

A. Recognise that hundredths arise from dividing an object by 100

B. Recognise that hundredths arise from dividing a one- or two-digit number by 100

C. Count up and down in hundredths

D. Recognise that hundredths arise from dividing tenths by 10

## Resources

Resource 24: Hundredths (per pupil)

coloured pencil (per pupil)

pencil and paper (per pupil)

## Assessment Task

**Success criterion A:** Recognise that hundredths arise from dividing an object by 100

| What to do | What to say | What to look out for |
|---|---|---|
| Provide the pupil with a copy of Resource 24 and a coloured pencil. | *Look at these grids. How many parts has each grid been divided into?* | Can the pupil recognise hundredths? |
| Draw the pupil's attention to the six grids in the top two rows. | *If each grid represents one, what does each small square on the grid represent?* | |
| Draw the pupil's attention to the first grid in the top row. | *Look at this grid. How many of the small squares on this grid have been shaded?* [68] <br><br> *If this grid represents one, what fraction of the grid is shaded?* [0·68/$\frac{68}{100}$] | Can the pupil recognise the hundredths represented on the grid? |
| Repeat for the second and third grids in the top row, | | |
| Draw the pupil's attention to the first blank grid in the second row. | *Look at this grid. Colour the grid so that it shows* [46] *hundredths.* | Can the pupil represent a given hundredths? |
| Repeat for the second and third grids in the second row, e.g. second grid: 0·81/$\frac{81}{100}$, third grid: 0·15/$\frac{15}{100}$. | | |

**Success criterion B:** Recognise that hundredths arise from dividing a one- or two-digit number by 100

| What to do | What to say | What to look out for |
|---|---|---|
| Provide the pupil with pencil and paper and draw their attention to the grid in the third row of Resource 24. | *This grid has been divided into 100 equal parts – it has been divided into hundredths.* <br><br> *One whole grid has been divided by 100.* <br><br> *What is one divided by 100?* <br><br> *How would you write this?* [0·01/$\frac{1}{100}$] | Does the pupil recognise that hundredths arise from dividing by 100? <br><br> Can the pupil write a given hundredths, i.e. 0·01 or $\frac{1}{100}$? |
| | *If one divided by 100 equals one hundredth, what is eight divided by 100?* <br> *How would you write this?* [0·08/$\frac{8}{100}$] <br><br> *What is 16 divided by 100?* <br> *How would you write this?* [0·16/$\frac{16}{100}$] <br><br> *How would you write 43 divided by 100?* [0·43/$\frac{43}{100}$] <br><br> *What about 81 divided by 100?* [0·81/$\frac{81}{100}$] | Does the pupil recognise that hundredths arise from dividing a one- or two-digit number by 100? <br><br> Can the pupil write a given hundredths? |

**Success criterion C:** Count up and down in hundredths

| What to do | What to say | What to look out for |
|---|---|---|
| Draw the pupil's attention back to the first grid in the top row of Resource 24. <br><br> | *What fraction of this grid is shaded?* [0·68/$\frac{68}{100}$] <br><br> *Starting at 68 hundredths, count on in hundredths until I say stop. Ready? Go!* | Can the pupil confidently count on in hundredths? |
| Draw the pupil's attention to the second grid in the top row. <br><br> | *What fraction of this grid is shaded?* [0·23/$\frac{23}{100}$] <br><br> *Starting at 23 hundredths, count back in hundredths until I say stop. Ready? Go!* | Can the pupil confidently count back in hundredths? |
| Draw the pupil's attention to the third grid in the top row. <br><br> | *What fraction of this grid is shaded?* [0·79/$\frac{79}{100}$] <br><br> *Starting at 79 hundredths, count on in hundredths until I say stop. Ready? Go!* <br><br> *This time count back in hundredths from 79 hundredths until I say stop. Ready? Go!* | Can the pupil confidently count on and back in hundredths? |
| Draw the pupil's attention to the first grid in the second row where the pupil shaded 0·46/$\frac{46}{100}$. <br><br> Repeat for the second and third grids in the second row, i.e. 0·81/$\frac{81}{100}$ and 0·15/$\frac{15}{100}$, asking the pupil to identify one hundredth more and one hundredth less than a given hundredth. | *What fraction of this grid is shaded?* [0·46/$\frac{46}{100}$] <br><br> *What is one hundredth more than [46] hundredths?* <br><br> *What is one hundredth less than [46] hundredths?* | Can the pupil identify the hundredth that is one hundredth more than a given hundredth? <br><br> Can the pupil identify the hundredth that is one hundredth less than a given hundredth? |

**Success criterion D:** Recognise that hundredths arise from dividing tenths by 10

| What to do | What to say | What to look out for |
|---|---|---|
| Draw the pupil's attention to the first grid in the penultimate row of Resource 24, i.e. | *This grid has been divided into ten equal parts – it has been divided into tenths.* <br><br> *What fraction of this grid is shaded?* [0·3/$\frac{3}{10}$] | Does the pupil recognise tenths? |
| Write 0·3 or $\frac{3}{10}$ to the right of the grid. | | |
| Draw the pupil's attention to the second grid in the penultimate row of Resource 24, i.e. | *Look at this grid. Each row on the tenths grid has now been divided into ten equal parts.* <br><br> *This grid has been divided into one hundred equal parts – it has been divided into hundredths.* <br><br> *So what fraction of this grid is shaded?* [0·03/$\frac{3}{100}$] <br><br> *How would you write this? Write it beside the grid.* | Does the pupil recognise that hundredths arise from dividing tenths by 10? <br><br> Can the pupil write a given hundredths, i.e. 0·03 or $\frac{3}{100}$? |
| Repeat above for the two grids in the bottom row of Resource 24, i.e. <br><br> 0.7　　　0.07 | | |
| | *So, if three tenths divided by ten is three hundredths, and seven tenths divided by ten is seven hundredths, what is two tenths divided by ten?* [0·02/$\frac{2}{100}$] <br><br> *What is nine tenths divided by ten?* [0·09/$\frac{9}{100}$] | Does the pupil recognise that hundredths arise from dividing tenths by 10? |

## What to do for those pupils working *below* or *above* expectations

Refer to the 'Tracking back and forward through the Mathematics National Curriculum attainment targets' charts on pages 310–320.

# Number – Fractions (including decimals)

## National Curriculum attainment target

- Solve problems involving increasingly harder fractions to calculate quantities, and fractions to divide quantities, including non-unit fractions where the answer is a whole number

## Prerequisite checklist

Can the pupil:

- recall and use multiplication and division facts for the multiplication tables up to 12 × 12?
- recognise, find, name and write unit fractions of a discrete set of objects?

- recognise, find, name and write non-unit fractions of a discrete set of objects?
- write simple fractions, for example $\frac{1}{2}$ of 6 = 3?

## Success criteria

A. Recognise, find and write unit fractions of numbers
B. Recognise, find and write non-unit fractions of numbers

## Resources

Resource 25: Fractions of numbers
pencil and paper (per pupil)

## Assessment Task

### Success criterion A: Recognise, find and write unit fractions of numbers

| What to do | What to say | What to look out for |
|---|---|---|
| Place Resource 25 on the table in front of the pupil.<br><br>Provide the pupil with pencil and paper. | *I'm going to point to a fraction on one of these arrows and a number on one of the targets, and I want you to find the fraction of that number.* | |
| Point to one of the unit fractions on the arrows, e.g. $\frac{1}{6}$, and a number that is a multiple of the fraction's denominator, i.e. 12, 18, 24, 30, 36, 42, 48, 54, 60, 72 or 96. | *What is [one sixth] of [54]?* | Can the pupil recognise and find a unit fraction of a number? |
| | *How did you work that out?* | Can the pupil explain how to find a unit fraction of a number? |
| | *How would you write this as a fraction calculation?* | Does the pupil write the corresponding fraction calculation? |

Repeat until the pupil has sufficiently demonstrated their ability to recognise, find and write unit fractions of numbers.

### Success criterion B: Recognise, find and write non-unit fractions of numbers

| What to do | What to say | What to look out for |
|---|---|---|
| Point to one of the non-unit fractions on the arrows, e.g. $\frac{3}{8}$, and a number that is a multiple of the fraction's denominator, i.e. 16, 24, 32, 40, 48, 72 or 96. | *What is [three eighths] of [32]?* | Can the pupil recognise and find a non-unit fraction of a number? |
| | *How did you work that out?* | Can the pupil explain how to find a non-unit fraction of a number? |
| | *How would you write this as a fraction calculation?* | Does the pupil write the corresponding fraction calculation? |

Repeat until the pupil has sufficiently demonstrated their ability to recognise, find and write non-unit fractions of numbers.

## What to do for those pupils working *below* or *above* expectations

Refer to the 'Tracking back and forward through the Mathematics National Curriculum attainment targets' charts on pages 310–320.

# Number – Fractions (including decimals)

## National Curriculum attainment target

• Add and subtract fractions with the same denominator

## Prerequisite checklist

Can the pupil:

• recall and use addition and subtraction facts to 20
• recognise and use fractions as numbers: unit fractions and non-unit fractions with small denominators?

• add fractions with the same denominator within one whole?

## Success criteria

**A.** Add fractions with the same denominator
**B.** Subtract fractions with the same denominator

## Resources

Resource 26: Adding fractions
Resource 27: Subtracting fractions

### NOTE

• Prior to the Assessment Task, cut out the 12 addition fraction cards from Resource 26 and the 12 subtraction fraction cards from Resource 27 and arrange them into two separate piles.

## Assessment Task

**Success criterion A:** Add fractions with the same denominator

| What to do | What to say | What to look out for |
| --- | --- | --- |
| Place one of the addition fraction cards from Resource 26 in front of the pupil. | *Read this fraction calculation to me.*<br><br>*What is the answer?* | Does the pupil answer the addition calculation correctly? |
| For more able pupils, if appropriate, encourage the pupil to reduce a fraction to its simplest form and to convert an improper fraction to a mixed number. | *What is […] reduced to its simplest form?*<br><br>*What is […] as a mixed number?* | Can the pupil reduce a fraction to its simplest form?<br><br>Can the pupil convert an improper fraction to a mixed number? |

Continue until the pupil has sufficiently demonstrated their ability to add fractions with the same denominator.

**Success criterion B:** Subtract fractions with the same denominator

| What to do | What to say | What to look out for |
| --- | --- | --- |
| Place one of the subtraction fraction cards from Resource 27 in front of the pupil. | *Read this fraction calculation to me.*<br><br>*What is the answer?* | Does the pupil answer the subtraction calculation correctly? |

Continue until the pupil has sufficiently demonstrated their ability to subtract fractions with the same denominator.

## What to do for those pupils working *below* or *above* expectations

Refer to the 'Tracking back and forward through the Mathematics National Curriculum attainment targets' charts on pages 310–320.

# Number – Fractions (including decimals)

**NOTE**

- This Assessment Task and Assessment Task 23: *Recognise and write decimal equivalents to $\frac{1}{4}$, $\frac{1}{2}$, $\frac{3}{4}$* both require the pupil to recognise the equivalence between fraction and decimal forms. It is recommended, therefore, that both these Assessment Tasks be undertaken with the pupil at the same time.

## National Curriculum attainment target

- Recognise and write decimal equivalents of any number of tenths or hundredths

## Prerequisite checklist

Can the pupil:

- recognise that tenths arise from dividing an object into 10 equal parts and from dividing one-digit numbers or quantities by 10?
- recognise that hundredths arise from dividing an object by 100 and dividing tenths by 10?
- recognise decimals in the context of measurement, including money?

## Success criteria

A. Partition decimals with up to two places, recognising the value of each digit

B. Recognise the equivalence between fraction and decimal forms of tenths or hundredths

C. Write fraction equivalents of any number of tenths

D. Write fraction equivalents of any number of hundredths

E. Write decimal equivalents of any number of tenths

F. Write decimal equivalents of any number of hundredths

G. Relate decimals with up to two places to measurement, including money

## Resources

Resource 28: Decimal cards – tenths

Resource 29: Decimal cards – hundredths

Resource 30: Fraction and decimal equivalents (preferably enlarged to A3)

Resource 31: Tenths and hundredths

small counter

pencil and paper (per pupil)

## Assessment Task

**Success criterion A:** Partition decimals with up to two places, recognising the value of each digit

| What to do | What to say | What to look out for |
|---|---|---|
| Place one of the decimal cards from Resources 28 or 29 in front of the pupil, e.g. 2·4. Pointing to one of the digits in the number, ask questions similar to the ones shown here: | *What does this digit represent?*<br><br>*What is the value of the two in this number?*<br><br>*What is the value of this digit?* | Can the pupil identify the value of a digit in a decimal with up to two decimal places? |
| Repeat several times using both the tenths decimal cards from Resource 28 and the hundredths decimal cards from Resource 29. | | |

| | | |
|---|---|---|
| Then place another card in front of the pupil, asking questions similar to the ones shown here: | *Point to the digit that shows how many ones are in this number.*<br><br>*Which digit shows how many hundredths there are?*<br><br>*Point to the digit that shows how many tenths are in this number.* | Can the pupil identify the ones digit in a decimal with up to two decimal places?<br><br>Can the pupil identify the tenths digit in a decimal with up to two decimal places?<br><br>Can the pupil identify the hundredths digit in a decimal with two decimal places? |

Repeat above until the pupil has sufficiently demonstrated their ability to partition decimals with up to two places, recognising the value of each digit.

## Success criterion B: Recognise the equivalence between fraction and decimal forms of tenths or hundredths

| What to do | What to say | What to look out for |
|---|---|---|
| Place Resource 30 on the table in front of the pupil.<br><br>Repeat several times. | *I'm going to put this counter onto one of these fractions. I then want you to point to the equivalent decimal. Ready? Let's begin.* | Can the pupil recognise the decimal equivalent for a given tenth when presented as a fraction?<br><br>Can the pupil recognise the decimal equivalent for a given hundredth when presented as a fraction? |
| | *I'm now going to put this counter onto one of the decimals and I want you to find an equivalent fraction. Ready? Let's begin.* | Can the pupil recognise the fraction equivalents for a given tenth when presented as a decimal? |
| When putting a counter onto one of the tenths expressed as a decimal, e.g. 0·5, ask the pupil if they can find two equivalent fractions, i.e. $\frac{5}{10}$ and $\frac{50}{100}$. | *What is the fraction equivalent to this decimal?*<br><br>*Can you find me another fraction that is equivalent to [zero point five/five tenths]?* | Can the pupil recognise the fraction equivalents for a given hundredth when presented as a decimal? |

Repeat until the pupil has sufficiently demonstrated their ability to recognise the equivalence between fraction and decimal forms of tenths or hundredths.

## Success criterion C: Write fraction equivalents of any number of tenths

| What to do | What to say | What to look out for |
|---|---|---|
| Place Resource 31 on the table in front of the pupil.<br><br>Provide the pupil with pencil and paper.<br><br>Draw the pupil's attention to the 0·3 decimal card on the sheet. | *Look at this decimal. How can you write this decimal as a fraction?* | Can the pupil express 0·3 as $\frac{3}{10}$? |
| If appropriate, ask the pupil if they can express the decimal as a different fraction with a denominator of 100. | *What is another fraction that is also equivalent to zero point three?* | Can the pupil express 0·3 as $\frac{30}{100}$? |
| Repeat for 0·8. | | |
| Draw the pupil's attention to the first tenths grid on the sheet. | *Look at this grid. It represents one whole. What fraction of this grid is shaded?*<br><br>*Can you write this for me as a fraction?* | Can the pupil interpret the grid as representing 2 tenths?<br><br>Can the pupil write the appropriate fraction, i.e. $\frac{2}{10}$? |
| Repeat for the $\frac{9}{10}$ / 0·9 grid. | | |

## Success criterion D: Write fraction equivalents of any number of hundredths

| What to do | What to say | What to look out for |
|---|---|---|
| Draw the pupil's attention to the 0·47 decimal card on Resource 31. | *Look at this decimal. How can you write this decimal as a fraction?* | Can the pupil express 0·47 as $\frac{47}{100}$? |
| Repeat for 0·98 and 0·64. | | |
| Draw the pupil's attention to the first hundredths grid on the sheet. | *Look at this grid. It represents one whole. What fraction of this grid is shaded?*<br><br>*Can you write this for me as a fraction?* | Can the pupil interpret the grid as representing 36 hundredths?<br><br>Can the pupil write the appropriate fraction, i.e. $\frac{36}{100}$? |
| Repeat for the $\frac{14}{100}$ / 0·14 and $\frac{78}{100}$ / 0·78 grids. | | |

## Success criterion E: Write decimal equivalents of any number of tenths

| What to do | What to say | What to look out for |
|---|---|---|
| Draw the pupil's attention to the $\frac{4}{10}$ fraction card on Resource 31. | *Look at this fraction. How can you write this fraction as a decimal?* | Can the pupil express $\frac{4}{10}$ as 0·4? |
| Repeat for $\frac{7}{10}$. | | |
| Draw the pupil's attention to the first tenths grid on the sheet. | *Look at this grid. It represents one whole. What fraction of this grid is shaded?*<br><br>*Can you write this for me as a decimal?* | Can the pupil interpret the grid as representing 2 tenths?<br><br>Can the pupil write the appropriate decimal, i.e. 0·2? |
| Repeat for the $\frac{9}{10}$ / 0·9 grid. | | |

## Success criterion F: Write decimal equivalents of any number of hundredths

| What to do | What to say | What to look out for |
|---|---|---|
| Draw the pupil's attention to the $\frac{27}{100}$ fraction card on Resource 31. | *Look at this fraction. How can you write this fraction as a decimal?* | Can the pupil express $\frac{27}{100}$ as 0·27? |
| Repeat for $\frac{56}{100}$ and $\frac{81}{100}$. | | |
| Draw the pupil's attention to the first hundredths grid on the sheet. | *Look at this grid. It represents one whole. What fraction of this grid is shaded?*<br><br>*Can you write this for me as a decimal?* | Can the pupil interpret the grid as representing 36 hundredths?<br><br>Can the pupil write the appropriate decimal 0·36? |
| Repeat for the $\frac{14}{100}$ / 0·14 and $\frac{78}{100}$ / 0·78 grids. | | |

**Success criterion 6:** Relate decimals with up to two places to measurement, including money

| What to do | What to say | What to look out for |
|---|---|---|
| Place one of the decimal cards from Resources 28 or 29 in front of the pupil, e.g. 2·5 or 3·01.<br><br>Ask questions similar to the ones shown here: | *If this number appeared as an answer on a calculator display and the calculation that you inputted into the calculator involved money, what would this mean? (£2.50)*<br><br>*What might two point five represent as a weight? (2 kg 500 g or $2\frac{1}{2}$ kg)*<br><br>*What does three point zero one mean in metres and centimetres? (3 m 1 cm)*<br><br>*What about in money? (£3.01)* | Can the pupil relate decimals with one or two decimal places to measurement, including money? |

Repeat several times using both the tenths decimal cards from Resource 28 and the hundredths decimal cards from Resource 29 until the pupil has sufficiently demonstrated their ability to relate decimals with up to two places to measurement, including money.

## What to do for those pupils working *below* or *above* expectations

Refer to the 'Tracking back and forward through the Mathematics National Curriculum attainment targets' charts on pages 310–320.

# Number – Fractions (including decimals)

## NOTE

• This Assessment Task and Assessment Task 22: *Recognise and write decimal equivalents of any number of tenths or hundredths* both require the pupil to recognise the equivalence between fraction and decimal forms. It is recommended, therefore, that both these Assessment Tasks be undertaken with the pupil at the same time.

## National Curriculum attainment target

• Recognise and write decimal equivalents to $\frac{1}{4}$, $\frac{1}{2}$, $\frac{3}{4}$

## Prerequisite checklist

Can the pupil:

• recognise decimals in the context of measurement, including money?

• recognise, find, name and write $\frac{1}{2}$, $\frac{1}{4}$ and $\frac{3}{4}$?

## Success criterion

**A.** Recognise the equivalence between fraction and decimal forms of one half and quarters

## Resources

Resource 30: Fraction and decimal equivalents (preferably enlarged to A3)

small counter

## Assessment Task

**Success criterion A:** Recognise the equivalence between fraction and decimal forms of one half and quarters

| What to do | What to say | What to look out for |
|---|---|---|
| Place Resource 30 on the table in front of the pupil.<br><br>Place the counter on $\frac{1}{4}$. | *What fraction have I put this counter on?*<br><br>*Point to the decimal that is equivalent to one quarter.* | Does the pupil recognise that 0·25 is equivalent to $\frac{1}{4}$? |
| | *Can you find another fraction on this sheet that represents one quarter?* | Does the pupil recognise that $\frac{25}{100}$ is equivalent to $\frac{1}{4}$ and 0·25? |
| Place the counter on 0·5. | *Point to a fraction that is equivalent to this decimal?*<br><br>*Can you find another fraction that represents a half?*<br><br>*Is there another fraction that represents a half?* | Does the pupil recognise that $\frac{1}{2}$, $\frac{5}{10}$ and $\frac{50}{100}$ are all equivalent to 0·5? |
| Place the counter on $\frac{3}{4}$. | *What fraction have I put this counter on?*<br><br>*Point to the decimal that is equivalent to three quarters.* | Does the pupil recognise that 0·75 is equivalent to $\frac{3}{4}$? |
| | *Can you find another fraction on this sheet that represents three quarters?* | Does the pupil recognise that $\frac{75}{100}$ is equivalent to $\frac{3}{4}$ and 0·75? |
| Conclude by assessing the pupil's understanding that two quarters equals a half. | *Look at all the fractions and decimals on this sheet.*<br><br>*Can you point to all the fractions and decimals that are equivalent to two quarters?*<br><br>*Can you find another fraction?*<br><br>*Are there any more?* | Does the pupil recognise that 0·5, $\frac{1}{2}$, $\frac{5}{10}$ and $\frac{50}{100}$ are all equivalent to two quarters? |

## What to do for those pupils working *below* or *above* expectations

Refer to the 'Tracking back and forward through the Mathematics National Curriculum attainment targets' charts on pages 310–320.

# Number – Fractions (including decimals)

## National Curriculum attainment target

- Find the effect of dividing a one- or two-digit number by 10 and 100, identifying the value of the digits in the answer as ones, tenths and hundredths

## Prerequisite checklist

Can the pupil:

- recognise that tenths arise from dividing an object into 10 equal parts and from dividing one-digit numbers or quantities by 10?
- recognise that hundredths arise from dividing an object by 100 and dividing tenths by 10?
- multiply a one- or two-digit number by 10 and 100, identifying the value of the digits in the answer?

## Success criteria

A. Divide a one-digit number by 10, understanding the effect and identifying the value of the digits in the answer as ones and tenths

B. Divide a one-digit number by 100, understanding the effect and identifying the value of the digits in the answer as ones, tenths and hundredths

C. Divide a two-digit number by 10, understanding the effect and identifying the value of the digits in the answer as ones and tenths

D. Divide a two-digit number by 100, understanding the effect and identifying the value of the digits in the answer as ones, tenths and hundredths

## Resources

Resource 32: Dividing by 10 and 100

pencil and paper clip (for the spinners)

pencil and paper (per pupil)

**NOTE**

- For this Assessment Task, the same activity is used to assess each of the four Success criteria listed above. As the pupil undertakes the activity, ask questions similar to those on pages 73 and 74 to assess the pupil's level of mastery in each of the four Success criteria.

# Assessment Task

**Success criterion A:** Divide a one-digit number by 10, understanding the effect and identifying the value of the digits in the answer as ones and tenths

**Success criterion B:** Divide a one-digit number by 100, understanding the effect and identifying the value of the digits in the answer as ones, tenths and hundredths

| What to do | What to say | What to look out for |
|---|---|---|
| Place Resource 32 and the pencil and paper clip on the table in front of the pupil.<br><br>Provide the pupil with pencil and paper.<br><br>Ensure that the pupil is familiar with how to use the spinner, i.e.<br><br><br><br>Hold the paper clip in the centre of the spinner using the pencil and gently flick the paper clip with your finger to make it spin.<br><br>Draw the pupil's attention to the one-digit number spinner and the ÷ 10 / ÷ 100 spinner. | *I want you to spin the one to nine spinner to generate a number.*<br><br>*I then want you to spin the divided by 10 and divided by 100 spinner.*<br><br>*As quickly as you can, I then want you to divide your one-digit number by 10 or 100 and write down the answer. Got the idea?* | |
| As the pupil undertakes the activity, ask questions similar to the ones shown here to assess their understanding of the effect of dividing a one-digit number by 10 or 100. | *What is nine divided by 10?*<br><br>*What is six divided by 100?*<br><br>*What is the value of this digit?*<br><br>*What is the value of the [ones/ tenths/hundredths] digit?*<br><br>*Which digit in your answer represents the [ones/tenths/ hundredths] digit?* | Can the pupil divide a one-digit number by 10?<br><br>Can the pupil identify the value of the digits in the answer as ones and tenths?<br><br>Can the pupil divide a one-digit number by 100?<br><br>Can the pupil identify the value of the digits in the answer as ones, tenths and hundredths? |

Repeat several times until the pupil has sufficiently demonstrated their ability to divide a one-digit number by 10 and 100, identifying the value of the digits in the answer as ones, tenths and when dividing by 100, hundredths.

**Success criterion C:** Divide a two-digit number by 10, understanding the effect and identifying the value of the digits in the answer as ones and tenths

**Success criterion D:** Divide a two-digit number by 100, understanding the effect and identifying the value of the digits in the answer as ones, tenths and hundredths

| What to do | What to say | What to look out for |
|---|---|---|
| Draw the pupil's attention to the two-digit number spinner and the ÷ 10 / ÷ 100 spinner. | *Now I want you to spin the two-digit numbers spinner to generate a number.*<br><br>*I then want you to spin the divided by 10 and divided by 100 spinner.*<br><br>*As quickly as you can, I then want you to divide your two-digit number by 10 or 100 and write down the answer. Got the idea?* | |
| As the pupil undertakes the activity, ask questions similar to the ones shown here to assess their understanding of the effect of dividing a two-digit number by 10 or 100. | *What is 45 divided by 10?*<br><br>*What is 39 divided by 100?*<br><br>*What is the value of this digit?*<br><br>*What is the value of the [ones/ tenths/hundredths] digit?*<br><br>*Which digit in your answer represents the [ones/tenths/ hundredths] digit?* | Can the pupil divide a two-digit number by 10?<br><br>Can the pupil identify the value of the digits in the answer as ones and tenths?<br><br>Can the pupil divide a two-digit number by 100?<br><br>Can the pupil identify the value of the digits in the answer as ones, tenths and hundredths? |

Repeat several times until the pupil has sufficiently demonstrated their ability to divide a two-digit number by 10 and 100, identifying the value of the digits in the answer as ones, tenths and when dividing by 100, hundredths.

## What to do for those pupils working *below* or *above* expectations

Refer to the 'Tracking back and forward through the Mathematics National Curriculum attainment targets' charts on pages 310–320.

# Number – Fractions (including decimals)

## National Curriculum attainment target

- Round decimals with one decimal place to the nearest whole number

## Prerequisite checklist

Can the pupil:

- round any whole number to the nearest 10, 100 or 1000?
- recognise that tenths arise from dividing an object into 10 equal parts and from dividing one-digit numbers or quantities by 10?

## Success criterion

A. Round decimals with one decimal place to the nearest whole number

## Resources

Resource 28: Decimal cards – tenths

**NOTE**

- Prior to the Assessment Task, cut out and shuffle the decimal cards and place them face down in a pile.

## Assessment Task

**Success criterion A:** Round decimals with one decimal place to the nearest whole number

| What to do | What to say | What to look out for |
|---|---|---|
| Place the pile of decimal cards on the table in front of the pupil.<br><br>Turn over the top card. Ask questions similar to the ones shown here that require the pupil to round the decimal to the nearest whole number. | *What is four point seven rounded to the nearest whole number?*<br><br>*Round six point three to the nearest whole number.* | Can the pupil round a tenth to the nearest whole number? |
| | *What do you look for when you round a tenth to the nearest whole number?* | Can the pupil explain how to round a decimal with one decimal place to the nearest whole number? |

Repeat until the pupil has sufficiently demonstrated their ability to round decimals with one decimal place to the nearest whole number.

## What to do for those pupils working *below* or *above* expectations

Refer to the 'Tracking back and forward through the Mathematics National Curriculum attainment targets' charts on pages 310–320.

# Number – Fractions (including decimals)

## National Curriculum attainment target

- Compare numbers with the same number of decimal places up to two decimal places

## Prerequisite checklist

Can the pupil:

- recognise that tenths arise from dividing an object into 10 equal parts and from dividing one-digit numbers or quantities by 10?
- recognise that hundredths arise from dividing an object by 100 and dividing tenths by 10?
- order and compare whole numbers to at least 1000?

## Success criteria

A. Compare decimals with one decimal place
B. Use the < and > symbols to compare decimals with one decimal place
C. Order decimals with one decimal place
D. Compare decimals with two decimal places
E. Use the < and > symbols to compare decimals with two decimal places
F. Order decimals with two decimal places
G. Position decimals with one decimal place on a number line
H. Position decimals with two decimal places on a number line

## Resources

Resource 5: Symbol cards
Resource 28: Decimal cards – tenths
Resource 29: Decimal cards – hundredths
pencil and paper (per pupil and teacher)

### NOTES

- Prior to the Assessment Task, cut out the tenths decimal cards from Resource 28 and the hundredths decimal cards from Resource 29 and arrange them into two separate piles.
- For this Assessment Task, you will only require the < and > symbol cards from Resource 5.

## Assessment Task

### Success criterion A: Compare decimals with one decimal place

| What to do | What to say | What to look out for |
|---|---|---|
| Place two tenths decimal cards with different ones digits face up in front of the pupil, e.g. 2·5 and 5·8. | *Point to the [larger/smaller] number.* | Can the pupil identify the larger/ smaller number? |
| Repeat above. | | |
| Place two tenths decimal cards with the same ones digit face up in front of the pupil, e.g. 4·7 and 4·9. | | |
| Repeat above. | | |

**Success criterion B:** Use the < and > symbols to compare decimals with one decimal place

| What to do | What to say | What to look out for |
|---|---|---|
| Provide the pupil with a 'greater than/less than' card from Resource 5. Ensure that the pupil realises that the 'greater than/less than' card can be used to represent either symbol by turning the card upside down.<br><br>Choose two tenths decimal cards and place them in front of the pupil, leaving a space between the two cards, e.g. $\boxed{3 \cdot 9}$ $\boxed{6 \cdot 3}$. | *Look at the two cards in front of you. I want you to place your symbol card between these two cards so that it makes a correct statement.* | Can the pupil correctly identify the greater than and less than symbols?<br><br>Can the pupil correctly use the greater than and less than symbols to compare two tenths? |
| When the pupil has done this, ask them to say their statement. | *Can you read this statement to me?* | |

Repeat above several times, including choosing two tenths decimal cards with the same ones digit, e.g. 4·7 and 4·9.

| What to do | What to say | What to look out for |
|---|---|---|
| Choose a tenths decimal card and a symbol card and place them in front of the pupil,<br><br>e.g. $\boxed{7 \cdot 6}$ $\boxed{<}$.<br><br>Randomly spread a selection of the other tenths decimal cards face up on the table. | *Look at the two cards in front of you. Choose a decimal number card from the table to put after the symbol card so that the statement is correct.* | Can the pupil correctly identify the greater than and less than symbols?<br><br>Can the pupil identify a tenth that correctly completes the statement? |
| When the pupil has done this, ask them to say their statement. | *Read me your statement.* | |
| Remove the decimal number card the pupil has used to complete the statement and place it with the other tenths decimal cards. | *Can you choose another decimal number card so that the statement is still correct?* | |

Repeat above several times, alternating the symbol card between $\boxed{<}$ and $\boxed{>}$.

**Success criterion C:** Order decimals with one decimal place

| What to do | What to say | What to look out for |
|---|---|---|
| Lay five tenths decimal cards face up in front of the pupil. | *Look at the decimal cards in front of you. I want you to place these cards in order, smallest decimal to largest decimal.* | Can the pupil order the set of tenths decimal cards? |
| Give the pupil another tenths decimal card. | *Look at the cards you have just put in order. Where would you put this card so that the order is still correct?* | |
| Referring to the set of six ordered tenths decimal cards, point to two consecutive numbers. | *Tell me a decimal that lies between these two decimals.* | Can the pupil identify a decimal that lies between two other decimals? |

Repeat until the pupil has sufficiently demonstrated their ability to order decimals with one decimal place.

**Success criterion D:** Compare decimals with two decimal places

| What to do | What to say | What to look out for |
|---|---|---|
| Place two hundredths decimal cards with different ones digits face up in front of the pupil, e.g. 3·65 and 6·26. | *Point to the [larger/smaller] number.* | Can the pupil identify the larger/smaller number? |
| Repeat above. | | |
| Place two hundredths decimal cards with the same ones digits face up in front of the pupil, e.g. 8·06 and 8·79. | | |
| Repeat above. | | |
| Place two hundredths decimal cards with the same ones and tenths digits face up in front of the pupil, e.g. 1·94 and 1·97. | | |
| Repeat above. | | |

**Success criterion E:** Use the < and > symbols to compare decimals with two decimal places

| What to do | What to say | What to look out for |
|---|---|---|
| Provide the pupil with a 'greater than/less than' card from Resource 5. Ensure that the pupil realises that the 'greater than/less than' card can be used to represent either symbol by turning the card upside down.<br><br>Choose two hundredths decimal cards and place them in front of the pupil, leaving a space between the two cards,<br><br>e.g. 4·59    3·01 . | *Look at the two cards in front of you. I want you to place your symbol card between these two cards so that it makes a correct statement.* | Can the pupil correctly identify the greater than and less than symbols?<br><br>Can the pupil correctly use the greater than and less than symbols to compare two hundredths? |
| When the pupil has done this, ask them to say their statement. | *Can you read this statement to me?* | |

Repeat above several times, including choosing two hundredths decimal cards with the same ones digits, e.g. 6·26 and 6·58; and the same ones and tenths digits, e.g. 7·32 and 7·37.

| What to do | What to say | What to look out for |
|---|---|---|
| Choose a hundredths decimal card and a symbol card and place them in front of the pupil,<br><br>e.g. 5·85    > .<br><br>Randomly spread a selection of the other hundredths decimal cards face up on the table. | *Look at the two cards in front of you. Choose a decimal number card from the table to put after the symbol card so that the statement is correct.* | Can the pupil correctly identify the greater than and less than symbols?<br><br>Can the pupil identify a hundredth that correctly completes the statement? |
| When the pupil has done this, ask them to say their statement. | *Read me your statement.* | |
| Remove the decimal number card the pupil has used to complete the statement and place it with the other hundredths decimal cards. | *Can you choose another decimal number card so that the statement is still correct?* | |

Repeat above several times, alternating the symbol card between < and > .

## Success criterion F: Order decimals with two decimal places

| What to do | What to say | What to look out for |
|---|---|---|
| Lay five hundredths decimal cards face up in front of the pupil. | *Look at the decimal cards in front of you. I want you to place these cards in order, smallest decimal to largest decimal.* | Can the pupil order the set of hundredths decimal cards? |
| Give the pupil another hundredths decimal card. | *Look at the cards you have just put in order. Where would you put this card so that the order is still correct?* | |
| Referring to the set of six ordered hundredths decimal cards, point to two consecutive numbers. | *Tell me a decimal that lies between these two decimals.* | Can the pupil identify a decimal that lies between two other decimals? |

Repeat until the pupil has sufficiently demonstrated their ability to order decimals with two decimal places.

## Success criterion G: Position decimals with one decimal place on a number line

| What to do |
|---|

On your sheet of paper, mark an empty number line with 0 at the left-hand end and 2 at the right-hand end, i.e.

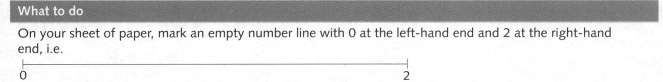

Ask the pupil to quickly copy the number line onto their sheet of paper.

Explain the following to the pupil:

- They are going to play a game called 'Guess the decimal'.
- You are going to think of a decimal with one place between 0 and 2 and secretly mark it on your number line, e.g. 1·4.
- The pupil then has to ask you questions to work out what your decimal number is, e.g. *Is your number less than 1?* (no)
- As you answer their questions the pupil records this information on the number line, e.g.

The game continues until the pupil guesses the decimal.

If appropriate, play several rounds, asking the pupil to think of a decimal between two other whole numbers, e.g. 3 and 5 or 6 and 10.

## Success criterion H: Position decimals with two decimal places on a number line

Repeat as for Success criterion G, asking the pupil to draw a number line between two tenths numbers and to guess the decimal with two decimal places that lies between the two tenths, e.g.

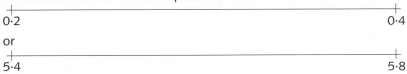

or

## What to do for those pupils working *below* or *above* expectations

Refer to the 'Tracking back and forward through the Mathematics National Curriculum attainment targets' charts on pages 310–320.

# Number – Fractions (including decimals)

## NOTE

- This Assessment Task, Assessment Tasks 12 and 17, and Assessment Task 33 all have the same four Success criteria. The difference between these Assessment Tasks is as follows:
  - Assessment Tasks 12 and 17: Solve problems involving all four operations
  - Assessment Task 27: Solve problems involving fractions and decimals to two decimal places
  - Assessment Task 33: Solve problems involving time

### National Curriculum attainment target

- Solve simple measure and money problems involving fractions and decimals to two decimal places

### Prerequisite checklist

Can the pupil:

- use decimal notation for tenths and hundredths and partition decimals; relate the notation to money and measurement; compare and order decimals to one and two places?
- find the effect of multiplying and dividing a one- or two-digit number by 10 and 100, identifying the value of the digits in the answer?
- solve problems involving addition, subtraction, multiplication or division in contexts of numbers or measures?
- identify and record the information or calculation needed to solve a problem?

- carry out the steps or calculations and check the solution in the context of the problem?
- present solutions to problems in an organised way, explaining decisions, methods and results?

### Success criteria

A. Read and understand the problem
B. Correctly identify which operation(s) to use
C. Carry out the calculation(s) to obtain the correct answer using an appropriate method
D. Check the answer using an effective method

### Resources

Resource 33: Fractions and decimals problems
pencil and paper (per pupil)

## Assessment Task

### Success criterion A: Read and understand the problem

| What to do | What to say | What to look out for |
|---|---|---|
| Provide the pupil with pencil and paper and one of the fractions or decimals word problem cards from Resource 33. | *Read the problem on your card.*<br><br>*What is your problem about?*<br><br>*What do you have to find out?* | Can the pupil read and understand the problem? |

### Success criterion B: Correctly identify which operation(s) to use

| What to do | What to say | What to look out for |
|---|---|---|
| Ask the pupil to suggest which operation(s) they need to use to work out the answer to the word problem. | *Which operation(s) do you need to use to work out the answer to your problem?* | Can the pupil correctly identify which operation(s) to use? |
| Ask the pupil to explain how they know which operation to use. | *How do you know you need to [add/ subtract/multiply/divide]? What clues are there in the problem?* | |

## Success criterion C: Carry out the calculation(s) to obtain the correct answer using an appropriate method

| What to do | What to say | What to look out for |
|---|---|---|
| Ask the pupil to write down the calculation(s) needed to solve the problem and work out the answer. | *On your sheet of paper I want you to write down the calculation(s) needed to solve your problem and then I want you to work out the answer.* | Can the pupil write the correct calculation(s)?<br><br>Does the pupil obtain the correct answer to the calculation(s)?<br><br>Does the pupil use an appropriate calculation method?<br><br>Can the pupil convert between different units of measure?<br><br>Does the pupil obtain the correct answer to the problem? |
| Encourage the pupil to talk about the method they used to obtain their answer. | *Explain to me how you worked out the answer to this problem.* | Can the pupil explain their method of working out the answer to the problem? |

## Success criterion D: Check the answer using an effective method

| What to do | What to say | What to look out for |
|---|---|---|
| Ask the pupil to check the answer to their problem. | *Are you sure that the answer to this problem is right?*<br><br>*How can you be so sure?* | Can the pupil check their answer using an effective method? |

Repeat Success criteria A–D until the pupil has sufficiently demonstrated their ability to solve measure and money problems involving fractions and decimals.

### Answers
Resource 33: Fractions and decimals problems

| | |
|---|---|
| 1. £150 | 2. Boris is 1·3 m tall and Harry is 1·8 m tall |
| 3. 20 paving stones | 4. 1 m 50 cm or $1\frac{1}{2}$ m or 1·5 m |
| 5. 50 days | 6. 3 large bottles |
| 7. 200 ml | 8. 220 g |
| 9. 3·61 kg | 10. 24 kg |
| 11. $18\frac{1}{10}$ m | 12. 4·8 kg |
| 13. 3 litres | 14. £21.90 |
| 15. $\frac{2}{7}$ | 16. £37.50 |
| 17. 84 km | 18. £8 |
| 19. $\frac{3}{5}$ | 20. 1 m 26 cm |

## What to do for those pupils working *below* or *above* expectations
Refer to the 'Tracking back and forward through the Mathematics National Curriculum attainment targets' charts on pages 310–320.

# Measurement

## National Curriculum attainment target

- Convert between different units of measure [for example, kilometre to metre; hour to minute]

## Prerequisite checklist

Can the pupil:

- choose and use appropriate standard units to estimate and measure length (m/cm/mm); mass (kg/g) and volume/capacity (litres/ml) to the nearest appropriate unit?
- compare and order lengths, mass and volume/capacity?

## Success criteria

**A.** Know the relationship between different units of measure: length (m/cm/mm); mass (kg/g), volume/capacity (litres/ml) and time (s, min, h, days, weeks, months)

**B.** Convert between different units of measure, including using decimals to two decimal places

## Resources

Resource 34: Relationship between different units of measure (1)

Resource 35: Relationship between different units of measure (2)

Resource 36: Convert between different units of measure (preferably enlarged to A3)

pencil and paper (optional)

## NOTE

- Prior to the Assessment Task, cut out the cards from Resources 34 and 35, and arrange the grey cards into one pile and the white cards into a separate pile. Shuffle each pile of cards.

## Assessment Task

**Success criterion A:** Know the relationship between different units of measure: length (m/cm/mm); mass (kg/g), volume/capacity (litres/ml) and time (s, min, h, days, weeks, months)

| What to do | What to say | What to look out for |
|---|---|---|
| Begin by asking the pupil to describe the relationship between the different units of measure.<br><br>Ask questions similar to the ones shown here: | *How many centimetres are there in a metre?*<br>*How many metres in a kilometre?*<br>*How many millimetres in a centimetre?*<br>*How many grams in a kilogram?*<br>*How many millilitres in a litre?*<br>*How many seconds in a minute?*<br>*How many minutes in an hour?* | Does the pupil know the relationship between different units of measure:<br>– length (m/cm/mm)<br>– mass (kg/g)<br>– volume/capacity (litres/ml)<br>– time (s, min, h, days, weeks, months)? |
| Place the 17 grey cards from Resources 34 and 35 face up on the table.<br><br>Give the pupil the pile of 19 white cards, face down, from Resources 34 and 35. | *I want you to turn over the top card from this pile and look at the grey cards. I then want you to match the white card to one of the grey cards. There are 17 grey cards and 19 white cards. So two of the grey cards will each match more than one white card. Turn over the top card. See if you can match the cards as quickly as possible. Ready? Go!* | Can the pupil match the cards to show the relationship between different units of measure:<br>– length (m/cm/mm)<br>– mass (kg/g)<br>– volume/capacity (litres/ml)<br>– time (s, min, h, days, weeks, months)? |

**Success criterion B:** Convert between different units of measure, including using decimals to two decimal places

| What to do | What to say | What to look out for |
|---|---|---|
| Place Resource 36 on the table in front of the pupil.<br><br>If appropriate, provide the pupil with pencil and paper.<br><br>Point to different statements, asking the pupil to convert between different units of measure, asking questions similar to the ones shown here: | *What is three point nine kilograms in grams?*<br><br>*How many centimetres equal five point two metres?* | Is the pupil able to use and apply the relationships between different units of measure to convert between different units? |
| Occasionally ask the pupil to explain how they were able to convert between the different units of measure. | *How did you work that out?*<br><br>*How did you know that there were [6400 millilitres in six point four litres]?* | Can the pupil explain the relationships between different units of measure to convert between different units? |

Repeat until the pupil has sufficiently demonstrated their ability to convert between different units of measure, including using decimals to two decimal places.

**Answers**

Resource 36: Convert between different units of measure

| | | |
|---|---|---|
| 5·3 km = 5300 m | 5 min = 300 sec | 6·4 $l$ = 6400 ml |
| 1·8 m = 1800 mm | 10 500 g = 10·5 kg | 8000 mm = 800 cm |
| 12 500 ml = 12·5 $l$ | 20 cm = 0·2 m | 144 h = 6 days |
| 3·9 kg = 3900 g | 2·6 cm = 26 mm | 4600 m = 4·6 km |
| $6\frac{1}{2}$ h = 390 min | 125 min = 2 h and 5 min | |
| 8·1 $l$ = 8100 ml | 880 cm = 8·8 m | 3200 g = 3·2 kg |
| 0·09 kg = 90 g | 2·9 km = 2900 m | 7 days = 168 h |
| 3 mm = 0·3 cm | 2200 ml = 2·2 $l$ | 46·8 kg = 46 800 g |
| 5·2 m = 520 cm | 12·2 kg = 12 200 g | 0·05 $l$ = 50 ml |
| 15·1 $l$ = 15 100 ml | 6 weeks = 42 days | 7 m = 700 cm |
| 14 cm = 140 mm | 7700 g = 7·7 kg | 30 sec = $\frac{1}{2}$ min |
| 5100 m = 5·1 km | 80 h = 3 days and 8 h | |
| 180 min = 3 h | 8500 ml = 8·5 $l$ | 500 mm = 0·5 m |

## What to do for those pupils working *below* or *above* expectations

Refer to the 'Tracking back and forward through the Mathematics National Curriculum attainment targets' charts on pages 310–320.

## Measurement

### National Curriculum attainment target

- Measure and calculate the perimeter of a rectilinear figure (including squares) in centimetres and metres

### Prerequisite checklist

Can the pupil:

- draw and measure lines to the nearest centimetre?
- add and subtract numbers mentally with increasingly large numbers?
- double numbers to at least 100?

### Success criteria

A. Find perimeters of rectilinear figures by measuring or counting

B. Calculate the perimeter of a rectilinear figure (including squares) in centimetres and metres

C. Measure and draw a rectangle and find its perimeter

D. Measure and draw a rectangle when its perimeter is known

### Resources

Resource 37: Rectilinear shapes (1) (per pupil)

Resource 38: Rectilinear shapes (2)

pencil and paper (per pupil)

ruler (per pupil)

1 cm squared paper (per pupil)

---

## Assessment Task

**Success criterion A:** Find perimeters of rectilinear figures by measuring or counting

| What to do | What to say | What to look out for |
|---|---|---|
| | *What does the word 'perimeter' mean?* | Does the pupil describe 'perimeter' as the distance all the way a round the edge of something/the boundary? |
| Provide the pupil with a copy of Resource 37, a pencil and a ruler.<br><br>Explain to the pupil how the shapes have been drawn on a 1 cm square grid. | *Look at the shapes on the sheet. They have been drawn using one centimetre squared paper.* | |
| Referring to individual shapes on the sheet, ask the pupil to find the shape's perimeter.<br><br>Choose which shapes to ask the pupil to find the perimeters of depending on their ability. See table below for guidance. | *I want you to find the perimeter of Shape One.* | Does the pupil use the ruler to measure the sides of the shape or do they realise that as each square is one square centimetre they can find the perimeter by counting the boundary (grid) lines around the shape?<br><br>Can the pupil accurately work out/calculate the perimeter of a rectilinear figure? |

Repeat above until the pupil has sufficiently demonstrated their ability to find the perimeter of rectilinear figures.

### Answers

Resource 37: Rectilinear shapes (1)

| Level of difficulty | Easy | | | Moderate | | | | Difficult | | |
|---|---|---|---|---|---|---|---|---|---|---|
| **Shape** | 1 | 2 | 3 | 4 | 5 | 6 | 7 | 8 | 9 | 10 |
| **Perimeter** | 12 cm | 16 cm | 20 cm | 18 cm | 28 cm | 14 cm | 14 cm | 24 cm | 24 cm | 34 cm |

**Success criterion B:** Calculate the perimeter of a rectilinear figure (including squares) in centimetres and metres

| What to do | What to say | What to look out for |
|---|---|---|
| Place Resource 38 on the table in front of the pupil and provide them with pencil and paper.<br><br>Referring to individual shapes on the sheet, ask the pupil to calculate the shape's perimeter. | *What is the perimeter of Shape One?* | Can the pupil use the rule: perimeter = twice (length + breadth) or $P = 2(l + b)$ to calculate the perimeter of a rectilinear figure? |
| Occasionally ask the pupil to explain how they calculated the shape's perimeter. | *What did you do to work out the perimeter of the shape?* | Can the pupil explain how to calculate the perimeter of a rectilinear figure (including squares) in centimetres or metres? |

Repeat above until the pupil has sufficiently demonstrated their ability to calculate the perimeter of a rectilinear figure (including squares) in centimetres and metres.

**Answers**

Resource 38: Rectilinear shapes (2)

| Shape | 1 | 2 | 3 | 4 | 5 | 6 | 7 | 8 | 9 | 10 |
|---|---|---|---|---|---|---|---|---|---|---|
| Perimeter | 16 cm | 18 m | 80 cm | 190 cm | 32 m | 260 cm | 44 m | 40 cm | 324 cm | 136 m |

**Success criterion C:** Measure and draw a rectangle and find its perimeter

| What to do | What to say | What to look out for |
|---|---|---|
| Provide the pupil with a sheet of 1 cm squared paper, a pencil and a ruler.<br><br>Ask the pupil to draw a rectangle of given dimensions, e.g. 7 cm × 3 cm. | *On your sheet of squared paper I want you to draw a rectangle for me with sides of [seven centimetres and three centimetres].* | Can the pupil measure and draw a rectangle? |
| Once the pupil has drawn their rectangle, ask them to find its perimeter. | *I want you now to work out what the perimeter of your rectangle is and write this inside the rectangle.* | Can the pupil calculate the perimeter of the rectangle? |

Repeat above, asking the pupil to measure and draw another rectangle of given dimensions and to then calculate the perimeter of the rectangle.

**Success criterion D:** Measure and draw a rectangle when its perimeter is known

| What to do | What to say | What to look out for |
|---|---|---|
| Ensure that the pupil has a sheet of 1 cm squared paper, a pencil and a ruler. | *The perimeter of a rectangle is 26 centimetres. On your sheet of one centimetre squared paper, I want you to draw what the rectangle might look like.* | Can the pupil work out the dimensions of a rectangle when its perimeter is given?<br><br>Can the pupil measure and draw the rectangle? |
| If appropriate, ask the pupil to suggest other possible dimensions for the rectangle. | *What else could the sides of a rectangle with a perimeter of 26 centimetres be?* | Can the pupil suggest another set of dimensions for a rectangle when its perimeter is known? |

Repeat above until the pupil has sufficiently demonstrated their ability to measure and draw a rectangle when its perimeter is known.

## What to do for those pupils working *below* or *above* expectations

Refer to the 'Tracking back and forward through the Mathematics National Curriculum attainment targets' charts on pages 310–320.

### National Curriculum attainment target

• Find the area of rectilinear shapes by counting squares

### Prerequisite checklist

Can the pupil:

• draw and measure lines to the nearest centimetre?
• add and subtract numbers mentally?
• recall and use multiplication and division facts for multiplication tables up to 12 × 12?

### Success criteria

A. Find the area of rectilinear shapes drawn on a square grid by counting squares
B. Measure and draw a rectangle and find its area
C. Measure and draw a rectangle when its area is known

### Resources

Resource 37: Rectilinear shapes (1)
pencil (per pupil)
ruler (per pupil)
1 cm squared paper (per pupil)

## Assessment Task

**Success criterion A:** Find the area of rectilinear shapes drawn on a square grid by counting squares

| What to do | What to say | What to look out for |
|---|---|---|
| | *What does the word 'area' mean?* | Does the pupil describe 'area' as the amount of surface space inside the perimeter? |
| Provide the pupil with a copy of Resource 37, a pencil and a ruler.<br><br>Explain to the pupil how the shapes have been drawn on a 1 cm square grid. | *Look at the shapes on the sheet. They have been drawn using one centimetre squared paper.* | |
| Referring to individual shapes on the sheet, ask the pupil to find the shape's area.<br><br>Choose which shapes to ask the pupil to find the areas of depending on their ability. See table below for guidance. | *I want you to find the area of Shape One.* | Does the pupil use the ruler to measure the sides of the shape or do they realise that as each square is one square centimetre they can find the area of the shape by counting the number of squares?<br><br>When working out the area of a rectangle, does the pupil count all the squares in the rectangle or do they count the number of squares in one row and one column and multiply together the two numbers? |

Repeat above until the pupil has sufficiently demonstrated their ability to find the area of rectilinear shapes drawn on a square grid by counting squares.

### Answers

Resource 37: Rectilinear shapes (1)

| Level of difficulty | Easy | | | Moderate | | | | Difficult | | |
|---|---|---|---|---|---|---|---|---|---|---|
| Shape | 1 | 2 | 3 | 4 | 5 | 6 | 7 | 8 | 9 | 10 |
| Perimeter | 9 cm² | 15 cm² | 24 cm² | 16 cm² | 31 cm² | 8 cm² | 10 cm² | 11 cm² | 15 cm² | 24 cm² |

## Success criterion B: Measure and draw a rectangle and find its area

| What to do | What to say | What to look out for |
|---|---|---|
| Provide the pupil with a sheet of 1 cm squared paper, a pencil and a ruler.<br><br>Ask the pupil to draw a rectangle of given dimensions, e.g. 5 cm × 4 cm. | *On your sheet of squared paper I want you to draw a rectangle for me with sides of [five centimetres and four centimetres].* | Can the pupil measure and draw a rectangle? |
| Once the pupil has drawn their rectangle, ask them to find its area. | *I want you now to work out what the area of your rectangle is and write this inside the rectangle.* | Does the pupil find the area of the rectangle by counting squares?<br><br>Does the pupil calculate the area of the rectangle by using and applying the rule:<br>area = (length x breadth)<br>or A = ($l$ x $b$)? |

Repeat above, asking the pupil to measure and draw another rectangle of given dimensions and to then calculate the area of the rectangle.

## Success criterion C: Measure and draw a rectangle when its area is known

| What to do | What to say | What to look out for |
|---|---|---|
| Ensure that the pupil has a sheet of 1 cm squared paper, a pencil and a ruler. | *The area of a rectangle is 12 centimetres squared. On your sheet of one centimetre squared paper, I want you to draw what the rectangle might look like.* | Can the pupil work out the dimensions of a rectangle when its area is given?<br><br>Can the pupil measure and draw the rectangle? |
| If appropriate, ask the pupil to suggest other possible dimensions for the rectangle. | *What else could the sides of a rectangle with an area of 12 cm² be?* | Can the pupil suggest another set of dimensions for a rectangle when its area is known? |

Repeat above until the pupil has sufficiently demonstrated their ability to measure and draw a rectangle when its area is known.

## What to do for those pupils working *below* or *above* expectations

Refer to the 'Tracking back and forward through the Mathematics National Curriculum attainment targets' charts on pages 310–320.

# Measurement

## National Curriculum attainment target

- Estimate, compare and calculate different measures, including money in pounds and pence

## Prerequisite checklist

Can the pupil:

- choose and use appropriate standard units to estimate and measure length/height in any direction (m/cm); mass (kg/g); capacity (litres/ml) to the nearest appropriate unit, using rulers, scales and measuring vessels?
- compare and order lengths, mass, volume/capacity and record the results using >, < and =?
- add and subtract lengths (m/cm/mm); mass (kg/g); volume/capacity (l/ml)?
- add and subtract amounts of money to give change, using both £ and p in practical contexts?
- convert between different units of measure?

## Success criteria

A. Estimate and compare length (m/cm/mm)
B. Read and interpret intervals and divisions on partially numbered scales, and record a given length accurately (cm/mm)
C. Calculate lengths (m/cm/mm)
D. Estimate and compare mass (kg/g)
E. Read and interpret intervals and divisions on partially numbered scales, and record a given mass accurately (kg/g)
F. Calculate masses (kg/g)
G. Estimate and compare capacity (l/ml)
H. Read and interpret intervals and divisions on partially numbered scales, and record a given volume accurately (l/ml)
I. Calculate volumes/capacities (l/ml)
J. Estimate and compare amounts of money
K. Calculate amounts of money, including £.p notation

## Resources

Resource 39: Length (per pupil)
Resource 40: Mass (per pupil)
Resource 41: Volume/capacity (per pupil)
Resource 42: Money (per pupil)
pencil and paper (per pupil)

## NOTES

- As this Assessment Task involves a number of Success criteria, it is advisable to focus on just one measure at a time.
- Prior to the Assessment Task:
  - provide each pupil with pencil and paper
  - mark different lengths, masses and capacities on each of the various scales on Resources 39 to 41, e.g.

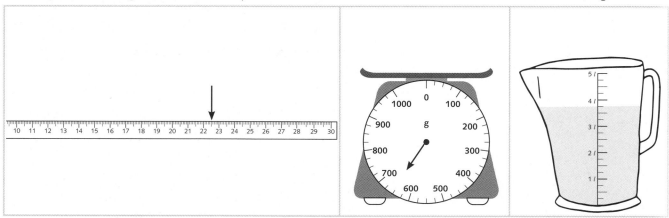

Vary the markings on the scales according to the ability of the pupil undertaking in the task, i.e.
  - mark a labelled division – easy
  - mark an unlabelled division – moderate
  - mark between two unlabelled divisions – difficult.
- You will also need blank copies of Resources 39 to 41 for the pupil to show a given measure.

## Assessment Task

### Success criterion A: Estimate and compare length (m/cm/mm)

| What to do | What to say | What to look out for |
|---|---|---|
| Place the marked-up copy of Resource 39 on the table and draw the pupil's attention to the objects at the top of the sheet.<br><br>Referring to each object in turn, ask the pupil to estimate the length/ height of the object and to write their estimate underneath the object. | *Look at the picture of the [man]. Imagine that this is a real [person]. Would you measure the height of a [man] in metres, centimetres or millimetres?*<br><br>*What would you use to measure the height of a [man]?* | Can the pupil suggest a suitable unit of measurement?<br><br>Can the pupil suggest a suitable instrument of measurement? |
| Repeat for the remaining objects on the sheet. | *What do you think might be the height of an average [man]?*<br><br>*Write your estimate under the picture of the [man].* | Can the pupil suggest a reasonable estimate? |
| Referring to two or more objects on the sheet, ask the pupil to compare the lengths/heights of the objects. | *Look at these two objects. Which one is the [smaller/larger]?* | Can the pupil compare the length/height of two or more objects? |
| Repeat several times. | *Look at these objects. Which is the [longest/tallest/shortest] object?*<br><br>*Can you tell me something on this sheet that is [smaller/larger] than the [street lamp]?* | |

**Answers**

Resource 39: Length

The following is the average length/height of the objects at the top of Resource 39. Accept a reasonable degree of flexibility in the responses offered by the pupil.
- adult male ≈ 1·75 m
- family car ≈ 4·5 m
- front door to a house ≈ 2 m
- large haulage truck ≈ 12 m
- pin ≈ 25 mm
- street light ≈ 12 m
- pencil ≈ 20 cm
- banana ≈ 18 cm

### Success criterion B: Read and interpret intervals and divisions on partially numbered scales, and record a given length accurately (cm/mm)

| What to do | What to say | What to look out for |
|---|---|---|
| Referring to the marked-up copy of Resource 39, ask questions similar to the one shown here that require the pupil to read and interpret the different readings. | *What length is the arrow pointing to on this ruler?* | Can the pupil read and interpret a length:<br>– to the nearest centimetre?<br>– to the nearest half centimetre?<br>– to the nearest millimetre? |
| Mark a second point on the ruler. | *What is the distance between these two arrows?* | Can the pupil calculate the interval between the two marked divisions? |
| Place the blank copy of Resource 39 on the table and ask the pupil to record a length on one of the rulers. | *Show me where 14·3 cm is on this ruler.* | Can the pupil record a length:<br>– to the nearest centimetre?<br>– to the nearest half centimetre?<br>– to the nearest millimetre? |

Continue until the pupil has demonstrated their ability to read and interpret intervals and divisions on partially numbered scales, and record a given length accurately.

## Success criterion C: Calculate lengths (m/cm/mm)

| What to do | What to say | What to look out for |
|---|---|---|
| Provide the pupil with pencil and paper.<br><br>Referring to the estimates of the lengths/heights of the objects and the lengths on the rulers on Resource 39, choose two (or more) estimates or rulers and ask questions similar to the ones shown here that require the pupil to calculate different lengths.<br><br>Be sure to ask questions that are appropriate to the calculating abilities of the pupil.<br><br>If the pupil has made unreasonable estimates of the objects, you may wish to discuss with them the more realistic estimates, writing these on the sheet, and asking the pupil to calculate using these estimates. | *Look at these two rulers. Ruler [1] shows a length [longer/shorter] than the length shown on ruler [2]. How much [longer/shorter] is the length?*<br><br>*Look at your estimates for the height of the front door and the height of the street lamp. Approximately how much taller is the street lamp than the door?*<br><br>*Approximately how many times longer is a large haulage truck than an average family-sized car?* | Can the pupil use mental and written methods to calculate lengths/heights, including using decimals to two decimal places?<br><br>Can the pupil make reasonable approximations when calculating lengths/heights?<br><br>Can the pupil convert between different units of measure? |

Continue until the pupil has sufficiently demonstrated their ability to calculate lengths/heights in metres, centimetres and millimetres, converting between different units of measure where necessary.

## Success criterion D: Estimate and compare mass (kg/g)

| What to do | What to say | What to look out for |
|---|---|---|
| Place the marked-up copy of Resource 40 on the table and draw the pupil's attention to the objects at the top of the sheet.<br><br>Referring to each object in turn, ask the pupil to estimate the mass of the object and to write their estimate underneath the object. | *Look at the picture of the [pineapple]. Which unit of measure would you use to measure the mass of a [pineapple]?*<br><br>*What instrument would you use to measure the mass of a [pineapple]?*<br><br>*What do you think might be the mass of an average [pineapple]?* | Can the pupil suggest a suitable unit of measurement?<br><br>Can the pupil suggest a suitable instrument of measurement?<br><br>Can the pupil suggest a reasonable estimate? |
| Repeat for the remaining objects on the sheet. | *Write your estimate under the picture of the [pineapple].* | |
| Referring to two or more objects on the sheet, ask the pupil to compare the masses of the objects.<br><br>Repeat several times. | *Look at these two objects. Which one is the [lighter/heavier]?*<br><br>*Look at these objects. Which is the [lightest/heaviest] object?*<br><br>*Can you tell me something on this sheet that is [lighter/heavier] than the [medium-sized dog]?* | Can the pupil compare the mass of two or more objects? |

**Answers**

Resource 40: Mass

The following is the average mass of the objects at the top of Resource 40. Accept a reasonable degree of flexibility in the responses offered by the pupil.

- pineapple ≈ 900 g
- baby ≈ 3·4 kg
- bag of 4 onions ≈ 400 g
- adult female ≈ 70 kg
- carry-on flight bag ≈ 20 kg
- addressed envelope with a stamp on it ≈ 80 g
- pupil's novel ≈ 200 g
- medium-sized dog ≈ 25 kg

## Success criterion E: Read and interpret intervals and divisions on partially numbered scales, and record a given mass accurately (kg/g)

| What to do | What to say | What to look out for |
|---|---|---|
| Referring to the marked-up copy of Resource 40, ask questions similar to the one shown here that require the pupil to read and interpret the different readings. | *What weight is the arrow pointing to on these weighing scales?* | Can the pupil read and interpret a mass:<br>– to the nearest labelled division?<br>– to the nearest unlabelled division?<br>– to a division that lies between two unlabelled divisions? |
| Place the blank copy of Resource 40 on the table and ask the pupil to record a mass on one of the weighing scales. | *If something weighed 750 grams, what would this look like on these weighing scales?*<br><br>*Show me what 3·6 kilograms would look like on this weighing scale.* | Can the pupil record a mass:<br>– to the nearest labelled division?<br>– to the nearest unlabelled division?<br>– to a division that lies between two unlabelled divisions? |

Continue until the pupil has demonstrated their ability to read and interpret intervals and divisions on partially numbered scales, and record a given mass accurately.

## Success criterion F: Calculate masses (kg/g)

| What to do | What to say | What to look out for |
|---|---|---|
| Provide the pupil with pencil and paper.<br><br>Referring to the estimates of the masses of the objects and the masses on the weighing scales on Resource 40, choose two (or more) estimates or scales and ask questions similar to the ones shown here that require the pupil to calculate different masses.<br><br>Be sure to ask questions that are appropriate to the calculating abilities of the pupil.<br><br>If the pupil has made unreasonable estimates of the objects, you may wish to discuss with them the more realistic estimates, writing these on the sheet, and asking the pupil to calculate using these estimates. | *Look at these two weighing scales. Weighing scale [1] shows a mass [lighter/heavier] than the mass shown on weighing scale [6]. How much [lighter/heavier] is the mass?*<br><br>*Look at your estimates for the woman and the bag that she is pulling. Approximately how much heavier is the woman than the bag?*<br><br>*Which is heavier, the pineapple or the bag of onions? How much heavier?* | Can the pupil use mental and written methods to calculate masses, including using decimals to two decimal places?<br><br>Can the pupil make reasonable approximations when calculating masses?<br><br>Can the pupil convert between different units of measure? |

Continue until the pupil has sufficiently demonstrated their ability to calculate masses in kilograms and grams, converting between different units of measure where necessary.

**Success criterion G:** Estimate and compare capacity (l/ml)

| What to do | What to say | What to look out for |
|---|---|---|
| Place the marked-up copy of Resource 41 on the table and draw the pupil's attention to the objects at the top of the sheet. | *Look at the picture of the [tin of soup]. Which unit of measure would you use to measure the capacity of this [tin]?* | Can the pupil suggest a suitable unit of measurement? |
| Referring to each object in turn, ask the pupil to estimate the capacity of the object and to write their estimate underneath the object. | *What instrument would you use to measure the capacity of the [tin of soup]?* | Can the pupil suggest a suitable instrument of measurement? |
| | *What do you think might be the capacity of an average [tin of soup]?* | Can the pupil suggest a reasonable estimate? |
| Repeat for the remaining objects on the sheet. | *Write your estimate under the picture of the [tin of soup].* | |
| Referring to two or more objects on the sheet, ask the pupil to compare the capacities of the objects. | *Look at these two objects. Which one has the [greater/smaller] capacity?* | Can the pupil compare the capacity of two or more objects? |
| Repeat several times. | *Look at these objects. Which object could hold the [most/least]?* | |
| | *Can you tell me something on this sheet that could hold [more/less] than the [bottle of soft drink]?* | |

**Answers**

Resource 41: Volume/capacity

The following is the average capacity of the objects at the top of Resource 41. Accept a reasonable degree of flexibility in the responses offered by the pupil.

- can of soft drink ≈ 330 ml
- teaspoon ≈ 5 ml
- tin of soup ≈ 280 ml
- bottle of soft drink ≈ 2 litres
- cup and saucer ≈ 260 ml
- bathroom hand basin ≈ 25 litres
- bath ≈ 120 litres
- household kettle ≈ 1·5 litres

**Success criterion H:** Read and interpret intervals and divisions on partially numbered scales, and record a given volume accurately (l/ml)

| What to do | What to say | What to look out for |
|---|---|---|
| Referring to the marked-up copy of Resource 41, ask questions similar to the one shown here that require the pupil to read and interpret the different readings. | *What is the volume of water that is in this container?* | Can the pupil read and interpret a volume:<br>– to the nearest labelled division?<br>– to the nearest unlabelled division?<br>– to a division that lies between two unlabelled divisions? |
| Place the blank copy of Resource 41 on the table and ask the pupil to record a volume on one of the containers. | *If this container had two and a half litres of liquid in it what would this look like?*<br><br>*Show me what [four point seven five] litres would look like on this container.* | Can the pupil record a volume:<br>– to the nearest labelled division?<br>– to the nearest unlabelled division?<br>– to a division that lies between two unlabelled divisions? |

Continue until the pupil has demonstrated their ability to read and interpret intervals and divisions on partially numbered scales, and record a given volume accurately.

## Success criterion I: Calculate volumes/capacities (*l*/ml)

| What to do | What to say | What to look out for |
|---|---|---|
| Provide the pupil with pencil and paper.<br><br>Referring to the estimates of the capacities of the objects and the volumes of the cylinders/measuring jugs on Resource 41, choose two (or more) estimates or cylinders/measuring jugs and ask questions similar to the ones shown here that require the pupil to calculate different volumes and capacities.<br><br>Be sure to ask questions that are appropriate to the calculating abilities of the pupil.<br><br>If the pupil has made unreasonable estimates of the objects, you may wish to discuss with them the more realistic estimates, writing these on the sheet, and asking the pupil to calculate using these estimates. | *Look at container [2] and container [6]. Container [2] shows a volume [greater than/ less than] that of container [6]. How much [more/less] water does container [2] show?*<br><br>*Look at all of these containers. What is the difference between the container with the greatest volume and the container with the smallest volume?*<br><br>*Look at your estimates for the tin of soup and the bottle of soft drink. Approximately how many more [litres/millilitres] does the bottle of soft drink hold?*<br><br>*Approximately how much more water can a bath tub hold than a hand basin?* | Can the pupil use mental and written methods to calculate volumes and capacities, including using decimals to two decimal places?<br><br>Can the pupil make reasonable approximations when calculating volumes and capacities?<br><br>Can the pupil convert between different units of measure? |

Continue until the pupil has sufficiently demonstrated their ability to calculate volumes and capacities in litres and millilitres, converting between different units of measure where necessary.

## Success criterion J: Estimate and compare amounts of money

| What to do | What to say | What to look out for |
|---|---|---|
| Place Resource 42 on the table in front of the pupil.<br><br>Ask questions similar to the ones shown here that require the pupil to estimate and compare the total cost of the receipts.<br><br>Ask the pupil to write their estimate in the bubble above the receipt. | *Look at these receipts. Which bill do you think will cost the least? Estimate how much the total of this bill is. Write your estimate in the bubble above the receipt.*<br><br>*Look at the receipts from Kidl and B-Mart. Which bill do you think will be [larger/ smaller]? Write your estimate in the bubble beside the receipt.*<br><br>*How much do you think the bill from Convenience Corner will add up to?*<br><br>*Which of these receipts do you think will total more than £20?*<br><br>*Write your estimates for these bills in the bubble beside each receipt.* | Can the pupil make a reasonable estimate of the total?<br><br>Can the pupil use estimates to compare amounts of money? |

## Success criterion K: Calculate amounts of money, including £.p notation

| What to do | What to say | What to look out for |
|---|---|---|
| Provide the pupil with pencil and paper.<br><br>Ask the pupil to find the total of one of the receipts. | *Look at the receipt from [Middletons]. Can you work out the exact total of this bill?*<br><br>*Write your answer beside the word 'Total' on the receipt.* | Can the pupil add amounts of money using pounds and pence notation? |
| | *How does the exact total compare with your estimated total?* | |
| In the space beside 'Cash', write an amount to indicate the amount of cash tendered, e.g. £30. Choose an amount appropriate to the ability of the pupil. | *So the total bill from [Middletons is £25.38]. If I handed over [£30] in cash to pay for this bill, how much change would I receive?*<br><br>*Write your answer beside the word 'CHANGE' on the receipt.* | Can the pupil subtract amounts of money using pounds and pence notation? |
| Repeat above several times for other receipts. | | |
| Conclude by asking questions similar to those shown here that require the pupil to calculate amounts of money. | *The total cost for three packets of Jammie Dodgers is £3.63. What is the cost of one packet?*<br><br>*The cornflakes from Middletons were bought on sale at half the normal price. What is the normal price?*<br><br>*Look at the receipt from Best For Less. How much more expensive are the courgettes than the carrots?*<br><br>*Look at the receipt from Greenway's Store. What would be the total cost of six yoghurts?*<br><br>*The Greek-style yoghurt from B-Mart costs £1.54. If next week they have a special promotion and offer it at half price, what will be the sale price?* | Can the pupil use all four operations to calculate amounts of money, including using pounds and pence notation? |

**Answers**

Resource 42: Money

| Supermarket/Shop | Receipt total |
|---|---|
| Middletons | £25.38 |
| Greenway's Store | £14.28 |
| Kidl | £16.44 |
| Convenience Corner | £15.44 |
| B-Mart | £19.67 |
| Best For Less | £26.63 |

## What to do for those pupils working *below* or *above* expectations

Refer to the 'Tracking back and forward through the Mathematics National Curriculum attainment targets' charts on pages 310–320.

# Measurement

## National Curriculum attainment target

• Read, write and convert time between analogue and digital 12- and 24-hour clocks

## Prerequisite checklist

Can the pupil:
• tell and write the time from a 12-hour analogue clock?
• tell and write the time from a 24-hour analogue clock?

## Success criteria

A. Read the time on a 12-hour analogue clock and display the time on a 12-hour digital clock

B. Read the time on a 12-hour analogue clock and display the time on a 24-hour digital clock

C. Read the time on a 12-hour digital clock and display the time on a 12-hour analogue clock

D. Read the time on a 12-hour digital clock and display the time on a 24-hour analogue clock

E. Read the time on a 12-hour digital clock and display the time on a 24-hour digital clock

F. Read the time on a 24-hour digital clock and display the time on a 12-hour analogue clock

G. Read the time on a 24-hour digital clock and display the time on a 12-hour digital clock

## Resources

12-hour analogue clock with geared hands
24-hour analogue clock with geared hands
Resource 43: Digital times
Resource 44: Blank digital clocks
pencil (per pupil)

## NOTE

Prior to the Assessment Task:
– Cut out the cards from Resource 43 and arrange the 12-hour digital times into one pile and the 24-hour digital times into a separate pile.
– Cut out the cards from Resource 44 and arrange the 12-hour blank digital clocks into one pile and the 24-hour blank digital clocks into a separate pile.

## Assessment Task

**Success criterion A:** Read the time on a 12-hour analogue clock and display the time on a 12-hour digital clock

| What to do | What to say | What to look out for |
|---|---|---|
| Place the pile of 12-hour blank digital clocks from Resource 44 on the table. Provide the pupil with a pencil. | | |
| Set a 'past the hour' time to the nearest minute on the 12-hour analogue clock, e.g. 6:18. | *What time does this clock show?* *How else could you say this time?* | Can the pupil accurately read a 'past the hour' time to the nearest minute on a 12-hour analogue clock? |

| | This clock shows a time that is in the morning. | Can the pupil use a.m. and p.m. notation to display the time on a 12-hour digital clock? |
| | | e.g. |
| | Using one of these blank digital clocks, what would this time look like on a 12-hour digital clock? | |
| Set a 'to the hour' time to the nearest minute on the 12-hour analogue clock, e.g. 4:41. | What time does this clock show? How else could you say this time? | Can the pupil accurately read a 'to the hour' time to the nearest minute on a 12-hour analogue clock? |
| | This clock shows a time that is in the afternoon. | Can the pupil use a.m. and p.m. notation to display the time on a 12-hour digital clock? |
| | | e.g. |
| | Using another one of these blank digital clocks, what would this time look like on a 12-hour digital clock? | |

Repeat several times until the pupil has sufficiently demonstrated their ability to read the time on a 12-hour analogue clock and display the time on a 12-hour digital clock.

**Success criterion B:** Read the time on a 12-hour analogue clock and display the time on a 24-hour digital clock

| What to do | What to say | What to look out for |
| --- | --- | --- |
| Place the pile of 24-hour blank digital clocks from Resource 44 on the table. | | |
| Set a 'past the hour' time to the nearest minute on the 12-hour analogue clock, e.g. 10:05. | What time does this clock show? How else could you say this time? | Can the pupil accurately read a 'past the hour' time to the nearest minute on a 12-hour analogue clock? |
| | This clock shows a time that is in the evening. Using one of these blank digital clocks, what would this time look like on a 24-hour digital clock? | Can the pupil display the time on a 24-hour digital clock? e.g. |
| Set a 'to the hour' time to the nearest minute on the 12-hour analogue clock, e.g. 7:54. | What time does this clock read? How else could you say this time? | Can the pupil accurately read a 'to the hour' time to the nearest minute on a 12-hour analogue clock? |
| | This clock shows a time that is in the morning. Using another one of the blank digital clocks, what would this time look like on a 24-hour digital clock? | Can the pupil display the time on a 24-hour digital clock? e.g. |

Repeat several times until the pupil has sufficiently demonstrated their ability to read the time on a 12-hour analogue clock and display the time on a 24-hour digital clock.

**Success criterion C:** Read the time on a 12-hour digital clock and display the time on a 12-hour analogue clock

| What to do | What to say | What to look out for |
|---|---|---|
| Place the pile of 12-hour digital clocks from Resource 43 on the table.<br><br>Provide the pupil with the 12-hour analogue clock. | | |
| Place one of the 12-hour digital clocks in front of the pupil.<br><br>`7:43` ● a.m. ○ p.m. | *What time does this clock show?*<br><br>*How else could you say this time?*<br><br>*Is this time in the morning or in evening?*<br><br>*How do you know?* | Can the pupil accurately read the time on a 12-hour digital clock?<br><br><br>Does the pupil understand a.m. and p.m. notation? |
| | *Show me what this time would look like on your 12-hour analogue clock?* | Can the pupil display the time on a 12-hour analogue clock? |

Repeat several times until the pupil has sufficiently demonstrated their ability to read the time on a 12-hour digital clock and display the time on a 12-hour analogue clock.

---

**Success criterion D:** Read the time on a 12-hour digital clock and display the time on a 24-hour analogue clock

| What to do | What to say | What to look out for |
|---|---|---|
| Provide the pupil with the 24-hour analogue clock. | | |
| Place one of the 12-hour digital clocks from Resource 43 in front of the pupil.<br><br>`8:22` ○ a.m. ● p.m. | *What time does this clock read?*<br><br>*How else could you say this time?*<br><br>*Is this time in the morning or the evening?*<br><br>*How do you know?* | Can the pupil accurately read the time on a 12-hour digital clock?<br><br><br>Does the pupil understand a.m. and p.m. notation? |
| | *Show me what this time would look like on your 24-hour analogue clock?* | Can the pupil display the time on a 24-hour analogue clock? |

Repeat several times until the pupil has sufficiently demonstrated their ability to read the time on a 12-hour digital clock and display the time on a 24-hour analogue clock.

**Success criterion E:** Read the time on a 12-hour digital clock and display the time on a 24-hour digital clock

| What to do | What to say | What to look out for |
|---|---|---|
| Place the pile of 24-hour blank digital clocks from Resource 44 on the table.<br><br>Place one of the 12-hour digital clocks from Resource 43 in front of the pupil.<br><br>**6:36** ○ a.m. ● p.m.<br><br>**:** | *What time does this clock show?*<br><br>*How else could you say this time?*<br><br>*Is this time in the morning or in the evening?*<br><br>*How do you know?* | Can the pupil accurately read the time on a 12-hour digital clock?<br><br>Does the pupil understand a.m. and p.m. notation? |
| | *This clock shows a time that is in the evening.*<br><br>*Using one of these blank digital clocks, what would this time look like on a 24-hour digital clock?* | Can the pupil display the time on a 24-hour digital clock?<br>e.g.<br><br>**18:36** |

Repeat several times until the pupil has sufficiently demonstrated their ability to read the time on a 12-hour digital clock and display the time on a 24-hour digital clock.

---

**Success criterion F:** Read the time on a 24-hour digital clock and display the time on a 12-hour analogue clock

| What to do | What to say | What to look out for |
|---|---|---|
| Place the pile of 24-hour digital clocks from Resource 43 on the table.<br><br>Provide the pupil with the 12-hour analogue clock. | | |
| Place one of the 24-hour digital clocks in front of the pupil.<br><br>**07:24** | *What time does this clock show?*<br><br>*How else could you say this time?*<br><br>*Is this time in the morning or in evening?*<br><br>*How do you know?* | Can the pupil accurately read the time on a 24-hour digital clock? |
| | *Show me what this time would look like on your 12-hour analogue clock?* | Can the pupil display the time on a 12-hour analogue clock? |

Repeat several times until the pupil has sufficiently demonstrated their ability to read the time on a 24-hour digital clock and display the time on a 12-hour analogue clock.

**Success criterion 6:** Read the time on a 24-hour digital clock and display the time on a 12-hour digital clock

| What to do | What to say | What to look out for |
|---|---|---|
| Place the pile of 12-hour blank digital clocks from Resource 44 on the table.<br><br>Place one of the 24-hour digital clocks from Resource 43 in front of the pupil<br><br>`16:21`<br><br>`:` | *What time does this clock read?*<br><br>*How else could you say this time?*<br><br>*Is this time in the morning or in the evening?*<br><br>*How do you know?* | Can the pupil accurately read the time on a 24-hour digital clock? |
|  | *This clock shows a time that is in the afternoon.*<br><br>*Using one of these blank digital clocks, what would this time look like on a 12-hour digital clock?* | Can the pupil display the time on a 12-hour digital clock?<br>e.g.<br><br>`4:21` ○ a.m. ● p.m. |

Repeat several times until the pupil has sufficiently demonstrated their ability to read the time on a 24-hour digital clock and display the time on a 12-hour digital clock.

## What to do for those pupils working *below* or *above* expectations

Refer to the 'Tracking back and forward through the Mathematics National Curriculum attainment targets' charts on pages 310–320.

# Measurement

**NOTE**

- This Assessment Task, Assessment Tasks 12 and 17, and Assessment Task 27 all have the same four Success criteria. The difference between these Assessment Tasks is as follows:
  - Assessment Tasks 12 and 17: Solve problems involving all four operations
  - Assessment Task 27: Solve problems involving fractions and decimals to two decimal places
  - Assessment Task 33: Solve problems involving time

## National Curriculum attainment target

- Solve problems involving converting from hours to minutes; minutes to seconds; years to months; weeks to days

## Prerequisite checklist

Can the pupil:

- use units of time (seconds, minutes, hours, days… ) and know the relationships between them?
- solve problems involving addition, subtraction, multiplication or division in contexts of numbers or measures?
- identify and record the information or calculation needed to solve a problem?

- carry out the steps or calculations and check the solution in the context of the problem?
- present solutions to problems in an organised way, explaining decisions, methods and results?

## Success criteria

A. Read and understand the problem
B. Correctly identify which operation(s) to use
C. Carry out the calculation(s) to obtain the correct answer using an appropriate method
D. Check the answer using an effective method

## Resources

Resource 45: Problems involving time
pencil and paper (per pupil)

## Assessment Task

### Success criterion A: Read and understand the problem

| What to do | What to say | What to look out for |
|---|---|---|
| Provide the pupil with pencil and paper and one of the time word problem cards from Resource 45. | *Read the problem on your card.*<br><br>*What is your problem about?*<br><br>*What do you have to find out?* | Can the pupil read and understand the problem? |

### Success criterion B: Correctly identify which operation(s) to use

| What to do | What to say | What to look out for |
|---|---|---|
| Ask the pupil to suggest which operation(s) they need to use to work out the answer to the word problem. | *Which operation(s) do you need to use to work out the answer to your problem?* | Can the pupil correctly identify which operation(s) to use? |
| Ask the pupil to explain how they know which operation to use. | *How do you know you need to [add/subtract/multiply/divide]? What clues are there in the problem?* | |

**Success criterion C:** Carry out the calculation(s) to obtain the correct answer using an appropriate method

| What to do | What to say | What to look out for |
|---|---|---|
| Ask the pupil to write down the calculation(s) needed to solve the problem and work out the answer. | *On your sheet of paper I want you to write down the calculation(s) needed to solve your problem and then I want you to work out the answer.* | Can the pupil write the correct calculation(s)?<br><br>Does the pupil obtain the correct answer to the calculation(s)?<br><br>Does the pupil use an appropriate calculation method?<br><br>Can the pupil convert between different units of time?<br><br>Does the pupil obtain the correct answer to the problem? |
| Encourage the pupil to talk about the method they used to obtain their answer. | *Explain to me how you worked out the answer to this problem.* | Can the pupil explain their method of working out the answer to the problem? |

**Success criterion D:** Check the answer using an effective method

| What to do | What to say | What to look out for |
|---|---|---|
| Ask the pupil to check the answer to their problem. | *Are you sure that the answer to this problem is right?*<br><br>*How can you be so sure?* | Can the pupil check their answer using an effective method? |

Repeat Success criteria A–D until the pupil has sufficiently demonstrated their ability to solve problems involving time, including converting between different units.

### Answers

Resource 45: Problems involving time

| | |
|---|---|
| 1.  1 day, 8 hours and 5 minutes | 2.  65 days |
| 3.  4 hours and 30 minutes | 4.  2 hours and 30 minutes |
| 5.  3 hours and 20 minutes | 6.  5 seconds |
| 7.  8 hours | 8.  6 days |
| 9.  41 years 8 months | 10.  210 seconds |
| 11.  222 seconds | 12.  8:15 a.m. |
| 13.  25 minutes | 14.  23 weeks |
| 15.  12 hours | 16.  122 days |
| 17.  8 minutes | 18.  720 months |
| 19.  42 days | 20.  475 minutes |

## What to do for those pupils working *below* or *above* expectations

Refer to the 'Tracking back and forward through the Mathematics National Curriculum attainment targets' charts on pages 310–320.

# Geometry – Properties of shapes

## National Curriculum attainment target

- Compare and classify geometric shapes, including quadrilaterals and triangles, based on their properties and sizes

## Prerequisite checklist

Can the pupil:
- recognise and name common 2-D and 3-D shapes?
- describe the properties of common 2-D and 3-D shapes?
- draw 2-D shapes and make 3-D shapes using modelling materials?
- recognise angles as a property of shape?
- recognise 3-D shapes in different orientations and describe them?

## Success criteria

A. Identify 2-D shapes, including quadrilaterals and triangles
B. Describe the properties of 2-D shapes, including quadrilaterals and triangles
C. Identify 3-D shapes in different orientations
D. Describe the properties of 3-D shapes
E. Compare and classify 2-D and 3-D shapes, based on their properties

## Resources

Resource 46: 2-D shapes

Resource 47: 3-D shapes (alternatively, a set of the following 3-D shapes: sphere, hemisphere (if available), cone, cylinder, cube, cuboid, triangular prism, square-based pyramid and triangular-based pyramid (tetrahedron))

## NOTES

- By this stage most pupils should be able to name and describe the properties of regular polygons and 3-D shapes. The focus of this Assessment Task, therefore, should be on identifying and describing the different types of triangles (i.e. equilateral, isosceles, right-angled isosceles and scalene) and quadrilaterals (i.e. rectangle, square, parallelogram, trapezium, rhombus and kite).
- For Success criterion D: *Describe the properties 3-D shapes*, either use the pictorial representations of the 3-D shapes on Resource 47 or, if available and appropriate, use the set of 3-D shapes.

## Assessment Task

**Success criterion A:** Identify 2-D shapes, including quadrilaterals and triangles

| What to do | What to say | What to look out for |
|---|---|---|
| Display Resource 46 and ask the pupil to identify a named 2-D shape. | *Point to a [heptagon].* | Does the pupil recognise a named 2-D shape? |
| Point to a particular shape and ask the pupil to name the shape. | *What is this shape called?* | Can the pupil name the 2-D shape? |

Continue until the pupil has sufficiently demonstrated their ability to identify the following 2-D shapes, and in particular the different types of triangles and quadrilaterals: circle, semicircle, equilateral triangle, right-angled isosceles triangle, isosceles triangle, scalene triangle, rectangle, square, parallelogram, trapezium, rhombus, kite, pentagon, hexagon, heptagon, octagon, nonagon, decagon and dodecagon.

**Success criterion B:** Describe the properties of 2-D shapes, including quadrilaterals and triangles

| What to do | What to say | What to look out for |
|---|---|---|
| Referring to the 2-D shapes on Resource 46, ask the pupil to describe the properties of a shape. | *Describe this shape to me.* | Can the pupil describe the properties of the 2-D shape including features such as: <br> – number of sides <br> – number of angles <br> – size of angles <br> – lines of symmetry <br> – whether opposite angles are equal <br> – whether opposite sides are equal <br> – whether adjacent sides are equal <br> – whether sides are parallel <br> – whether sides are perpendicular? |
| If the pupil has difficulty in describing the properties of the shape, ask questions similar to the ones shown here. <br><br> The main focus of your questioning should be on encouraging the pupil to describe the properties of different types of triangles and quadrilaterals. | *How many [sides/vertices] does this shape have?* <br><br> *What can you tell me about the angles in this shape?* <br><br> *What can you tell me about the opposite angles in a parallelogram?* <br><br> *What can you tell me about the opposite sides in a rhombus?* | Does the pupil describe the properties of different types of triangles and quadrilaterals as shown below? |

Continue until the pupil has sufficiently demonstrated their ability to describe the properties of the following 2-D shapes, and in particular the different types of triangles and quadrilaterals: circle, semicircle, equilateral triangle, right-angled isosceles triangle, isosceles triangle, scalene triangle, rectangle, square, parallelogram, trapezium, rhombus, kite, pentagon, hexagon, heptagon, octagon, nonagon, decagon and dodecagon.

### Properties of different types of triangles

A triangle is a polygon with three sides and three angles. The three angles in a triangle always add up to 180°.

- An equilateral triangle has three equal sides and three equal angles. Each angle measures 60°.
- A right-angled triangle has an angle of 90° (a right angle). The longest side is opposite the right angle.
- An isosceles triangle has two equal sides. The angles opposite these two sides are also equal.
- A scalene triangle has no equal sides or angles. All three sides are of different lengths and all three angles are different sizes.

### Properties of different types of quadrilaterals

A quadrilateral is a polygon with four straight sides. The four angles in a quadrilateral always add up to 360°.

- A rectangle has four right angles (90°). Its opposite sides are of equal length and are parallel to each other.
- A square has four equal sides. Each of its four angles is a right angle (90°). The opposite sides of a square are parallel.
- A parallelogram has two pairs of parallel sides. Its opposite sides are of equal length and its opposite angles are equal.
- A rhombus has four equal sides. The opposite angles are equal and the opposite sides are parallel.
- A trapezium, also called a trapezoid, has one pair of parallel sides. These sides are not the same length.
- A kite has two pairs of adjacent sides that are equal in length. Opposite sides are not of equal length. One pair of opposite angles are equal. The other pair of angles are different sizes.

## Success criterion C: Identify 3-D shapes in different orientations

| What to do | What to say | What to look out for |
|---|---|---|
| Display Resource 47 (or the set of 3-D shapes) and ask the pupil to identify a named 3-D shape. | *Point to a [cuboid].* | Does the pupil recognise a named 3-D shape? |
| Point to a particular shape and ask the pupil to name the shape. | *What is this shape called?* | Can the pupil name the 3-D shape? |

Continue until the pupil has sufficiently demonstrated their ability to identify the following 3-D shapes in different orientations: sphere, hemisphere, cone, cylinder, cube, cuboid, triangular prism, square-based pyramid and triangular-based pyramid (tetrahedron).

## Success criterion D: Describe the properties of 3-D shapes

| What to do | What to say | What to look out for |
|---|---|---|
| Referring to the 3-D shapes on Resource 47 (or the set of 3-D shapes), ask the pupil to describe the properties of a shape. | *Describe this shape to me.* | Can the pupil describe the properties of the 3-D shape including features such as:<br>– number of faces<br>– number of edges<br>– number of vertices? |
| If the pupil has difficulty in describing the properties of the shape, ask questions similar to the ones shown here: | *How many faces does this shape have?*<br><br>*How many vertices does this shape have?*<br><br>*How many edges does this shape have?* | |

Continue until the pupil has sufficiently demonstrated their ability to describe the properties of the following 3-D shapes: sphere, hemisphere, cone, cylinder, cube, cuboid, triangular prism, square-based pyramid and triangular-based pyramid (tetrahedron).

## Success criterion E: Compare and classify 2-D and 3-D shapes, based on their properties

| What to do | What to say | What to look out for |
|---|---|---|
| Referring to the 2-D and 3-D shapes on Resources 46 and 47, ask the pupil to compare two or classify more than two shapes. Ask questions similar to the ones shown here: | *Look at these two triangles. What is similar about them? What is different?*<br>*What can you tell me about these two shapes? How are they different? How are they the same?*<br>*What do these shapes have in common?*<br>*Which of these shapes have at least one pair of opposite sides parallel?*<br>*Which of these shapes have at least one pair of perpendicular sides?*<br>*Which of these shapes have adjacent sides that are equal?*<br>*Which of these shapes have opposite sides that are equal?*<br>*Which of these shapes have opposite angles that are equal?* | Can the pupil compare and classify 2-D and 3-D shapes based on their properties? |

Repeat, referring to different pairs or sets of 2-D and/or 3-D shapes until the pupil has sufficiently demonstrated their ability to compare and classify 2-D and 3-D shapes based on their properties.

## What to do for those pupils working *below* or *above* expectations

Refer to the 'Tracking back and forward through the Mathematics National Curriculum attainment targets' charts on pages 310–320.

# Geometry – Properties of shapes

## National Curriculum attainment target

- Identify acute and obtuse angles and compare and order angles up to two right angles by size

## Prerequisite checklist

Can the pupil:
- identify right angles?
- identify whether angles are greater than or less than a right angle?
- recognise and name common 2-D shapes?
- describe the properties of common 2-D shapes?

## Success criteria

A. Identify right angles, acute angles and obtuse angles
B. Identify right angles, acute angles and obtuse angles in regular polygons
C. Compare angles less than 180°
D. Order angles less than 180°

## Resources

Resource 46: 2-D shapes
Resource 48: Angle cards
right-angle tester (per pupil)
pencil and paper (per pupil)
ruler (per pupil)

## NOTES

- Prior to the Assessment Task, cut out the angle cards from Resource 48 and arrange them in a pile.
- Provide the pupil with a right-angle tester for each of the Success criteria. However, at this stage, pupils should be able to identify most acute angles, obtuse angles and certainly right angles by sight. However, for angles that are close to 90°, you may want to encourage the pupil to use the right-angle tester.

## Assessment Task

**Success criterion A:** Identify right angles, acute angles and obtuse angles

| What to do | What to say | What to look out for |
|---|---|---|
| Place the pile of angle cards from Resource 48 face down on the table in front of the pupil.<br><br>Repeat until all 12 angles have been identified. | *Turn over the top card.*<br><br>*Is this angle a right angle, an acute angle or an obtuse angle?* | Can the pupil identify right angles, acute angles and obtuse angles? |
| | *What makes an angle a right angle?* | Does the pupil describe a right angle as having 90°? |
| | *How do you know an angle is an acute angle?* | Does the pupil describe an acute angle as having less than 90°? |
| | *How do you know an angle is an obtuse angle?* | Does the pupil describe an obtuse angle as having more than 90° but less than 180°? |

**Success criterion B:** Identify right angles, acute angles and obtuse angles in regular polygons

| What to do | What to say | What to look out for |
|---|---|---|
| Display Resource 46.<br><br>Briefly name and discuss some of the 2-D shapes on the sheet. | *Point to [an octagon].*<br><br>*What is this shape called?* | Does the pupil recognise a named 2-D shape?<br><br>Can the pupil name the 2-D shape? |
| | *Look at all the 2-D shapes on the sheet. Point to a right angle in one of the shapes.*<br><br>*Can you find another shape that has a right angle?*<br><br>*What makes this angle a right angle?* | Can the pupil identify right angles in regular polygons?<br><br><br><br>Does the pupil describe a right angle as having 90°? |
| | *Point to an angle in one of these 2-D shapes that is an acute angle?*<br><br>*Can you find another shape that has an acute angle?*<br><br>*How do you know that this angle is an acute angle?* | Can the pupil identify acute angles in regular polygons?<br><br><br><br>Does the pupil describe an acute angle as having less than 90°? |
| | *Now point to an angle in one of the 2-D shapes that is an obtuse angle.*<br><br>*Can you find another shape that has an obtuse angle?*<br><br>*What makes this an obtuse angle?* | Can the pupil identify obtuse angles in regular polygons?<br><br><br><br>Does the pupil describe an obtuse angle as having more than 90° but less than 180°? |

Repeat until each pupil has sufficiently demonstrated their ability to identify right angles, acute angles and obtuse angles in regular polygons.

## Success criterion C: Compare angles less than 180°

| What to do | What to say | What to look out for |
|---|---|---|
| Spread the angle cards from Resource 48 face up on the table. | *Point to an angle that is bigger than a right angle.*<br>*What do we call this angle?* | Can the pupil identify and name an obtuse angle? |
| Ask the pupil to compare the size of the angles by asking questions similar to the ones shown here: | *Point to an angle that is smaller than a right angle.*<br>*What is this angle called?* | Can the pupil identify and name an acute angle? |
| Point to different angle cards, asking questions similar to the ones shown here: | *Point to a card that shows an angle bigger than this angle.*<br><br>*Point to an angle that is smaller than the angle on this card.* | Can the pupil compare the size of two angles? |
| Provide the pupil with a pencil, paper and a ruler and ask them to draw a right angle, an acute angle and an obtuse angle. | *Can you draw me a right angle?*<br><br>*Draw an acute angle.*<br><br>*Draw an angle for me that is larger than a right angle.*<br><br>*Draw me an angle of 180 degrees.* | Can the pupil draw:<br>  – a right angle<br>  – an acute angle<br>  – an obtuse angle<br>  – a straight angle? |

## Success criterion D: Order angles less than 180°

| What to do | What to say | What to look out for |
|---|---|---|
| Collect the angle cards from Resource 48 and place them in a pile.<br><br>Take four to six cards and place them face up on the table in front of the pupil. | *Look at these angles.*<br><br>*Which is the smallest angle?*<br><br>*Which is the largest angle?*<br><br>*Can you place these angles in order of size, starting with the smallest angle?* | Can the pupil compare angles less than 180°?<br><br>Can the pupil order angles less than 180°? |

Collect the angle cards, shuffle them and repeat the above using another set of four to six cards.
Continue until each pupil has sufficiently demonstrated their ability to order angles less than 180°.

## What to do for those pupils working *below* or *above* expectations

Refer to the 'Tracking back and forward through the Mathematics National Curriculum attainment targets' charts on pages 310–320.

# Geometry – Properties of shapes

## National Curriculum attainment target

- Identify lines of symmetry in 2-D shapes presented in different orientations

## Prerequisite checklist

Can the pupil:

- identify and describe the properties of 2-D shapes, including the number of sides and line symmetry in a vertical line?
- identify reflective symmetry in patterns?

## Success criteria

**A.** Identify lines of symmetry in regular 2-D shapes

**B.** Identify lines of symmetry in 2-D shapes and recognise shapes with no lines of symmetry

## Resources

Resource 46: 2-D shapes (alternatively, a set of the following 2-D shapes: circle, equilateral triangle, rectangle, square, regular pentagon, regular hexagon and regular octagon; also, if available, any of the following additional 2-D shapes: semicircle, right-angled isosceles triangle, isosceles triangle, scalene triangle, parallelogram, trapezium, rhombus, kite, regular heptagon, regular nonagon, regular decagon and regular dodecagon)

Resource 49: Lines of symmetry (enlarged to A3)

mirror

0–9 dice

1–6 dice

ruler

pencil

## Assessment Task

**Success criterion A:** Identify lines of symmetry in regular 2-D shapes

| What to do | What to say | What to look out for |
|---|---|---|
| Place Resource 46 (or the set of 2-D shapes) and the mirror on the table in front of the pupil. | | |
| Pointing to a shape, ask the pupil to identify a line of symmetry. | *Can you show me a line of symmetry in this shape?*<br><br>*Can you find another line of symmetry in this square?*<br><br>*Show me a line of symmetry in this pentagon.* | Can the pupil identify lines of symmetry in regular 2-D shapes? |
| If appropriate, ask questions similar to the ones shown here to assess whether the pupil can identify the total number of lines of symmetry in regular 2-D shapes. | *How many lines of symmetry are there in a square?*<br><br>*How many lines of symmetry are there in this triangle?*<br><br>*How many lines of symmetry are there in a regular pentagon?* | Can the pupil identify the total number of lines of symmetry in regular 2-D shapes? |

Continue until the pupil has sufficiently demonstrated their ability to identify lines of symmetry in regular 2-D shapes.

**Success criterion B:** Identify lines of symmetry in 2-D shapes and recognise shapes with no lines of symmetry

### What to do

Place Resource 49, the mirror, the two dice, the ruler and the pencil on the table in front of the pupil.

Explain the following to the pupil:
- The 1–6 dice represents the horizontal axis and the 0–9 dice represents the vertical axis.
- The pupil rolls the dice (or takes turns to roll the dice if more than one pupil is undertaking the Assessment Task) and finds the corresponding shape on the sheet.
- The pupil then uses their ruler and pencil to draw a line of symmetry on the shape if it has one.
- If the shape does not have a line of symmetry, they write 0 on the shape.
- If the pupil rolls the dice and lands on a shape that has already been drawn on, they roll the dice again.

| What to do | What to say | What to look out for |
|---|---|---|
| If appropriate, for those shapes with more than one line of symmetry, once a pupil has drawn one line of symmetry on the shape, ask questions similar to the ones shown here to assess whether the pupil can identify the total number of lines of symmetry in regular 2-D shapes. | *Does this shape have another line of symmetry?*<br><br>*Does this shape have any more lines of symmetry?*<br><br>*How many lines of symmetry does this shape have?* | Can the pupil identify the total number of lines of symmetry in regular 2-D shapes? |

Continue until the pupil has sufficiently demonstrated their ability to identify lines of symmetry in 2-D shapes and recognise shapes with no lines of symmetry.

**Answers**

Resource 49: Lines of symmetry

### What to do for those pupils working *below* or *above* expectations

Refer to the 'Tracking back and forward through the Mathematics National Curriculum attainment targets' charts on pages 310–320.

# Geometry – Properties of shapes

## National Curriculum attainment target

- Complete a simple symmetric figure with respect to a specific line of symmetry

## Prerequisite checklist

Can the pupil:

- identify and describe the properties of 2-D shapes, including the number of sides and line symmetry in a vertical line?
- identify reflective symmetry in patterns?
- draw and complete shapes with reflective symmetry?
- draw the reflection of a simple shape in a mirror line along one side?

## Success criteria

A. Draw and complete shapes in a vertical or horizontal line of symmetry where the edges of the shape are parallel or perpendicular to the mirror line

B. Draw and complete shapes in a vertical or horizontal line of symmetry where the edges of the shape are not all parallel or perpendicular to the mirror line

C. Draw and complete shapes in a diagonal line of symmetry

D. Complete symmetrical patterns with up to two lines of symmetry

## Resources

Resource 50: Reflections (1)

Resource 51: Reflections (2)

pencil (per pupil)

ruler (per pupil)

mirror (optional) (per pupil)

## NOTE

- For this Assessment Task, the same activity is used to assess each of the four Success criteria listed above and in the table below. As the pupil undertakes the activity, ask questions similar to those overleaf to assess the pupil's level of mastery in each of the four Success criteria.

| Success criterion A | An edge of the shape touching the mirror line. | Shapes A and B |
| | Edges of the shape not touching the mirror line. | Shapes C and D |
| Success criterion B | An edge of the shape touching the mirror line. | Shapes E and F |
| | Edges of the shape not touching the mirror line. | Shapes G and H |
| Success criterion C | Shape in a diagonal line of symmetry. | Shapes I and J |
| Success criterion D | Pattern with two lines of symmetry at right angles. | Shape K |
| | Pattern with one diagonal line of symmetry. | Shape L |

## Assessment Task

**Success criterion A:** Draw and complete shapes in a vertical or horizontal line of symmetry where the edges of the shape are parallel or perpendicular to the mirror line

| What to do | What to say | What to look out for |
|---|---|---|
| Provide the pupil with a ruler and a pencil and, if appropriate, a mirror.<br><br>Place Resource 50 on the table in front of the pupil and draw their attention to Shape A or B. | *Use the ruler to carefully draw the [vertical/horizontal] reflection of the shape in the line of symmetry.* | Can the pupil draw and complete the shape in a vertical or horizontal line of symmetry where the edges of the shape are parallel or perpendicular to the mirror line, and where an edge of the shape touches the mirror line? |

| | | |
|---|---|---|
| Draw the pupil's attention to Shape C or D. | *Use the ruler to carefully draw the [vertical/horizontal] reflection of the shape in the line of symmetry.* | Can the pupil draw and complete the shape in a vertical or horizontal line of symmetry where the edges of the shape are parallel or perpendicular to the mirror line, and where the edges of the shape do not touch the mirror line? |

If appropriate, use whichever shapes (A to D) have not been used to assess the pupil's level of mastery in drawing and completing shapes in a vertical or horizontal line of symmetry where the edges of the shape are parallel or perpendicular to the mirror line.

**Success criterion B:** Draw and complete shapes in a vertical or horizontal line of symmetry where the edges of the shape are not all parallel or perpendicular to the mirror line

| What to do | What to say | What to look out for |
|---|---|---|
| Draw the pupil's attention to Shape E or F on Resource 50. | *Use the ruler to carefully draw the [vertical/horizontal] reflection of the shape in the line of symmetry.* | Can the pupil draw and complete the shape in a vertical or horizontal line of symmetry where the edges of the shape are not all parallel or perpendicular to the mirror line, and where an edge of the shape touches the mirror line? |
| Place Resource 51 on the table in front of the pupil and draw their attention to Shape G or H. | | Can the pupil draw and complete the shape in a vertical or horizontal line of symmetry where the edges of the shape are not all parallel or perpendicular to the mirror line, and where the edges of the shape do not touch the mirror line? |

If appropriate, use whichever shapes (E to H) have not been used to assess the pupil's level of mastery in drawing and completing shapes in a vertical or horizontal line of symmetry where the edges of the shape are not all parallel or perpendicular to the mirror line.

**Success criterion C:** Draw and complete shapes in a diagonal line of symmetry

| What to do | What to say | What to look out for |
|---|---|---|
| Draw the pupil's attention to Shape I or J on Resource 51. | *Use the ruler to carefully draw the reflection of the shape in the diagonal line of symmetry.* | Can the pupil draw and complete the shape in a diagonal line of symmetry? |

If appropriate, use whichever shape (I or J) has not been used to assess the pupil's level of mastery in drawing and completing shapes in a diagonal line of symmetry.

**Success criterion D:** Complete symmetrical patterns with up to two lines of symmetry

| What to do | What to say | What to look out for |
|---|---|---|
| Draw the pupil's attention to Shape K on Resource 51. | *Colour squares on this grid to make the symmetrical pattern.* | Can the pupil complete the symmetrical pattern with two lines of symmetry at right angles? |
| Draw the pupil's attention to Shape L on Resource 51. | | Can the pupil complete the symmetrical pattern with a diagonal line of symmetry? |

## What to do for those pupils working *below* or *above* expectations

Refer to the 'Tracking back and forward through the Mathematics National Curriculum attainment targets' charts on pages 310–320.

# Geometry – Position and direction

## National Curriculum attainment target

- Describe positions on a 2-D grid as coordinates in the first quadrant

## Prerequisite checklist

Can the pupil:
- identify horizontal and vertical lines?
- identify pairs of perpendicular and parallel lines?

## Success criteria

A. Read and write coordinates in the first quadrant
B. Plot coordinates in the first quadrant

## Resources

Resource 52: Coordinates (per pupil)
pencil and paper (per pupil)

### NOTE

- Prior to the Assessment Task, cut out the coordinates cards from the bottom of Resource 52 and arrange them in a pile.

## Assessment Task

### Success criterion A: Read and write coordinates in the first quadrant

| What to do | What to say | What to look out for |
| --- | --- | --- |
| Place the coordinates grid from Resource 52 on the table in front of the pupil.<br><br>Provide the pupil with pencil and paper. | Look at this grid.<br><br>What are the coordinates of Point A on this grid?<br><br>Can you write these coordinates down for me? | Can the pupil read coordinates in the first quadrant?<br><br>Can the pupil write coordinates in the first quadrant? |

Repeat for Points B to H or until the pupil has sufficiently demonstrated their ability to read and write coordinates in the first quadrant.

### Success criterion B: Plot coordinates in the first quadrant

| What to do | What to say | What to look out for |
| --- | --- | --- |
| Place the pile of coordinates cards from Resource 52 face down on the table beside the coordinates grid. | Turn over the top card.<br><br>Can you plot this point on the coordinates grid? | Can the pupil plot coordinates in the first quadrant? |

Repeat for Points I to P or until the pupil has sufficiently demonstrated their ability to plot coordinates in the first quadrant.

**Answers**

Resource 52: Coordinates

A (7, 10)
B (9, 3)
C (8, 5)
D (3, 6)
E (1, 9)
F (2, 1)
G (5, 8)
H (6, 2)

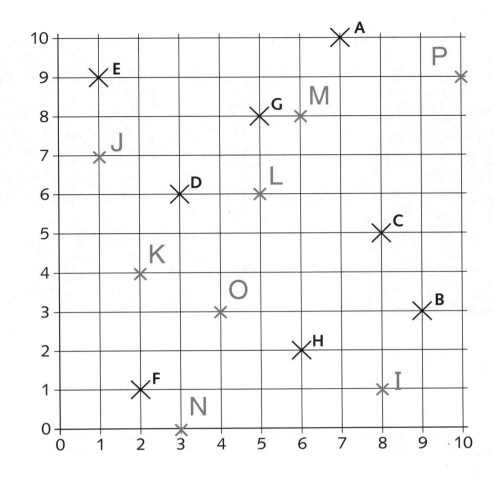

## What to do for those pupils working *below* or *above* expectations

Refer to the 'Tracking back and forward through the Mathematics National Curriculum attainment targets' charts on pages 310–320.

# Geometry – Position and direction

## National Curriculum attainment target

- Describe movements between positions as translations of a given unit to the left/right and up/down

## Prerequisite checklist

Can the pupil:

- identify horizontal and vertical lines?
- identify pairs of perpendicular and parallel lines?
- use mathematical vocabulary to describe position, direction and movement, including movement in a straight line?

## Success criteria

**A.** Describe the movement of a shape after one translation

**B.** Describe the movement of a shape after two translations

**C.** Draw the position of a shape after one translation

**D.** Draw the position of a shape after two translations

## Resources

Resource 53: Translations (1)

Resource 54: Translations (2) (per pupil)

pencil (per pupil)

ruler (per pupil)

## Assessment Task

### Success criterion A: Describe the movement of a shape after one translation

| What to do | What to say | What to look out for |
|---|---|---|
| Place Resource 53 on the table in front of the pupil. | Look at Shape A.<br><br>How has Shape A been translated to Shape A$^l$? | Does the pupil describe the movement of Shape A to Shape A$^l$ as 4 squares/units to the right? |
| | Look at Shape B.<br><br>How has Shape B been translated to Shape B$^l$? | Does the pupil describe the movement of Shape B to Shape B$^l$ as 7 squares/units up? |

### Success criterion B: Describe the movement of a shape after two translations

| What to do | What to say | What to look out for |
|---|---|---|
| Draw the pupil's attention to Shape C on Resource 53. | Look at Shape C.<br><br>How has Shape C been translated to Shape C$^l$? | Does the pupil describe the movement of Shape C to Shape C$^l$ as 4 squares/units to the left and 5 squares units down? |
| | Look at Shape D.<br><br>How has Shape D been translated to Shape D$^l$? | Does the pupil describe the movement of Shape D to Shape D$^l$ as 1 square/unit to the right and 7 squares/units up? |
| | Look at Shape E.<br><br>How has Shape E been translated to Shape E$^l$? | Does the pupil describe the movement of Shape E to Shape E$^l$ as 5 squares/units to the left and 3 squares/units up? |

**Success criterion C:** Draw the position of a shape after one translation

| What to do | What to say | What to look out for |
|---|---|---|
| Place Resource 54 on the table in front of the pupil.<br><br>Provide the pupil with a pencil and a ruler. | *Look at Shape F.*<br><br>*I want you to translate this shape eight [squares/units] to the right.* | Can the pupil draw the position of a shape after one translation? |
| | *Look at Shape G.*<br><br>*This time I want you to translate this shape seven [squares/units] down.* | |

**Success criterion D:** Draw the position of a shape after two translations

| What to do | What to say | What to look out for |
|---|---|---|
| Draw the pupil's attention to Shape H on Resource 54.<br><br>Ensure that the pupil still has access to a pencil and a ruler. | *Now look at Shape H.*<br><br>*Translate this shape one [square/unit] down and six [squares/units] to the left.* | Can the pupil draw the position of a shape after two translations? |
| | *This time look at Shape I.*<br><br>*I want you to translate this shape four [squares/units] down and five [squares/units] to the right.* | |
| | *Finally look at Shape J.*<br><br>*Translate this shape ten [squares/units] to the left and three [squares/units] up.* | |

## What to do for those pupils working *below* or *above* expectations

Refer to the 'Tracking back and forward through the Mathematics National Curriculum attainment targets' charts on pages 310–320.

# Geometry – Position and direction

## National Curriculum attainment target

- Plot specified points and draw sides to complete a given polygon

## Prerequisite checklist

Can the pupil:

- identify horizontal and vertical lines?
- identify pairs of perpendicular and parallel lines?
- recognise and name common 2-D shapes, including quadrilaterals?
- describe the properties of common 2-D shapes, including quadrilaterals?
- describe positions on a 2-D grid as coordinates in the first quadrant?

## Success criteria

**A.** Plot specified points and draw sides to complete a given polygon

**B.** Write a set of coordinates to draw a given polygon

## Resources

Resource 55: Plotting points to make quadrilaterals (per pupil)

pencil (per pupil)

ruler (per pupil)

................................................................................

## Assessment Task

**Success criterion A:** Plot specified points and draw sides to complete a given polygon

| What to do | What to say | What to look out for |
|---|---|---|
| Place Resource 55 on the table in front of the pupil. | *Look at these four pairs of lines on the sheet.* | |
| Provide the pupil with a pencil and a ruler. | *Each pair of lines is two sides of a quadrilateral.* | |
| Draw the pupil's attention to the two sides of Shape A. | *Look at the two sides that form Shape A. These are two sides of a rectangle.* | |
| | *What are the coordinates for the missing vertex of the rectangle?* | Does the pupil give the correct coordinates for the missing vertex, i.e. (10, 13)? |
| | *Mark this point on the grid and then use the ruler to complete the rectangle.* | Can the pupil draw the sides to complete the rectangle? |
| Draw the pupil's attention to the two sides of Shape B. | *Look at the two sides that form Shape B. Shape B is a parallelogram.* | |
| | *What are the coordinates for the missing vertex of this parallelogram?* | Does the pupil give the correct coordinates for the missing vertex, i.e. (6, 5)? |
| | *Mark this point on the grid and then use the ruler to complete the parallelogram.* | Can the pupil draw the sides to complete the parallelogram? |
| Draw the pupil's attention to the two sides of Shape C. | *Look at the two sides that form Shape C. Shape C is a square.* | |
| | *What are the coordinates for the missing vertex of this square?* | Does the pupil give the correct coordinates for the missing vertex, i.e. (15, 11)? |
| | *Mark this point on the grid and then use the ruler to complete the square.* | Can the pupil draw the sides to complete the square? |

| Draw the pupil's attention to the two sides of Shape D. | Look at the two sides that form Shape D. Shape D is a trapezium.<br><br>What are the coordinates for the missing vertex of the trapezium?<br><br>Mark this point on the grid and then use the ruler to complete the trapezium. | Does the pupil give the correct coordinates for the missing vertex, i.e. (10, 3)?<br>Can the pupil draw the sides to complete the trapezium? |
|---|---|---|
| | You now need to listen carefully. I'm going to give you some coordinates to plot. Mark each pair of coordinates with an x. There are four pairs of coordinates altogether. Ready? Let's go. | |
| Slowly read out the four pairs of coordinates, allowing sufficient time for the pupil to plot each point. | (13, 1)<br>(11, 3)<br>(13, 8)<br>(15, 3) | Can the pupil plot coordinates in the first quadrant? |
| Once the pupil has plotted all four points, ask them to join these points in the order in which you said them. | These four points are the four vertices of another quadrilateral.<br><br>Do you know which quadrilateral this is?<br><br><br>Using your ruler, I want you to join together these four points in the same order that you plotted them on the grid to draw the kite. | Does the pupil recognise that the four pairs of coordinates are the four vertices of a kite?<br><br>Can the pupil draw the sides to complete the kite? |
| If necessary, ensure that the pupil realises that the last point (15, 3) needs to connect with the first point (13, 1) in order to complete the four sides of the kite. | You have joined together all the points you plotted on the grid, but this still hasn't made a kite. What do you need to do to make a closed shape and complete the kite? | Does the pupil realise that the last point (15, 3) needs to connect with the first point (13, 1) in order to complete the four sides of the kite? |

**Success criterion B:** Write a set of coordinates to draw a given polygon

| What to do | What to say | What to look out for |
|---|---|---|
| Draw the pupil's attention to the completed rectangle at the top of Resource 55 (Shape A). | Look at Shape A: the rectangle.<br><br>In the same way as I gave you a set of coordinates to plot the vertices of a kite, at the bottom of this sheet I want you to write a set of coordinates that would help someone plot the vertices of the rectangle.<br><br>Make sure you write the coordinates in an order that will complete the rectangle. | Can the pupil write a set of four [or five] coordinates in an acceptable order, e.g. (4, 13), (4, 15), (10, 15), (10, 13), (4, 13)? |

If appropriate, repeat for Shapes B, C and D until the pupil has sufficiently demonstrated their ability to write a set of coordinates to draw a given polygon.

## What to do for those pupils working *below* or *above* expectations

Refer to the 'Tracking back and forward through the Mathematics National Curriculum attainment targets' charts on pages 310–320.

## Statistics

### National Curriculum attainment target

- Interpret and present discrete and continuous data using appropriate graphical methods, including bar charts and time graphs

### Prerequisite checklist

Can the pupil:

- interpret and construct simple pictograms, tally charts, block diagrams, bar charts and simple tables?
- ask and answer simple questions?

### Success criteria

A. Identify what data to collect
B. Collect data using frequency tables or tally charts
C. Organise data
D. Present data in pictograms, bar charts or time (line) graphs
E. Analyse data
F. Interpret data

### Resources

Resource 56: Collecting, organising and presenting data (per pupil)

squared paper (per pupil)

pencil (per pupil)

ruler (per pupil)

ICT data handling package – optional (per pupil)

### NOTES

- Prior to the Assessment Task, write a question in the box at the top of Resource 56. Choose a topic to investigate that is relevant to your particular circumstances and of interest to the pupil(s), e.g. *How far do most pupils travel to school? What is the most common type of transport that pupils use to travel to school? Which school lunch tastes best? Which school lunch is best for you? Which job do you think is the most important? Who is Year 4's favourite author? Is it true that most advertisements on television are for cars?* Alternatively, you may wish the pupil(s) to suggest their own line of enquiry.
- If this Assessment Task is being undertaken with more than one pupil, it is advisable for the pupils to work in pairs.

## Assessment Task

**Success criterion A:** Identify what data to collect

**Success criterion B:** Collect data using frequency tables or tally charts

**Success criterion C:** Organise data

**Success criterion D:** Present data in pictograms, bar charts or time (line) graphs

**Success criterion E:** Analyse data

**Success criterion F:** Interpret data

| What to do | What to say | What to look out for |
|---|---|---|
| Provide the pupil (or pair of pupils) with a copy of Resource 56, some squared paper, a pencil and a ruler. | | |
| Briefly discuss the question with the pupil(s). | | |
| Discuss the first five questions on the resource sheet. | *What data do you need to collect?*<br><br>*How are you going to collect the data?*<br><br>*How are you going to organise the data?*<br><br>*How are you going to present the data?*<br><br>*Why are you going to present it this way?* | Can the pupil:<br>– identify what data to collect?<br>– collect the data using a frequency table or tally chart?<br>– organise the data?<br>– present the data in a pictogram, bar chart or time (line) graph?<br>– analyse the data?<br>– interpret the data? |
| Ask the pupil(s) to collect, organise and present the data. | | |
| When the pupil(s) have completed the investigation, ask questions similar to the ones shown here: | *What does this [bar chart/ pictogram/table/time (line) graph] tell you?*<br><br>*What makes the information easy or difficult to interpret?*<br><br>*Make up three questions that can be answered using the data in this [bar chart/pictogram/table/time (line) graph].*<br><br>*What further information could you collect to answer the question more fully?* | |
| Ask the pupil(s) to write about what they found out and what things they would do differently and the same if they were asked to investigate the same question again. | | |

## What to do for those pupils working *below* or *above* expectations

Refer to the 'Tracking back and forward through the Mathematics National Curriculum attainment targets' charts on pages 310–320.

## Statistics

### National Curriculum attainment target

- Solve comparison, sum and difference problems using information presented in bar charts, pictograms, tables and other graphs

### Prerequisite checklist

Can the pupil:

- interpret and construct simple tables, tally charts, pictograms, block diagrams and bar charts?
- ask and answer simple questions?

### Success criteria

A. Answer and ask questions using information presented in a table

B. Answer and ask questions using information presented in a scaled pictogram

C. Answer and ask questions using information presented in a scaled bar chart

D. Answer and ask questions using information presented in a time graph

E. Interpret and infer information presented in a table, pictogram, bar chart and time graph

### Resources

Resource 57: Statistics (preferably enlarged to A3)

### NOTE

- Prior to the Assessment task, in the key underneath the 'Travelling to work' pictogram on Resource 57, write the number that each symbol ( 👤 ) in the pictogram represents. Use an even number so that the symbol ( 👤 ) has meaning. It is recommend that the symbol 👤 represents 2 or 10, but for some pupils it may be more appropriate if the symbol represents another number.

## Assessment Task

**Success criterion A:** Answer and ask questions using information presented in a table

| What to do | What to say | What to look out for |
|---|---|---|
| Display Resource 57 and explain to the pupil that this sheet shows four different types of data, all concerning transport. | *This sheet shows four different ways of displaying data – in a table, pictogram, bar chart and time graph. All these forms of data presentation are about transport.* | |
| Draw the pupil's attention to the table. | *Look at the table. It shows how a group of pupils travel to school each day. The pupils were asked two questions: how they travel to school on most days, and also if there have been any days so far this year when they have come to school a different way. This table shows the results.* | |

| Ask questions similar to the ones shown here that require the pupil to interpret the data in the table. | How do most pupils come to school? Why do you think this is? On most days, how many pupils do not walk to school? Why do you think some pupils may not always travel to school the same way? | Can the pupil read the data presented in the table and answer related questions? |
|---|---|---|
| | Look at the table and ask me a question about the information presented in it. | Does the pupil ask a suitable question from the data presented in the table? |

Ask further questions until the pupil has sufficiently demonstrated their ability to answer questions using the information presented in the table.

## Success criterion B: Answer and ask questions using information presented in a scaled pictogram

| What to do | What to say | What to look out for |
|---|---|---|
| Draw the pupil's attention to the pictogram.<br><br>Ensure that you have included a number in the key to indicate the number of employees that the symbol 👤 represents (see Note). | This pictogram shows how the employees of a company travel to work. | |
| Ask questions similar to the ones shown here that require the pupil to interpret the data in the pictogram. | How do most of the employees travel to work? How many employees is this? Approximately how many employees are there in the company? Which type of transport do [20] employees travel to work by? Which type of transport do the smallest number of employees travel to work by? How many employees is this? Altogether how many of the employees travel to work by train or underground? | Can the pupil read the data presented in the pictogram and answer related questions? |
| | Look at the information shown in the pictogram and ask me a question about it. | Does the pupil ask a suitable question from the data presented in the pictogram? |

Ask further questions until the pupil has sufficiently demonstrated their ability to answer questions using the information presented in the pictogram.

**Success criterion C:** Answer and ask questions using information presented in a scaled bar chart

| What to do | What to say | What to look out for |
|---|---|---|
| Draw the pupil's attention to the bar chart. | *This bar chart shows the approximate distance that the employees of a company travel to work.* | |
| Ask questions similar to the ones shown here that require the pupil to interpret the data in the bar chart. | *How far do most people travel to work? How many people is this? How far do 11 people have to travel each day to get to work? Altogether, how many people travel more than ten miles to get to work each day? Altogether, how many people travel less than five miles to get to work each day?* | Can the pupil read the data presented in the bar chart and answer related questions? |
| | *Ask me a question about the information in the bar chart.* | Does the pupil ask a suitable question from the data presented in the bar chart? |

Ask further questions until the pupil has sufficiently demonstrated their ability to answer questions using the information presented in the bar chart.

**Success criterion D:** Answer and ask questions using information presented in a time graph

| What to do | What to say | What to look out for |
|---|---|---|
| Draw the pupil's attention to the time graph. | *This time graph shows the distance Tom travelled from his home on a day's cycling trip.* | |
| Ask questions similar to the ones shown here that require the pupil to interpret the data in the time graph. | *When did Tom leave home? When did he return home? How far away from home was Tom at [10:00 a.m./11:00 a.m./2:00 p.m./2:30 p.m./3:00 p.m./4:30 p.m./5:00 p.m.]? At what times did Tom take a rest?* | Can the pupil read the data presented in the time graph and answer related questions? |
| | *Ask me a question about the information in the time graph.* | Does the pupil ask a suitable question from the data presented in the time graph? |

Ask further questions until the pupil has sufficiently demonstrated their ability to answer questions using the information presented in the time graph.

## Success criterion E: Interpret and infer information presented in a table, pictogram, bar chart and time graph

| What to do | What to say | What to look out for |
|---|---|---|
| Draw the pupil's attention to the entire sheet. | *This sheet shows four different ways of displaying data – in a table, pictogram, bar chart and time graph. All these forms of data presentation are about transport.*<br><br>*Look at all the information on this sheet to answer these questions.* | |
| Ask questions similar to the ones shown here that require the pupil to interpret and infer the data in the table, pictogram, bar chart and time graph. | **Table**<br>*Two pupils said that they occasionally come to school not by foot, car, cycle or bus, but by some other method of transport. What type of transport might this be?*<br>*Why might a pupil who usually comes to school by foot occasionally come via a different form of transport?*<br>*Does this table tell us exactly how many pupils always travel to school by car?*<br>**Pictogram**<br>*Do you think the company has a car park? Why do you think that?*<br>*Altogether, how many employees take public transport to work?*<br>*Would you say that this is a large company or a small company? Why?*<br>**Bar chart**<br>*How might the 13 people who travel less than one mile to work each day travel to work?*<br>*What about the two people who have to travel 15 or more miles each day? How might they travel to work? Why do you think this?*<br>*Approximately how many people does this company employ?*<br>**Time graph**<br>*When was Tom travelling the fastest? How does the graph show this?*<br>*When do you think Tom may have stopped and had some lunch? How long did he stop for?*<br>**General**<br>*Which type of data presentation do you think is the easiest to read and interpret? Why?* | Can the pupil read the data presented in the table, pictogram, bar chart and time graph, and answer related questions and make inferences about the data? |

Ask further questions until the pupil has sufficiently demonstrated their ability to interpret and infer the information presented in the table, pictogram, bar chart and time graph.

## What to do for those pupils working *below* or *above* expectations
Refer to the 'Tracking back and forward through the Mathematics National Curriculum attainment targets' charts on pages 310–320.

Domain: _____

National Curriculum attainment target (NC AT): _____

_____

Teacher: _____ Class: _____ Date: _____

| Success criteria | Name | | | |
|---|---|---|---|---|
| A | | | | |
| B | | | | |
| C | | | | |
| D | | | | |
| E | | | | |
| F | | | | |
| G | | | | |
| H | | | | |
| I | | | | |
| J | | | | |
| K | | | | |
| Other observations | | | | |

| Level of mastery of NC AT* | NYA | A | A&E | NYA | A | A&E | NYA | A | A&E | NYA | A | A&E |
|---|---|---|---|---|---|---|---|---|---|---|---|---|
| Future action | | | | | | | | | | | | |

Level of mastery key: NYA – Not yet achieved | A – Achieved | A&E – Achieved and exceeded

Name: _____     Date: _____

# Number and place value

Write the missing multiples.

**1** 12, ☐, 24, ☐, ☐, 42, ☐, ☐, 60, ☐, ☐     ☐ **1**
   1 mark

**2** 9, 18, ☐, ☐, 45, ☐, ☐, 72, ☐, ☐, ☐     ☐ **2**
   1 mark

**3** 14, 21, ☐, 35, ☐, ☐, 56, ☐, ☐, 77, ☐     ☐ **3**
   1 mark

**4** 25, ☐, 75, ☐, ☐, 150, ☐, ☐, ☐, ☐, 275     ☐ **4**
   1 mark

**5** ☐, 2000, 3000, ☐, ☐, ☐, 7000, ☐,     ☐ **5**

   ☐, ☐, 11 000
   1 mark

Complete each number line.

**6**     7     14     21     ☐ ☐ ☐ ☐ ☐ ☐ ☐ ☐ ☐     ☐ **6**
   1 mark

**7**     9     18     27     ☐ ☐ ☐ ☐ ☐ ☐ ☐ ☐ ☐     ☐ **7**
   1 mark

**8**     1000     2000     ☐ ☐ ☐ ☐ ☐ ☐ ☐     ☐ **8**
   1 mark

**9**     25     50     ☐ ☐ ☐ ☐ ☐ ☐ ☐ ☐ ☐     ☐ **9**
   1 mark

**10**     6     12     18     ☐ ☐ ☐ ☐ ☐ ☐ ☐ ☐ ☐     ☐ **10**
   1 mark

● count in multiples of 6, 7, 9, 25 and 1000     Total: ☐ out of 10     Mastery:  NYA | A | A&E

Name: _____ Date: _____

## Number and place value

**1** Write 1000 more than each number.

a) 6000 → [　　]      b) 3000 → [　　]

c) 2000 → [　　]      d) 5800 → [　　]

e) 9700 → [　　]      f) 4280 → [　　]

g) 8650 → [　　]      h) 1046 → [　　]

i) 7724 → [　　]      j) 3692 → [　　]

**1**
10 marks

**2** Write 1000 less than each number.

a) 4000 → [　　]      b) 8000 → [　　]

c) 7000 → [　　]      d) 2400 → [　　]

e) 6300 → [　　]      f) 9500 → [　　]

g) 3548 → [　　]      h) 1526 → [　　]

i) 5507 → [　　]      j) 8414 → [　　]

**2**
10 marks

● find 1000 more or less than a given number      Total: [　] out of 20    Mastery: NYA | A | A&E

Name: _____     Date: _____

# Number and place value

**1** Write the numbers on each number line.

a)
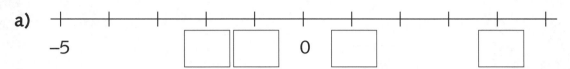
−5 [ ] [ ] 0 [ ] [ ]

b)
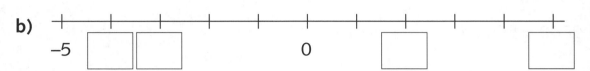
−5 [ ] [ ] 0 [ ] [ ]

c)
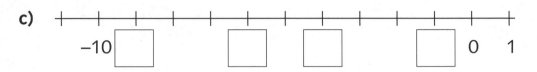
−10 [ ] [ ] [ ] [ ] 0  1

d)
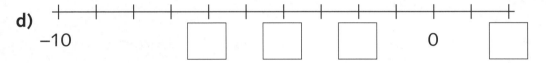
−10 [ ] [ ] [ ] 0 [ ]

e)
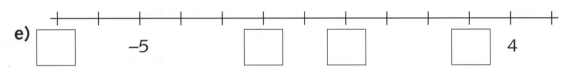
[ ] −5 [ ] [ ] [ ] 4

f)
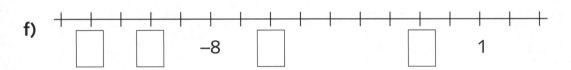
[ ] [ ] −8 [ ] [ ] 1

[ ] **1**
6 marks

**2** Count backwards from each of these numbers. Write the next number.

a) [ ] ← −8          b) [ ] ← −12

[ ] **2**
2 marks

**3** Count forwards from each of these numbers. Write the next number.

a) −15 → [ ]          b) −10 → [ ]

[ ] **3**
2 marks

Name: _____     Date: _____

## Number and place value

**1** a) 6857 = 6000 + 800 + 50 + ☐

b) 4192 = 4000 + 100 + ☐ + 2

c) 2483 = ☐ + 400 + 80 + 3

d) 5346 = 5000 + ☐ + 40 + 6

**1** 4 marks

**2** a) 8000 + 600 + 70 + 1 = ☐     b) 50 + 3000 + 9 + 100 = ☐

c) 7 + 30 + 800 + 4000 = ☐     d) 400 + 8 + 3000 + 60 = ☐

**2** 4 marks

**3** a) 3956 → ☐ thousands     b) 2674 → ☐ thousands

→ ☐ hundreds     → ☐ hundreds

→ ☐ tens     → ☐ tens

→ ☐ ones     → ☐ ones

**3** 2 marks

**4** Write the value of the **bold** digit in each of these numbers.

a) 5**2**89 → ☐     b) **3**421 → ☐

c) 8**3**75 → ☐     d) 29**4**3 → ☐

**4** 4 marks

**5** Write the value of the 8 in each of these numbers.

a) 2**3**85 → ☐     b) **8**712 → ☐     c) 4**8**29 → ☐

**5** 3 marks

**6** Write the number shown on each abacus.

a)     b)     c)

Th H T O     Th H T O     Th H T O

☐     ☐     ☐

**6** 3 marks

● recognise the place value of each digit in a four-digit number (thousands, hundreds, tens, and ones)

Total: ☐ out of 20     Mastery:  NYA | A | A&E

Name: _____     Date: _____

# Number and place value

**1** Write any number that lies between each pair of number cards.

a) 3857 [ ] 3852     b) 1458 [ ] 1456

c) 7209 [ ] 7230

**1**
3 marks

**2** Use the < or > sign to make each statement correct.

a) 5548 [ ] 5458     b) 6023 [ ] 6043     c) 1678 [ ] 1677

**2**
3 marks

**3** Order the numbers, smallest to largest.

3427, 3247, 3742, 3542, 3274, 3472, 3724, 3172

[ ] [ ] [ ] [ ] [ ] [ ] [ ] [ ]

**3**
1 mark

**4** Order the numbers, largest to smallest.

5734, 5764, 5768, 5731, 5738, 5761, 5732, 5762

[ ] [ ] [ ] [ ] [ ] [ ] [ ] [ ]

**4**
1 mark

**5** Order the distances, shortest to longest.

1106 m, 1060 m, 1100 m, 1160 m, 1006 m, 1066 m

[ ] [ ] [ ] [ ] [ ] [ ]

**5**
1 mark

**6** Order the masses, heaviest to lightest.

2350 g, 2575 g, 2300 g, 2525 g, 2550 g, 2500 g

[ ] [ ] [ ] [ ] [ ] [ ]

**6**
1 mark

● order and compare numbers beyond 1000     Total: [ ] out of 10     Mastery: NYA | A | A&E

Name: _____  Date: _____

## Number and place value

**1** Write these numbers on the number line.

┼────┼────┼────┼────┼────┼────┼────┼────┼────┼────┼────┼────┼

2490    2495

**1** 2 marks

**2** **a)** 4375 = 4000 + 200 + ☐ + 5  **b)** 8463 = 8000 + ☐ + 260 + 3

**2** 2 marks

**3** Write the numbers shown by the Base 10 material.

**a)**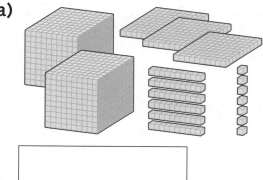

**b)**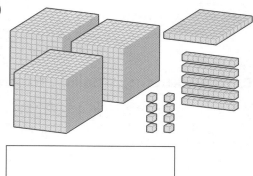

☐

☐

**3** 2 marks

**4** Draw beads on each abacus to represent the number.

**a)** 7634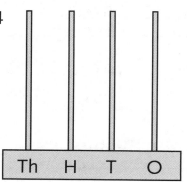

**b)** 5819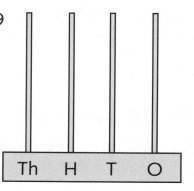

**4** 2 marks

**5** Circle the fewest number of weights you would need to make each mass.

**a)** 2745 g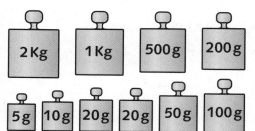

**b)** 3680 g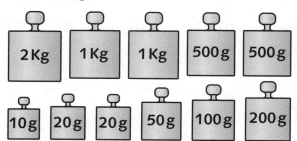

**5** 2 marks

● identify, represent and estimate numbers using
different representations

Total: ☐ out of 10    Mastery:  NYA | A | A&E

Name: _____   Date: _____

## Number and place value

**1** Round each number to the nearest 10.

a) 84 → ▢     b) 67 → ▢

c) 368 → ▢     d) 423 → ▢

e) 4635 → ▢     f) 1982 → ▢

1

6 marks

**2** Round each number to the nearest 100.

a) 549 → ▢     b) 275 → ▢

c) 3651 → ▢     d) 8237 → ▢

2

4 marks

**3** Round each number to the nearest 1000.

a) 7436 → ▢     b) 5808 → ▢

c) 2595 → ▢     d) 6163 → ▢

3

4 marks

**4** a) Write a two-digit number that rounds to 30 when rounded to the nearest multiple of 10. ▢

b) Write a three-digit number that rounds to 160 when rounded to the nearest multiple of 10. ▢

c) Write a three-digit number that rounds to 400 when rounded to the nearest multiple of 100. ▢

d) Write a four-digit number that rounds to 5720 when rounded to the nearest multiple of 10. ▢

e) Write a four-digit number that rounds to 2300 when rounded to the nearest multiple of 100. ▢

f) Write a four-digit number that rounds to 7000 when rounded to the nearest multiple of 1000. ▢

4

6 marks

● round any number to the nearest 10, 100 or 1000     Total: ▢ out of 20     Mastery:  NYA | A | A&E

© HarperCollins*Publishers* Ltd. 2015

**Name:** _____     **Date:** _____

# Number and place value

**1** Arrange these digits to make a 4-digit number where the:

- 100s digit is twice the 1s digit;
- 10s digit is $\frac{1}{3}$ of the 100s digit;
- 10s digit is twice the 1000s digit.

**1**
1 mark

**2** **a)** Which number on the right fits all the descriptions below?

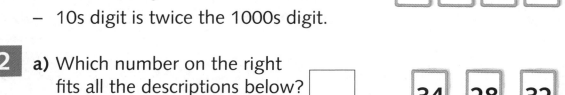

- It is a multiple of 6.
- It is a multiple of 4.
- It is less than 40.

**b)** Write another number that fits all the descriptions above.

**2**
2 marks

**3** Write the missing numbers in each of these number sequences.

**a)** −14, ☐ , −8, −5, ☐ , ☐     **b)** −8, ☐ , ☐ , 1, ☐ , 7

**3**
2 marks

**4** In the triangle on the right, the number in the middle of each side of the triangle is the difference between the numbers at the points of the triangle.

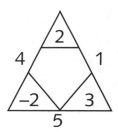

Work out the missing numbers in the triangles below.

**a)**

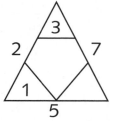

**b)**

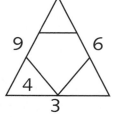

**4**
2 marks

**5** Fill in the missing digits to make two 4-digit numbers that both round to 6000, 5600 and 5630.

**5**
2 marks

**6** Write the answer in Roman numerals. LXIII + XXVIII = ☐

**6**
1 mark

● solve number and practical problems that involve all of the above and with increasingly large positive numbers

Total: ☐ out of 10     Mastery:  NYA | A | A&E

Name: _____     Date: _____

## Number and place value

**1** Write each of these Hindu-Arabic numbers in Roman numerals.

**a)** 9 →  [    ]          **b)** 64 → [    ]

**c)** 25 → [    ]          **d)** 13 → [    ]

**e)** 31 → [    ]          **f)** 76 → [    ]

**g)** 98 → [    ]          **h)** 42 → [    ]

**1**
8 marks

**2** Write each of these Roman numerals as a Hindu-Arabic number.

**a)** XIX → [    ]          **b)** XVI → [    ]

**c)** LIX → [    ]          **d)** XCIX → [    ]

**e)** VII → [    ]          **f)** LXXXVIII → [    ]

**g)** XXIX → [    ]          **h)** LXIV → [    ]

**2**
8 marks

**3** Explain the purpose of the zero in each of these numbers.

**a)** 3408

[                                                      ]

**b)** 3480

[                                                      ]

**3**
4 marks

● read Roman numerals to 100 (I to C) and know that over time, the numeral system changed to include the concept of zero and place value

Total: [    ] out of 20     Mastery:  NYA  |  A  |  A&E

**Name:** _____ **Date:** _____

## Addition and subtraction

For each calculation:

• Estimate the answer.
• Calculate the answer using a written method.
• Check your answer.

**1** 5487 + 2352

| Estimate | Calculate | Check |
|---|---|---|
| | | |

**2** 2538 + 4285

| Estimate | Calculate | Check |
|---|---|---|
| | | |

**3** 1946 + 3527

| Estimate | Calculate | Check |
|---|---|---|
| | | |

**4** 7485 + 2966

| Estimate | Calculate | Check |
|---|---|---|
| | | |

**5** 5577 + 1659

| Estimate | Calculate | Check |
|---|---|---|
| | | |

● add numbers with up to 4 digits using the formal written method of columnar addition where appropriate

● estimate and use inverse operations to check answers to a calculation

Total: _____ out of 10   Mastery: NYA | A | A&E

Total: _____ out of 10   Mastery: NYA | A | A&E

Name: _____    Date: _____

# Addition and subtraction

For each calculation:

- Estimate the answer.
- Calculate the answer using a written method.
- Check your answer.

**1** 4867 − 1524

| Estimate | Calculate | Check |
|---|---|---|
| | | |

1
4 marks

**2** 3376 − 1453

| Estimate | Calculate | Check |
|---|---|---|
| | | |

2
4 marks

**3** 9527 − 4848

| Estimate | Calculate | Check |
|---|---|---|
| | | |

3
4 marks

**4** 8234 − 5785

| Estimate | Calculate | Check |
|---|---|---|
| | | |

4
4 marks

**5** 6036 − 2657

| Estimate | Calculate | Check |
|---|---|---|
| | | |

5
4 marks

Name: _____ Date: _____

# Addition and subtraction

**1** This table shows the distances in kilometres between 4 towns.

|  | Birmingham | Edinburgh | London | Newcastle |
|---|---|---|---|---|
| Birmingham |  | 473 | 192 | 335 |
| Edinburgh | 473 |  | 641 | 180 |
| London | 192 | 641 |  | 446 |
| Newcastle | 335 | 180 | 446 |  |

Simon goes from London to Birmingham, and then on to Newcastle. How many kilometres does he travel?

**1**
2 marks

**2** Lisa throws three darts at this board. Every dart lands on a different number.

Lisa scores exactly 184 points. Which numbers do the darts land on?

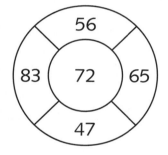

56
83 72 65
47

**2**
2 marks

**3**

Holiday to
Australia
Adult: £1896
Child: £1248

**a)** How much more expensive is an adult ticket to Australia than a child ticket?

**b)** What is the total cost of two adult tickets and one child ticket to Australia?

**3**
4 marks

**4** There are 8432 spectators at a football match between Winston Warriers and Morcella Mavericks. 3867 of the spectators support Winston Warriers. The rest support Morcella Mavericks. How many Morcella Mavericks supporters are there at the match?

**4**
2 marks

● solve addition and subtraction two-step problems in contexts, deciding which operations and methods to use and why

Total: ___ out of 10    Mastery:  NYA   A   A&E

Name: _____  Date: _____

## Multiplication and division

**1** Complete the table.

| x | 4 | 7 | 2 | 6 | 9 | 5 | 3 | 8 |
|---|---|---|---|---|---|---|---|---|
| 6 | | | | | | | | |
| 11 | | | | | | | | |
| 7 | | | | | | | | |
| 12 | | | | | | | | |
| 9 | | | | | | | | |

1
40 marks

**2**
a) 40 ÷ 5 =

b) 144 ÷ 12 =

c) 24 ÷ 8 =

d) 36 ÷ 9 =

e) 14 ÷ 2 =

f) 12 ÷ 4 =

g) 24 ÷ 3 =

h) 10 ÷ 5 =

i) 12 ÷ 4 =

j) 60 ÷ 6 =

k) 90 ÷ 10 =

l) 64 ÷ 8 =

m) 48 ÷ 6 =

n) 12 ÷ 3 =

o) 99 ÷ 11 =

p) 8 ÷ 2 =

q) 28 ÷ 7 =

r) 20 ÷ 5 =

s) 33 ÷ 3 =

t) 132 ÷ 12 =

2
20 marks

● recall multiplication and division facts for multiplication tables up to 12 × 12

Total: ____ out of 60    Mastery: NYA | A | A&E

Name: _____     Date: _____

# Multiplication and division

**1**   **a)** $6 \times 7 =$ ☐     **b)** $4 \times 9 =$ ☐     **c)** $8 \times 3 =$ ☐

   $60 \times 7 =$ ☐     $4 \times 900 =$ ☐     $80 \times 30 =$ ☐

   **d)** $50 \times 12 =$ ☐     **e)** $300 \times 6 =$ ☐     **f)** $90 \times 0 =$ ☐

   $50 \times 120 =$ ☐     $3 \times 60 =$ ☐     $900 \times 1 =$ ☐

☐ **1**
12 marks

**2**   **a)** $9^2 =$ ☐     **b)** $12^2 =$ ☐     **c)** $7^2 =$ ☐     **d)** $6^2 =$ ☐

☐ **2**
4 marks

**3**   **a)** $210 \div 3 =$ ☐     **b)** $560 \div 8 =$ ☐

   **c)** $480 \div 6 =$ ☐     **d)** $270 \div 9 =$ ☐

   **e)** $140 \div 1 =$ ☐     **f)** $600 \div 5 =$ ☐

   **g)** $560 \div 7 =$ ☐     **h)** $400 \div 4 =$ ☐

☐ **3**
8 marks

**4**   **a)** $4 \times 7 \times 3 =$ ☐     **b)** $8 \times 2 \times 3 =$ ☐

   **c)** $6 \times 8 \times 5 =$ ☐     **d)** $4 \times 2 \times 9 =$ ☐

   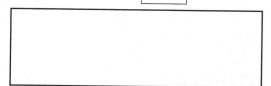

   **e)** $9 \times 5 \times 8 =$ ☐     **f)** $6 \times 4 \times 4 =$ ☐

☐ **4**
6 marks

● use place value, known and derived facts to multiply and divide mentally, including: multiplying by 0 and 1; dividing by 1; multiplying together three numbers

Total: ☐ out of 30     Mastery:   NYA   A   A&E

Name: _____   Date: _____

# Multiplication and division

**1** Use the three numbers in this trio to write two multiplication facts.

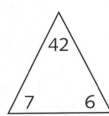

**2** Here are four number cards.

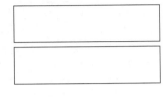

Draw a ring around the two number cards that are factors of 42.

**3** Write the missing numbers.

Factors of 20 =

1, ☐, ☐, ☐, ☐, 20

**4** Draw a ring around the numbers that are factors of 40.

4   5   6   8   20   60   80

**5** Draw a ring around the numbers that are **not** factors of 500.

20      25      75      120

100      125      250

**6** Write the missing numbers in this multiplication grid.

| × | 2 | | |
|---|---|---|---|
| 8 | 16 | 56 | 72 |
| | 10 | 35 | 45 |
| | 12 | 42 | 54 |

**7** Work out the answer to these calculations.

8 × 7 × 5 = ☐

8 × 5 × 7 = ☐

Circle the calculation that is easier to work out mentally. Explain why.

**8** Write each of these numbers in the correct place on the Venn diagram.

8      12      15      40

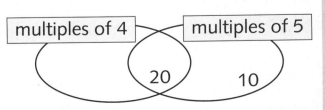

1 mark  1

1 mark  2

1 mark  3

1 mark  4

1 mark  5

1 mark  6

3 marks  7

1 mark  8

● recognise and use factor pairs and commutativity in mental calculations

Total: ☐ out of 10   Mastery: NYA | A | A&E

Name: _____    Date: _____

# Multiplication and division

Work out the answer to each calculation using a written method.

**1**   76 × 3

|  |
|  |

1

2 marks

**2**   49 × 6

|  |
|  |

2

2 marks

**3**   94 × 8

|  |
|  |

3

2 marks

**4**   368 × 4

|  |
|  |

4

2 marks

**5**   237 × 9

|  |
|  |

5

2 marks

● multiply two-digit and three-digit numbers by a one-digit
number using formal written layout

Total: [ ] out of 10     Mastery:   NYA   A   A&E

Name: _____ Date: _____

# Multiplication and division

**1** A shop sells packets of biscuits.

Sunita buys 4 packets of cream biscuits and 2 packets of plain biscuits. How much does she pay altogether?

**1**
2 marks

**2**

Sky hire: £46 per day
Chair lift pass: £32 per day

**a)** How much does it cost to hire a set of skis for 7 days?

**b)** What is the total cost to hire a set of skis and buy a chair lift pass for 3 days?

**2**
4 marks

**3** A shop sells batteries in packs of 4 and packs of 2.

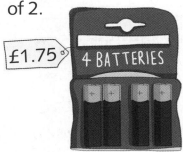
£1.75

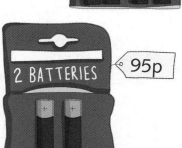
95p

**a)** Hayley buys 3 packs of 4 batteries. How much does she pay?

**b)** Leo and Ruby each want 6 batteries. Leo buys 3 packs of 2 batteries. Ruby buys 1 pack of 4 batteries and 1 pack of 2 batteries. How much more does Leo pay than Ruby?

**3**
4 marks

● solve problems involving multiplying and adding, including using the distributive law to multiply two digit numbers by one digit, integer scaling problems and harder correspondence problems such as n objects are connected to m objects

Total: ____ out of 10    Mastery: NYA | A | A&E

Name: _____  Date: _____

## Fractions (including decimals)

**1** Look at the diagrams below. Write two fractions that are equivalent to a half.

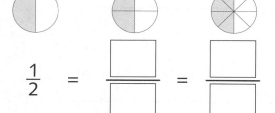

$\dfrac{1}{2}$ = $\dfrac{\Box}{\Box}$ = $\dfrac{\Box}{\Box}$

**2** Look at the circles below. Colour the circle on the right to show a fraction that is equivalent to three-quarters. Then write the fraction.

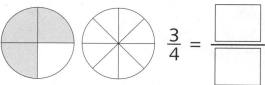

$\dfrac{3}{4}$ = $\dfrac{\Box}{\Box}$

**3** Look at the number line below. Fill in the missing numbers to show fractions that are equivalent to one third.

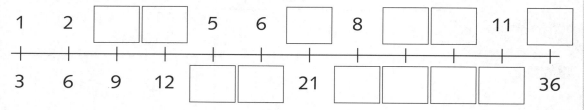

1   2   $\Box$ $\Box$   5   6   $\Box$   8   $\Box$ $\Box$   11   $\Box$

3   6   9   12   $\Box$ $\Box$   21   $\Box$ $\Box$ $\Box$   36

**4** Look at the diagrams below. Fill in the missing numbers to show fractions that are equivalent to one quarter.

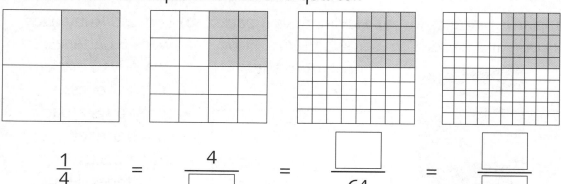

$\dfrac{1}{4}$ = $\dfrac{4}{\Box}$ = $\dfrac{\Box}{64}$ = $\dfrac{\Box}{\Box}$

**5** Complete the families of equivalent fractions.

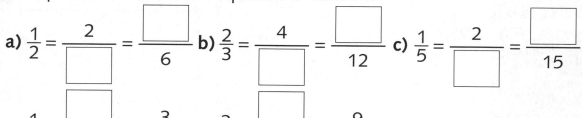

a) $\dfrac{1}{2} = \dfrac{2}{\Box} = \dfrac{\Box}{6}$   b) $\dfrac{2}{3} = \dfrac{4}{\Box} = \dfrac{\Box}{12}$   c) $\dfrac{1}{5} = \dfrac{2}{\Box} = \dfrac{\Box}{15}$

d) $\dfrac{1}{4} = \dfrac{\Box}{8} = \dfrac{3}{\Box}$   e) $\dfrac{3}{4} = \dfrac{\Box}{8} = \dfrac{9}{\Box}$

● recognise and show, using diagrams, families of common equivalent fractions

Total: [   ] out of 10    Mastery:  NYA | A | A&E

Name: _____    Date: _____

## Fractions (including decimals)

**1**  $\dfrac{34}{100}$, $\dfrac{\ \ }{\ \ }$, $\dfrac{\ \ }{\ \ }$, $\dfrac{37}{100}$, $\dfrac{38}{100}$, $\dfrac{\ \ }{\ \ }$, $\dfrac{\ \ }{\ \ }$, $\dfrac{\ \ }{\ \ }$, $\dfrac{\ \ }{\ \ }$, $\dfrac{43}{100}$, $\dfrac{\ \ }{\ \ }$, $\dfrac{\ \ }{\ \ }$

**1**
1 mark

**2**  What fraction of each grid is shaded?

a) 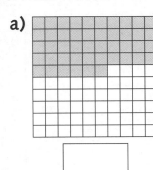    b) 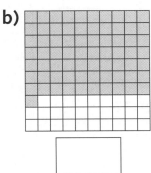    c)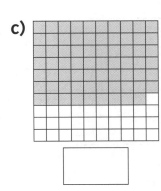

**2**
3 marks

**3**  Write a tenth and a hundredth to describe what fraction of each grid is shaded.

a) 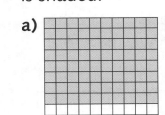    b) 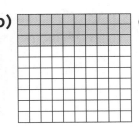    c) 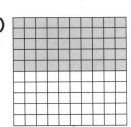    d)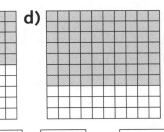

☐ = ☐    ☐ = ☐    ☐ = ☐    ☐ = ☐

**3**
8 marks

**4**  a) 5 ÷ 100 = ☐    b) 28 ÷ 100 = ☐

c) 67 ÷ 100 = ☐    d) 80 ÷ 100 = ☐

**4**
4 marks

**5**  a) 0·3 ÷ 10 = ☐    b) 0·8 ÷ 10 = ☐

c) 0·6 ÷ 10 = ☐    d) 0·1 ÷ 10 = ☐

**5**
4 marks

● count up and down in hundredths; recognise that hundredths arise when dividing an object by one hundred and dividing tenths by ten

Total: ☐ out of 20    Mastery:  NYA  |  A  |  A&E

Name: _____  Date: _____

## Fractions (including decimals)

**1**  a) $\frac{1}{5}$ of 20 = ☐  b) $\frac{1}{3}$ of 27 = ☐  c) $\frac{1}{8}$ of 96 = ☐

d) $\frac{1}{4}$ of 104 = ☐  e) $\frac{1}{6}$ of 96 = ☐  f) $\frac{1}{7}$ of 98 = ☐

1
6 marks

**2**  a) $\frac{3}{4}$ of 32 = ☐  b) $\frac{3}{5}$ of 95 = ☐  c) $\frac{4}{7}$ of 63 = ☐

d) $\frac{5}{6}$ of 84 = ☐  e) $\frac{7}{10}$ of 150 = ☐  f) $\frac{2}{3}$ of 75 = ☐

2
6 marks

**3**  Alice has some pocket money. She spends three-quarters of it. She has £2 left. How much pocket money did she have?

**4**  In a sale, everything is half price. A chair costs £99 in the sale. How much was it before the sale?

3
2 marks

4
2 marks

**5**  Willis had £270. He gave two-thirds of it to charity. How much did he give?

**6**  What is the cost of the monitor during the sale?

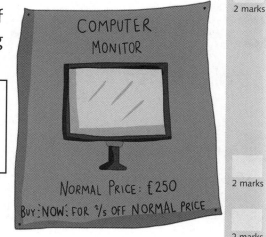

COMPUTER MONITOR

NORMAL PRICE: £250

BUY NOW FOR ⅖ OFF NORMAL PRICE

5
2 marks

6
2 marks

● solve problems involving increasingly harder fractions to calculate quantities, and fractions to divide quantities, including non-unit fractions where the answer is a whole number

Total: ☐ out of 20   Mastery:  NYA | A | A&E

Name: _____ Date: _____

# Fractions (including decimals)

**1**  a) $\dfrac{1}{5} + \dfrac{3}{5} = \dfrac{\Box}{\Box}$    b) $\dfrac{2}{7} + \dfrac{3}{7} = \dfrac{\Box}{\Box}$

c) $\dfrac{7}{9} + \dfrac{5}{9} = \dfrac{\Box}{\Box}$    d) $\dfrac{11}{12} + \dfrac{5}{12} = \dfrac{\Box}{\Box}$    **1**
4 marks

**2**  a) $\dfrac{7}{10} - \dfrac{3}{10} = \dfrac{\Box}{\Box}$    b) $\dfrac{8}{11} - \dfrac{7}{11} = \dfrac{\Box}{\Box}$

c) $\dfrac{4}{5} - \dfrac{3}{5} = \dfrac{\Box}{\Box}$    d) $\dfrac{7}{8} - \dfrac{5}{8} = \dfrac{\Box}{\Box}$    **2**
4 marks

**3**  a) $\dfrac{4}{11} + \dfrac{\Box}{\Box} = \dfrac{7}{11}$    b) $\dfrac{\Box}{\Box} + \dfrac{1}{6} = \dfrac{5}{6}$

c) $\dfrac{\Box}{\Box} + \dfrac{5}{8} = \dfrac{12}{8}$    d) $\dfrac{3}{10} + \dfrac{\Box}{\Box} = 1$    **3**
4 marks

**4**  a) $\dfrac{8}{9} - \dfrac{\Box}{\Box} = \dfrac{2}{9}$    b) $\dfrac{\Box}{\Box} - \dfrac{2}{5} = \dfrac{1}{5}$

c) $\dfrac{\Box}{\Box} - \dfrac{3}{7} = \dfrac{2}{7}$    d) $\dfrac{7}{12} - \dfrac{\Box}{\Box} = \dfrac{5}{12}$    **4**
4 marks

**5**  a) $\dfrac{1}{5} + \dfrac{1}{5} + \dfrac{1}{5} = \dfrac{\Box}{\Box}$    b) $\dfrac{3}{10} + \dfrac{5}{10} - \dfrac{1}{10} = \dfrac{\Box}{\Box}$

c) $\dfrac{2}{7} + \dfrac{5}{7} - \dfrac{\Box}{\Box} = \dfrac{1}{7}$    d) $\dfrac{11}{12} - \dfrac{\Box}{\Box} + \dfrac{1}{12} = \dfrac{5}{12}$    **5**
4 marks

● add and subtract fractions with the same denominator     Total: ▢ out of 20     Mastery:  NYA   A   A&E

Name: _____    Date: _____

# Fractions (including decimals)

**1** What fraction of each grid is shaded?

Write a fraction and a decimal fraction to describe each grid.

a)

[ ] = [ ]

b)
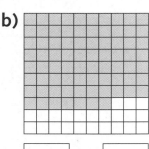

[ ] = [ ]

c)
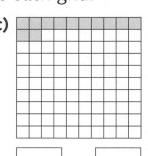

[ ] = [ ]

d)
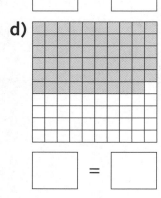

[ ] = [ ]

e)
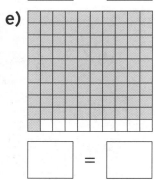

[ ] = [ ]

**1** 5 marks

**2** Write the decimal fraction that is equivalent to these fractions.

a) $\frac{3}{10}$ = [ ]     b) $\frac{44}{100}$ = [ ]     c) $\frac{91}{100}$ = [ ]

d) $\frac{7}{10}$ = [ ]     e) $\frac{52}{100}$ = [ ]

**2** 5 marks

**3** Write a fraction that is equivalent to these decimal fractions.

a) 0·9 = [ ]     b) 0·71 = [ ]     c) 0·38 = [ ]

d) 0·5 = [ ]     e) 0·12 = [ ]

**3** 5 marks

**4** Write the decimal values for the arrows marked on the number line.

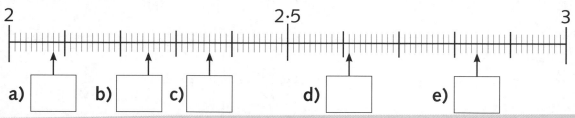

a) [ ]     b) [ ]     c) [ ]     d) [ ]     e) [ ]

**4** 5 marks

● recognise and write decimal equivalents of any number of tenths or hundredths

Total: [ ] out of 20     Mastery: NYA | A | A&E

Name: _____     Date: _____

## Fractions (including decimals)

**1**  What fraction of each shape is shaded?

a)

b)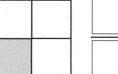

c)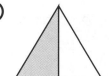

**1** 3 marks

**2**  Write the decimal fraction that is equivalent to these fractions.

a) $\frac{1}{4}$ = [ ]     b) $\frac{1}{2}$ = [ ]     c) $\frac{3}{4}$ = [ ]

**2** 3 marks

**3**  Draw lines to match the equivalent fractions and decimals in each set.

| 0·75 | $\frac{1}{2}$ | $\frac{25}{100}$ |
| 0·5  | $\frac{1}{4}$ | $\frac{50}{100}$ |
| 0·25 | $\frac{3}{4}$ | $\frac{75}{100}$ |

**3** 1 mark

**4**  Look at the three sets of fractions and decimals that you have joined together in Question 3.

Write each set of three fractions and decimals on the number line below.

0                                                                 1

**4** 3 marks

Name: _____    Date: _____

# Fractions (including decimals)

For each question below write your answer as a decimal.

**1**  Divide each of these numbers by 10.

a) 6 → ☐          b) 2 → ☐          c) 13 → ☐

d) 9 → ☐          e) 58 → ☐         f) 25 → ☐

1
6 marks

**2**  Divide each of these numbers by 100.

a) 5 → ☐          b) 12 → ☐         c) 34 → ☐

d) 7 → ☐          e) 61 → ☐         f) 89 → ☐

2
6 marks

**3**  Divide each of these numbers by 10.
Then look at the answer and circle the digit that is in the tenths place.

a) 8 → ☐                    b) 52 → ☐

3
2 marks

**4**  Divide each of these numbers by 10.
Then look at the answer and circle the digit that is in the ones place.

a) 96 → ☐                   b) 2 → ☐

4
2 marks

**5**  Divide each of these numbers by 100.
Then look at the answer and circle the digit that is in the hundredths place.

a) 78 → ☐                   b) 3 → ☐

5
2 marks

**6**  Divide each of these numbers by 100.
Then look at the answer and circle the digit that is in the tenths place.

a) 4 → ☐                    b) 49 → ☐

6
2 marks

● find the effect of dividing a one- or two-digit number by 10
and 100, identifying the value of the digits in the answer as    Total: ☐ out of 20    Mastery:   NYA   A   A&E
ones, tenths and hundredths

Name: ______________________ Date: ____________

# Fractions (including decimals)

**1** Round each decimal to the nearest whole number.

a) 0·8 → [ ]   b) 0·5 → [ ]

c) 1·9 → [ ]   d) 12·1 → [ ]

e) 8·2 → [ ]   f) 24·3 → [ ]

g) 61·6 → [ ]   h) 84·7 → [ ]

1 — 8 marks

**2** Write two decimals that round to 4. [ ] and [ ]

2 — 2 marks

**3** Write two decimals that round to 46. [ ] and [ ]

3 — 2 marks

**4** Write the two whole numbers that each of these decimals lie between.

Then circle the whole number that the decimal rounds to.

a) [ ] 7·6 [ ]   b) [ ] 16·3 [ ]

c) [ ] 39·5 [ ]   d) [ ] 73·4 [ ]

4 — 8 marks

- round decimals with one decimal place to the nearest whole number

Total: [ ] out of 20   Mastery: NYA A A&E

Name: _____     Date: _____

## Fractions (including decimals)

**1** Write any decimal that lies between each pair of numbers.

a) **5.5** ☐ **6.5**      b) **18.7** ☐ **19.1**

c) **2.47** ☐ **2.53**      d) **36.27** ☐ **36.34**

**1**
4 marks

**2** Use the < or > sign to make each statement correct.

a) 45·8 ☐ 48·5      b) 12·27 ☐ 12·07

c) 37·14 ☐ 37·18      d) 71·52 ☐ 71·55

**2**
4 marks

**3** Order each set of decimals, smallest to largest.

a) 5·9,  5·2,  5·1,  4·5,  4·9,  5·4,  4·2,  4·1

☐ ☐ ☐ ☐ ☐ ☐ ☐ ☐

b) 7·84,  8·44,  7·44,  8·84,  7·88,  8·88,  8·48,  7·48

☐ ☐ ☐ ☐ ☐ ☐ ☐ ☐

c) 10·6,  10·1,  10·9,  10·5,  10·7,  10·2,  10·8,  10·3

☐ ☐ ☐ ☐ ☐ ☐ ☐ ☐

d) 45·37,  45·17,  45·03,  45·33,  45·71,  45·07,  45·77,  45·73

☐ ☐ ☐ ☐ ☐ ☐ ☐ ☐

**3**
4 marks

**4** Write the decimal that is one tenth **smaller** than each of these decimals.

a) 7·6 → ☐      b) 12·53 → ☐

**4**
2 marks

**5** Write the decimal that is one tenth **larger** than each of these decimals.

a) 58·49 → ☐      b) 26·8 → ☐

**5**
2 marks

**6** Write the decimal that is one hundredth **smaller** than each of these decimals.

a) 81·67 → ☐      b) 3·44 → ☐

**6**
2 marks

**7** Write the decimal that is one hundredth **larger** than each of these decimals.

a) 19·85 → ☐      b) 60·06 → ☐

**7**
2 marks

● compare numbers with the same number of decimal places up to two decimal places

Total: ☐ out of 20     Mastery:  NYA  |  A  |  A&E

Name: _____     Date: _____

# Fractions (including decimals)

**1** The table shows the cost of train tickets to different cities.

| | | Birmingham | Manchester | Glasgow |
|---|---|---|---|---|
| Adult | Single | £21.75 | £38.90 | £61.20 |
| | Return | £36.80 | £80.25 | £112.50 |
| Child | Single | £16.40 | £26.10 | £48.75 |
| | Return | £28.95 | £59.40 | £96.90 |

**a)** What is the total cost for a return journey to Birmingham for one adult and two children?

**b)** How much more does it cost for two adults to make a single journey to Glasgow than to Manchester?

1

4 marks

**2** Ellis jumped 2·45 metres on his second attempt at the long jump. This was 65 centimetres longer than on his first attempt. How far in metres did Ellis jump on his first attempt?

**3** A school is aiming to raise £1200 for charity. So far they have raised $\frac{3}{4}$ of this. How much money has the school already raised?

2

2 marks

3

2 marks

**4** Lakshmi is making an orange drink. The drink is made up of $\frac{1}{3}$ cordial and $\frac{2}{3}$ water. Lakshmi puts 100 ml of cordial in a glass.

**a)** How much water should Lakshmi put in the glass?

**b)** What is the total volume of orange drink in the glass?

4

2 marks

● solve simple measure and money problems involving fractions and decimals to two decimal places

Total: ____ out of 10     Mastery:  NYA  |  A  |  A&E

Name: _____     Date: _____

## Measurement

**1**  **a)** 4·2 km = [        ] m     **b)** 1·6 km = [        ] m

    **c)** 5·8 km = [        ] m     **d)** 84·1 km = [        ] m

                                                          [   ] **1**
     4 marks

**2**  **a)** 5600 m = [        ] km     **b)** 8300 m = [        ] km

    **c)** 12 500 m = [        ] km     **d)** 7100 m = [        ] km

                                                            [   ] **2**
     4 marks

**3**  **a)** 6 m = [        ] cm     **b)** 19 m = [        ] cm

    **c)** 3·7 m = [        ] cm     **d)** 5000 mm = [        ] cm

                                                            [   ] **3**
     4 marks

**4**  **a)** 70 cm = [        ] m     **b)** 600 mm = [        ] m

    **c)** 450 cm = [        ] m     **d)** 200 mm = [        ] m

                                                            [   ] **4**
     4 marks

**5**  **a)** 4·7 kg = [        ] g     **b)** 5·1 kg = [        ] g

    **c)** 12·9 kg = [        ] g     **d)** 24·6 kg = [        ] g

                                                            [   ] **5**
     4 marks

**6**  **a)** 6800 g = [        ] kg     **b)** 1900 g = [        ] kg

    **c)** 2400 g = [        ] kg     **d)** 5600 g = [        ] kg

                                                            [   ] **6**
     4 marks

**7**  **a)** 1·9 $l$ = [        ] ml     **b)** 3·7 $l$ = [        ] ml

    **c)** 2·5 $l$ = [        ] ml     **d)** 12·3 $l$ = [        ] ml

                                                            [   ] **7**
     4 marks

**8**  **a)** 3800 ml = [        ] $l$     **b)** 5400 ml = [        ] $l$

    **c)** 1600 ml = [        ] $l$     **d)** 2900 ml = [        ] $l$

                                                            [   ] **8**
     4 marks

**9**  **a)** $4\frac{1}{2}$ h = [   ] min     **b)** 240 min = [   ] h     **c)** 3 days = [   ] h

    **d)** 120 h = [   ] days     **e)** 4 weeks = [   ] days

    **f)** 42 days = [   ] weeks     **g)** 250 min = [   ] h and [   ] min

    **h)** 60 h = [   ] days and [   ] h

                                                            [   ] **9**
     8 marks

● convert between different units of measure [for example, kilometre to metre; hour to minute]     Total: [   ] out of 40     Mastery:  NYA | A | A&E

Name: _____ Date: _____

## Measurement

You will need:
• ruler

**1** Find the perimeter of each shape.

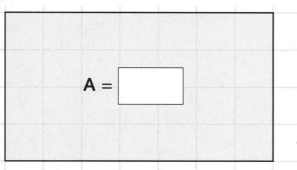
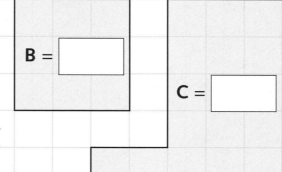

A = [ ]

B = [ ]

C = [ ]

**1**
3 marks

**2** Measure the sides of each shape and then calculate its perimeter.

a) 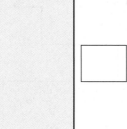 [ ]

b)  [ ]

c) 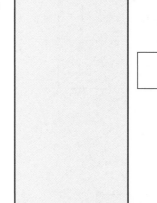 [ ]

**2**
3 marks

**3** Calculate the perimeter of each shape.

a)
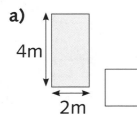
4m
2m
[ ]

b)
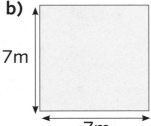
7m
7m
[ ]

c)
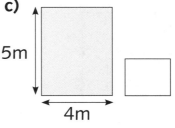
5m
4m
[ ]

**3**
3 marks

**4** Draw a rectangle with a perimeter of 20 cm.

**4**
1 mark

● measure and calculate the perimeter of a rectilinear figure (including squares) in centimetres and metres

Total: [ ] out of 10    Mastery:  NYA | A | A&E

Name: _____    Date: _____

You will need:
• ruler

## Measurement

**1**  Find the area of each shape A to I.

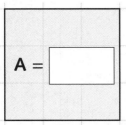
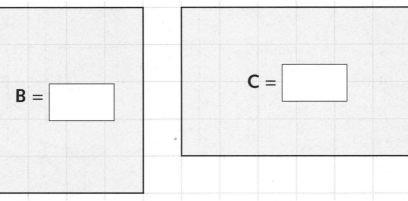

A = [ ]

B = [ ]

C = [ ]

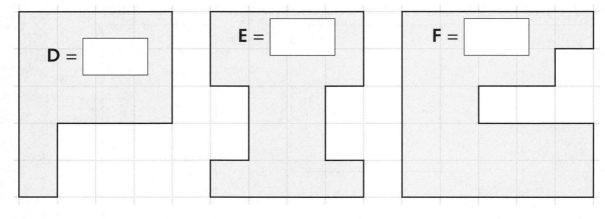

D = [ ]

E = [ ]

F = [ ]

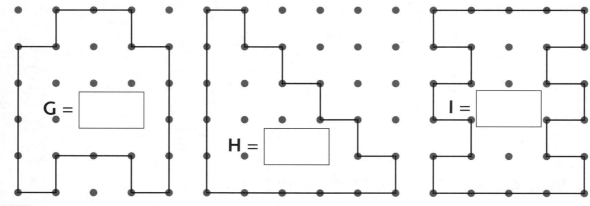
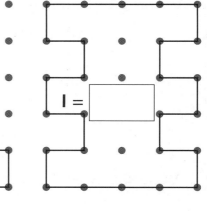

G = [ ]

H = [ ]

I = [ ]

**1**
9 marks

**2**  What is the area of Shape J? [ ]

J

**2**
1 mark

● find the area of rectilinear shapes by counting squares      Total: [ ] out of 10      Mastery:  NYA   A   A&E

Name: _____    Date: _____

## Measurement

**1** Estimate the mass shown on each scale to the nearest 100 g.

A    B    C    D

     1

4 marks

**2** Use the < or > sign to compare each pair of scales.

Scale A ☐ Scale D      Scale C ☐ Scale B

     2

2 marks

**3** Estimate the volume of liquid in each jug to the nearest 100 ml.

A    B    C    D

     3

4 marks

**4** Use the < or > sign to compare each pair of jugs.

Jug C ☐ Jug A      Jug B ☐ Jug D

     4

2 marks

**5** School sweatshirts cost £12.85 each. Mrs Singh buys 2 for her son. How much change does she get from £50?

     5

2 marks

**6** A colouring book plus a pack of 10 pencils cost £3.80. The book costs £2.40. What does each pencil cost?

     6

2 marks

**7** A python is 8·7 m long. A cobra is 3·5 m shorter than the python, but double the length of the grass snake. What is the length of the grass snake?

     7

2 marks

**8** A bottle of oil holds 330 ml. A tablespoon holds 15 ml. 6 tablespoons of oil are poured out of the bottle. How many millilitres of oil are left in the bottle?

     8

2 marks

● estimate, compare and calculate different measures, including money in pounds and pence

Total: ☐ out of 20    Mastery: NYA | A | A&E

Name: _____  Date: _____

## Measurement

**1** Draw hands to match the 12-hour digital times.

a)

b)

c)

d)

**1**
4 marks

**2** Write the 12-hour digital time to match the time on each clock.

a)

b)

c)

d)

**2**
4 marks

**3** Draw hands to match the 24-hour digital times. Circle a.m. or p.m.

a)

b)

c)

d)

a.m.   p.m.     a.m.   p.m.     a.m.   p.m.     a.m.   p.m.

**3**
4 marks

**4** Write the 24-hour digital time to match these times.

a)

b)

c)

d)

**4**
4 marks

**5** Write the 24-hour digital time to match these times.

a) a.m.: 25 past 2 [ ]          b) p.m.: Quarter to 5 [ ]

c) a.m.: 13 minutes past 7 [ ]   d) p.m.: 18 minutes to 9 [ ]

**5**
4 marks

● read, write and convert time between analogue and
digital 12- and 24-hour clocks

Total: [ ] out of 20    Mastery:  NYA   A   A&E

Name: _____ Date: _____

# Measurement

**1** A tap drips once every 6 s. How many times does it drip in 5 min?

**2** The 8:52 train is 1 h 25 min late. At what time does it arrive?

**3** Ava pays £2.25 per day on a return train ticket. How much does she pay in a 4-week month if she works 5 days a week?

**4** Bob works 5 days a week. Each day he spends 35 min travelling to and from work. Approximately how many h is this per week?

**5** A ride on the dodgem cars lasts 6 minutes. There is a 2 min break at the end of each ride to get people off and on. If the first ride starts at 10:30 a.m., when does the 8th ride start?

**6** A film lasts for 1 h and 45 min and is shown twice a day with a 4 h break between screenings. Complete the timetable.

|  | Start | Finish |
|---|---|---|
| Screening 1 | 11:20 | |
| Screening 2 | | |

**7** A plane takes off on Friday at 20:38. It lands on Saturday at 06:05. How long in h and min is the flight?

**8** Simon says that he is 103 months old. How old is he in years and months?

**9** Morning Radio.

| 6:00 | Wake Up |
|---|---|
| 6:55 | Weather |
| 7:00 | News |
| 7:15 | Sport |
| 7:25 | Traffic Report |
| 7:30 | On Your Way |

**a)** Leo wakes at 6:15. How many min does he have to wait for the news?

**b)** 'On Your Way' finishes at 9:00. How long does it last?

1 mark (1), 1 mark (2), 1 mark (3), 1 mark (4), 1 mark (5), 1 mark (6), 1 mark (7), 1 mark (8), 2 marks (9)

● solve problems involving converting from hours to minutes; minutes to seconds; years to months; weeks to days

Total: ___ out of 10   Mastery: NYA  A  A&E

© HarperCollins*Publishers* Ltd. 2015

Name: _____ Date: _____

## Properties of shapes

**1** Look at the triangles below. Write the letter of each shape in the correct column.

| equilaterial triangle | isosceles triangle | scalene triangle |
|---|---|---|
|  |  |  |

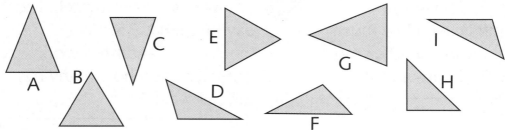

**2** Look at the quadrilaterals below. Write the letter of each shape in the correct column.

| square | rectangle | parallelogram | rhombus | trapezium | kite |
|---|---|---|---|---|---|
|  |  |  |  |  |  |

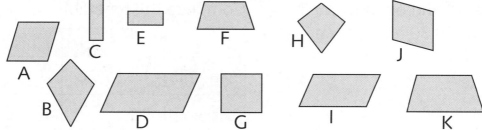

**3** Complete the table. Write ✓ for yes and ✗ for no.

|  | square | rectangle | parallelogram | rhombus | trapezium | kite |
|---|---|---|---|---|---|---|
| opposite angles equal |  |  |  |  |  |  |
| opposite sides equal |  |  |  |  |  |  |
| adjacent sides equal |  |  |  |  |  |  |
| at least one pair of opposite sides parallel |  |  |  |  |  |  |
| at least one pair of perpendicular sides |  |  |  |  |  |  |

1
9 marks

2
11 marks

3
30 marks

● compare and classify geometric shapes, including quadrilaterals and triangles, based on their properties and sizes

Total: _____ out of 50    Mastery:  NYA | A | A&E

Name: _____    Date: _____

## Properties of shapes

**You will need:**
- right-angle tester
- ruler

**1** Label each acute angle 'a' and each obtuse angle 'o'.

1
8 marks

**2** Label the marked angle in each shape as 'a' for an acute angle or 'o' for an obtuse angle.

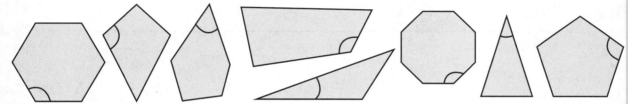

2
8 marks

**3** Order each set of angles, smallest to largest.

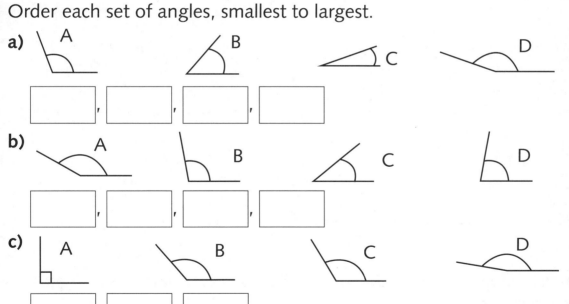

a) ▢ , ▢ , ▢ , ▢

b) ▢ , ▢ , ▢ , ▢

c) ▢ , ▢ , ▢ ,

3
3 marks

**4** Order the shapes, smallest to largest, according to the size of the shape's angle.

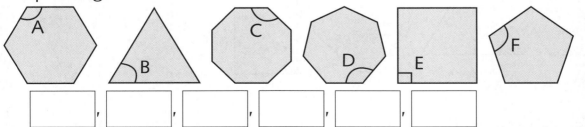

▢ , ▢ , ▢ , ▢ , ▢ , ▢

4
1 mark

● identify acute and obtuse angles and compare and order angles up to two right angles by size

Total: ▢ out of 20    Mastery:  NYA | A | A&E

Name: _____    Date: _____

## Properties of shapes

**1** Look at shapes A to N below. Use a mirror to check for lines of symmetry. Write each letter in the appropriate row in the table.

|  | shapes |
|---|---|
| no lines of symmetry |  |
| 1 line of symmetry |  |
| more than 1 line of symmetry |  |

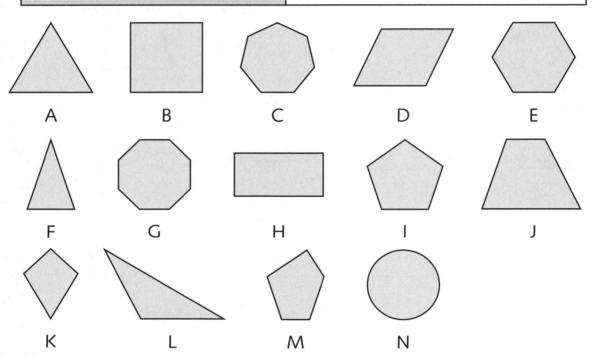

A      B      C      D      E

F      G      H      I      J

K      L      M      N

**1**
14 marks

**2** Look at shapes A to F below. Use a ruler to draw 1 line of symmetry on each shape.

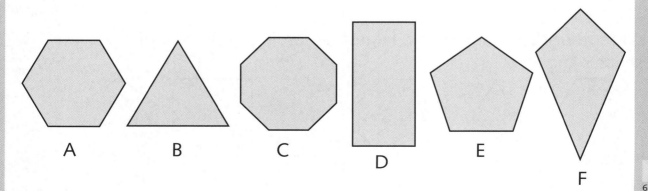

A      B      C      D      E      F

**2**
6 marks

● identify lines of symmetry in 2-D shapes presented in different orientations

Total: [  ] out of 20    Mastery:  NYA    A    A&E

Name: _____     Date: _____

You will need:
• mirror
• ruler

# Properties of shapes

**1** Reflect each of these shapes.

a)

b)
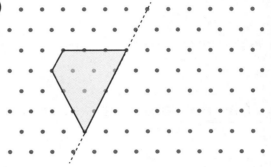

c)
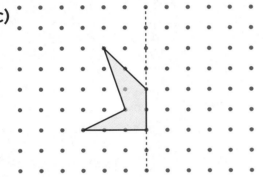

d)
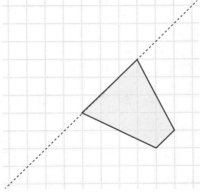

**1**
4 marks

**2** Shade the squares to make a symmetrical image.

a)
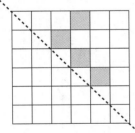

b)
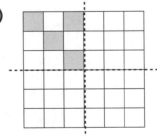

**2**
2 marks

**3** Reflect each of these shapes.

a)

b)
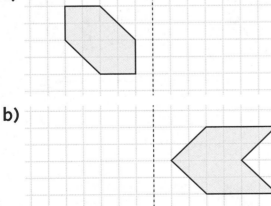

c)
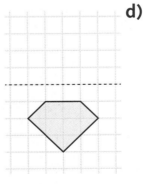

d)

**3**
4 marks

● complete a simple symmetric figure with respect to a specific line of symmetry

Total: [    ] out of 10     Mastery:  NYA   A   A&E

# Position and direction

**1** **a)** Write the coordinates of point **A**.

**b)** Write the coordinates of point **B**.

**c)** Write the coordinates of point **C**.

**d)** Write the coordinates of point **D**.

Plot these points on the grid:

**E** (5, 7)    **F** (9, 8)    **G** (3, 4)    **H** (8, 5)

**1**

8 marks

**2** (9, 8) are coordinates of a point on the line. Circle the coordinates of any other points on the line.

(6, 4)    (6, 6)    (5, 6)

(6, 5)    (3, 4)    (4, 3)

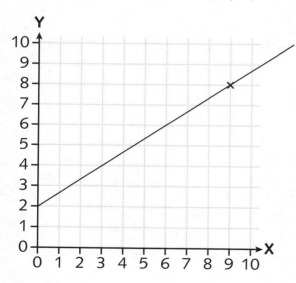

**3** Here is a shaded square.

Write the coordinates of point **B**.

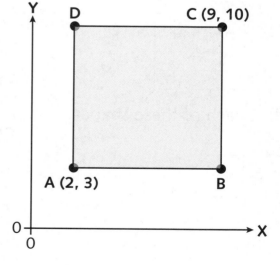

A (2, 3)    B

**2**

1 mark

**3**

1 mark

● describe positions on a 2-D grid as coordinates in the first quadrant

Total: ____ out of 10    Mastery:    NYA    A    A&E

© HarperCollins*Publishers* Ltd. 2015

Name: _____     Date: _____

# Position and direction

**You will need:**
• ruler

**1** **a)** Translate shape A 4 dots to the left.

**c)** Translate shape C 9 dots to the right and 3 dots up.

**b)** Translate shape B 3 dots down.

**d)** Translate shape D 7 dots to the left and 2 dots up.

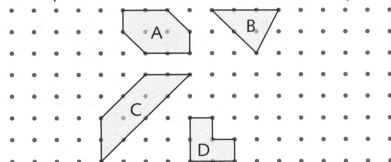

**1**
4 marks

**2** **a)** Describe how shape E has been translated to shape E'.

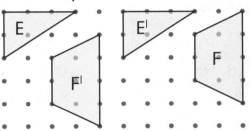

**b)** Describe how shape F has been translated to shape F'.

**2**
2 marks

**4** **a)** Describe how shape I has been translated to shape I'.

**b)** Describe how shape J has been translated to shape J'.

**3** **a)** Translate shape G 3 squares to the right and 5 squares up.

**b)** Translate shape H 2 squares to the left and 6 squares down.

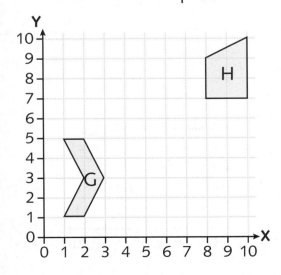

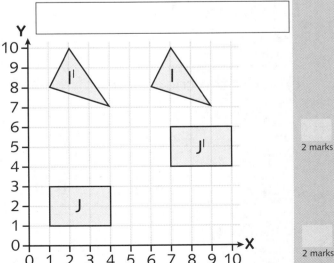

**3**
2 marks

**4**
2 marks

● describe movements between positions as translations of a given unit to the left/right and up/down

Total: _____ out of 10     Mastery:  NYA  |  A  |  A&E

Name: _____     Date: _____

## Position and direction

You will need:
• ruler

**1** The coordinates are joined to make a shape.

Write the coordinates in order.

(0, 5) → ( ☐ , ☐ ) → ( ☐ , ☐ )

→ ( ☐ , ☐ ) → ( ☐ , ☐ )

→ ( ☐ , ☐ ) → ( ☐ , ☐ )

→ ( ☐ , ☐ ) → ( ☐ , ☐ )

→ ( ☐ , ☐ ) → (0, 5)

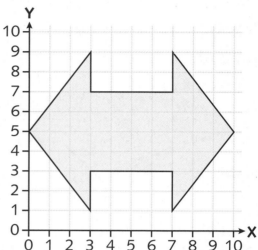

**1**
9 marks

**2** Plot these points on the grid.

**A** (2, 5)          **B** (4, 9)

**C** (8, 9)          **D** (10, 5)

**E** (8, 1)          **F** (4, 1)

Then join the points to make a
2-D shape. Join A to B, B to C,
C to D, D to E, E to F and F to A.

Name the shape. ☐

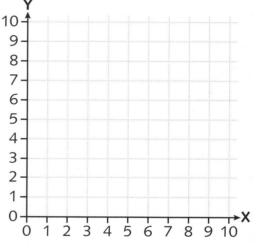

**2**
8 marks

**3** **a)** Reflect this shape in the dotted line of symmetry.

**b)** Name the whole shape.

☐

**c)** Write the coordinates of the shape.

(3, 1) → ( 2 , 5 )

→ ( ☐ , ☐ ) → ( ☐ , ☐ )

→ ( ☐ , ☐ ) → ( ☐ , ☐ )

→ (3, 1)

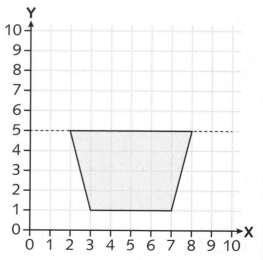

**3**
3 marks

● plot specified points and draw sides to complete
a given polygon

Total: ☐ out of 20     Mastery:  NYA | A | A&E

Name: _____     Date: _____

## Statistics

You will need:
• ruler

**1** Complete each diagram below using the data presented.

**Books borrowed from the library in one week**     Key: 📖 = 10 books

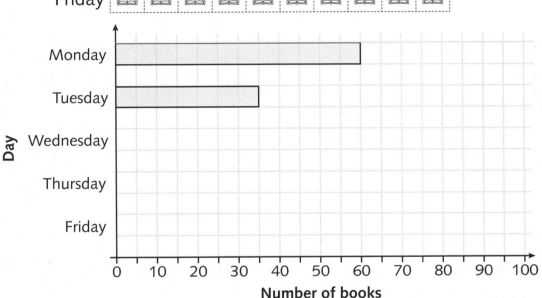

**Number of books**

1

5 marks

**2** Use the data in the pictogram and bar chart to answer the questions.

**a)** How many more books were borrowed on Thursday than on Monday?

**b)** On which day of the week were twice as many books borrowed than were borrowed on Tuesday?

**c)** Altogether how many books were borrowed during the week?

**d) i)** On which day of the week were most books borrowed?

**ii)** How many books was this?

**iii)** Give a possible reason as to why most books were borrowed on this day.

2

6 marks

Name: _____     Date: _____

## Statistics

You will need:
• ruler

**3** Use the data in the table to complete the line graph.

The first four months are shown on the graph.

| Temperature outside at midday on the last day of each month (May to Dec) | | | | | | | |
|---|---|---|---|---|---|---|---|
| May | Jun | Jul | Aug | Sep | Oct | Nov | Dec |
| 18 | 20 | 26 | 23 | 20 | 16 | 9 | 7 |

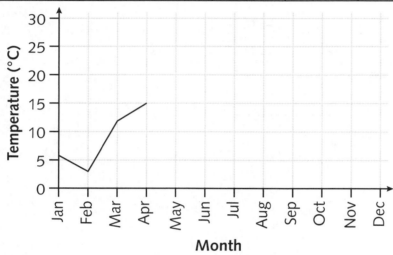

**4** Use the data above to answer the questions.

**a)** What was the midday temperature on 30th April? ☐

**b)** What was the midday temperature for the coldest month? ☐

**c)** How many months had a temperature between 10°C and 20°C? ☐

**d)** What was the difference in temperature between December and July? ☐

**e) i)** Which two consecutive months showed the greatest change in temperature? ☐ and ☐

**ii)** By how many degrees did the temperature change between these two months? ☐

3

3 marks

4

6 marks

● Interpret and present discrete and continuous data using appropriate graphical methods, including bar charts and time graphs

Total: ☐ out of 20   Mastery: NYA  A  A&E

Page 2 of 2                    © HarperCollinsPublishers Ltd. 2015

**Name:** _____  **Date:** _____

# Statistics

**1** Use the data in the pictogram to answer the questions.

**Number of flights sold (March)**   Key: ✈ = 2 tickets

| | | | | | | |
|---|---|---|---|---|---|---|
| North America | ✈ | ✈ | ✈ | ⊥ | | |
| South America | ✈ | ✈ | | | | |
| Europe | ✈ | ✈ | ✈ | ✈ | ✈ | ✈ |
| Middle East | ✈ | ✈ | ✈ | ✈ | ⊥ | |
| South and Central Asia | ✈ | ✈ | ✈ | ✈ | | |
| Far East and Australia | ✈ | ✈ | ✈ | | | |
| Africa | ✈ | ✈ | ⊥ | | | |

**a)** To which destination were most flights sold?

**b)** How many flights were sold to the Middle East?

**c)** How many more flights were sold to North America than were sold to South America?

**d)** Three times as many flights were sold to Europe than to which other destination?

**e)** Not including Europe, altogether how many flights were sold in March?

**1**
5 marks

**2** Use the data in the tally chart to answer the questions.

**a)** How many people prefer salad for lunch?

**b)** How many more people prefer a sandwich to soup?

**c)** Which type of lunch is less popular than soup?

**d)** Altogether how many people were asked about their preferred lunch?

**e)** Name two different types of food not already on the chart that could be included in the 'other' category. _____ and _____

| Preferred lunch | |
|---|---|
| sandwich | ⳾⳾⳾⳾ ⳾⳾⳾⳾ ⳾⳾⳾⳾ ⳾⳾⳾⳾ III |
| salad | ⳾⳾⳾⳾ ⳾⳾⳾⳾ ⳾⳾⳾⳾ II |
| jacket potato | ⳾⳾⳾⳾ |
| soup | ⳾⳾⳾⳾ IIII |
| other | ⳾⳾⳾⳾ ⳾⳾⳾⳾ I |

**2**
5 marks

Name: _____    Date: _____

## Statistics

**3** Last week members of the Gilroy Swimming Club kept a record of the number of laps they swam. Use the data in the bar chart to answer the questions.

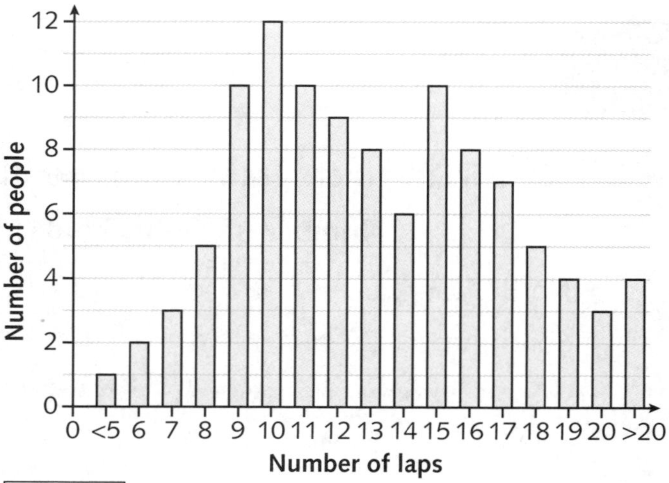

a) How many people swam more than 15 laps? ☐

b) 9 people swam the same number of laps. How many laps was this? ☐

c) How many people swam 10 laps or fewer? ☐

d) i) How many laps did more people swim than any other? ☐

   ii) How many people swam this number of laps? ☐

**3**

5 marks

**4** The graph shows the journey of a glider. Use the data to answer the questions.

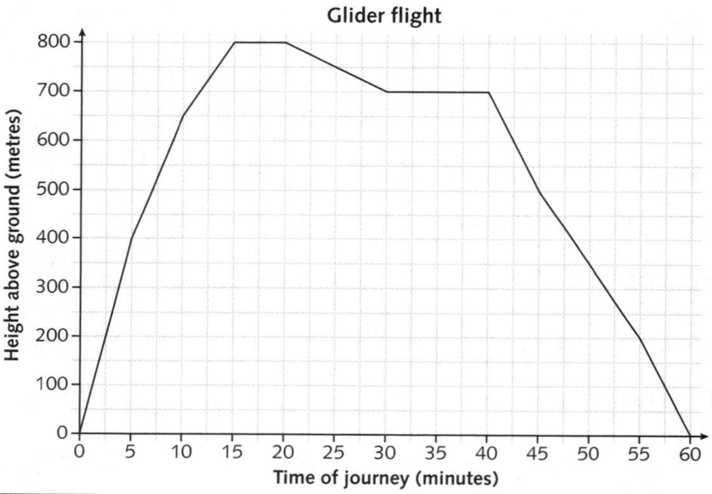

a) At what height above the ground was the glider after 10 minutes? ☐

b) How long did it take the glider to reach a height of 800 metres above the ground? ☐

c) For how many minutes did the glider stay at 700 metres above the ground? ☐

d) After how many minutes of the journey did the glider begin its landing? ☐

e) Altogether, how many minutes was the glider 500 metres or more above the ground? ☐

**4**

5 marks

● Solve comparison, sum and difference problems using information presented in bar charts, pictograms, tables and other graphs

Total: ☐ out of 20    Mastery:  NYA │ A │ A&E

**Exercise 1: Number - Number and place value**

**1** 18, 30, 36, 48, 54, 66, 72

**2** 27, 36, 54, 63, 81, 90, 99

**3** 28, 42, 49, 63, 70, 84

**4** 50, 100, 125, 175, 200, 225, 250

**5** 1000, 4000, 5000, 6000, 8000, 9000, 10 000

**6** 7 14 21 28 35 42 49 56 63 70 77 84

**7** 9 18 27 36 45 54 63 72 81 90 99 108

**8** 1000 2000 3000 4000 5000 6000 7000 8000 9000

**9** 25 50 75 100 125 150 175 200 225 250 275 300

**10** 6 12 18 24 30 36 42 48 54 60 66 72

**Exercise 2: Number - Number and place value**

**1 a)** 7000  **b)** 4000  **c)** 3000  **d)** 6800

**e)** 10700  **f)** 5280  **g)** 9650  **h)** 2046

**i)** 8724  **j)** 4692

**2 a)** 3000  **b)** 7000  **c)** 6000  **d)** 1400

**e)** 5300  **f)** 8500  **g)** 2548  **h)** 526

**i)** 4507  **j)** 7414

**Exercise 3: Number - Number and place value**

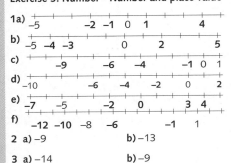

**1a)** −5  −2 −1 0 1  4

**b)** −5 −4 −3  0  2  5

**c)** −9  −6  −4  −1 0 1

**d)** −10  −6  −4  −2  0  2

**e)** −7  −5  −2  0  3 4

**f)** −12 −10 −8 −6  −1  1

**2 a)** −9  **b)** −13

**3 a)** −14  **b)** −9

**Exercise 4: Number - Number and place value**

**1 a)** 7  **b)** 90  **c)** 2000  **d)** 300

**2 a)** 8671  **b)** 3159  **c)** 4837  **d)** 3468

**3 a)** 3, 9, 5, 6  **b)** 2, 6, 7, 4

**4 a)** 9  **b)** 3000  **c)** 70  **d)** 900

**5 a)** 80  **b)** 8000  **c)** 800

**6 a)** 2485  **b)** 5317  **c)** 7624

**Exercise 5: Number - Number and place value**

**1** Answers will vary

**2 a)** 5548 > 5458

**b)** 6023 < 6043

**c)** 1678 > 1677

**3** 3172, 3247, 3274, 3427, 3472, 3542, 3724, 3742

**4** 5731, 5732, 5734, 5738, 5761, 5762, 5764, 5768

**5** 1006 m, 1060 m, 1066 m, 1100 m, 1106 m, 1160 m

**6** 2575 g, 2550 g, 2525 g, 2500 g, 2350 g, 2300 g

**Exercise 6: Number - Number and place value**

**1** 2475  2490 2495  2510

**2 a)** 170  **b)** 200

**3 a)** 2367  **b)** 3158

**4 a)**

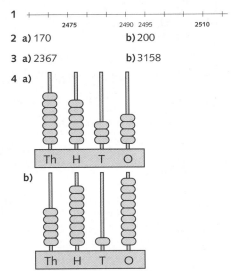

Th  H  T  O

**b)**

Th  H  T  O

**5 a)** 2 kg, 500 g, 200 g, 20 g, 20 g, 5 g masses circled

**b)** 2 kg, 1 kg, 500 g, 100 g, 50 g, 20 g, 10 g masses circled

**Exercise 7: Number - Number and place value**

**1 a)** 80  **b)** 70  **c)** 370

**d)** 420  **e)** 4640  **f)** 1980

**2 a)** 500  **b)** 300  **c)** 3700  **d)** 8200

**3 a)** 7000  **b)** 6000  **c)** 3000  **d)** 6000

**4** Answers will vary as follows:

**a)** A number from 25 to 34

**b)** A number from 155 to 164

**c)** A number from 350 to 449

**d)** A number from 5715 to 5724

**e)** A number from 2250 to 2349

**f)** A number from 6500 to 7499

**Exercise 8: Number - Number and place value**

**1** 1623

**2 a)** 36  **b)** 12 or 24

**3 a)** −11, −2, 1  **b)** −5, −2, 4

**4 a)** −4

**b)** −5 at the top, 1 at the bottom right

**5** A number from 5625 to 5629, and a number from 5630 to 5634

**6** XCI

**Exercise 9: Number - Number and place value**

**1 a)** IX  **b)** LXIV  **c)** XXV  **d)** XIII

**e)** XXXI  **f)** LXXVI  **g)** XCVIII  **h)** XLII

**2 a)** 19  **b)** 16  **c)** 59  **d)** 99

**e)** 7  **f)** 88  **g)** 29  **h)** 64

**3** Award up to 2 marks for each part for a suitable explanation of the value of the zero digit in each number, and how it represents the placeholder.

**a)** It is a placeholder for zero tens.

**b)** It is a place holder for zero units.

**Exercise 10: Number - Addition and subtraction**

Q1–5: For each question:

Award 1 mark for evidence of working out an estimate.

Award 2 marks for the correct answer. If the answer is incorrect, award 1 mark for evidence of using an appropriate method of calculation.

Award 1 mark for evidence of checking the answer using an appropriate method, e.g. using the inverse operation.

**1** 7839

**2** 6823

**3** 5473

**4** 10 451

**5** 7236

**Exercise 11: Number - Addition and subtraction**

Q1–5: For each question:
- Award 1 mark for evidence of working out an estimate.
- Award 2 marks for the correct answer. If the answer is incorrect, award 1 mark for evidence of using an appropriate method of calculation.
- Award 1 mark for evidence of checking the answer using an appropriate method, e.g. using the inverse operation.

**1** 3343

**2** 1923

**3** 4679

**4** 2449

**5** 3379

**Exercise 12: Number - Addition and subtraction**

Q1–4: Award 2 marks per question for the correct answer. If the answer is incorrect, award 1 mark for identifying the correct calculation(s).

**1** 192 + 335 = 527 km

**2** 65, 72 and 47

**3 a)** £648  **b)** £5040

**4** 4565 Morcella Mavericks supporters

**Exercise 13: Number - Multiplication and division**

**1**

| × | 4 | 7 | 2 | 6 | 9 | 5 | 3 | 8 |
|---|---|---|---|---|---|---|---|---|
| 6 | 24 | 42 | 12 | 36 | 54 | 30 | 18 | 48 |
| 11 | 44 | 77 | 22 | 66 | 99 | 55 | 33 | 88 |
| 7 | 28 | 49 | 14 | 42 | 63 | 35 | 21 | 56 |
| 12 | 48 | 84 | 24 | 72 | 108 | 60 | 36 | 96 |
| 9 | 36 | 63 | 18 | 54 | 81 | 45 | 27 | 72 |

2 a) 8    b) 12    c) 3    d) 4

   e) 7    f) 3    g) 8    h) 2

   i) 3    j) 10    k) 9    l) 8

   m) 8    n) 4    o) 9    p) 4

   q) 4    r) 4    s) 11    t) 11

### Exercise 14: Number - Multiplication and division

1 a) 42, 420    b) 36, 3600

   c) 24, 2400    d) 600, 6000

   e) 1800, 180    f) 0, 900

2 a) 81    b) 144    c) 49    d) 36

3 a) 70    b) 70    c) 80    d) 30

   e) 140    f) 120    g) 80    h) 100

4 a) 84    b) 48    c) 240

   d) 72    e) 360    f) 96

### Exercise 15: Number - Multiplication and division

1  $6 \times 7 = 42$

   $7 \times 6 = 42$

2  3 and 7 circled

3  2, 4, 5, 10

4  4, 5, 8, 20 circled

5  75 and 120 circled

6  7, 9 in the top row

   5, 6 in the first column

7  Award 1 mark for a correct answer to both calculations. Award 1 mark for identifying $8 \times 5 \times 7$ as the more effective, efficient and appropriate calculation.

   Award 1 mark for a suitable explanation as to why $8 \times 5 \times 7$ is the more effective, efficient and appropriate calculation.

**280, 280**

   Explanations will vary.

**8**

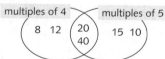

### Exercise 16: Number - Multiplication and division

Q1–5: Award 1 mark per question for using an effective, efficient and appropriate method. Award 1 mark per question for calculating the correct answer.

1  228

2  294

3  752

4  1472

5  2133

### Exercise 17: Number - Multiplication and division

Q1–3: Award 2 marks per question for the correct answer. If the answer is incorrect, award 1 mark for identifying the correct calculation(s).

---

1  £4.84

2 a) £322    b) £234

3 a) £5.25    b) 15p

### Exercise 18: Number - Fractions (including decimals)

1  $\frac{2}{4}$, $\frac{4}{8}$

2  Award 1 mark for shading 6 of the 8 sectors. Award 1 mark for identifying the equivalent fraction as $\frac{6}{8}$.

   Six of the eight sectors coloured; $\frac{6}{8}$

3  a/w: Y4 Sheet 18 Q3

4  $\frac{4}{16}$, $\frac{16}{24}$, $\frac{25}{100}$

5 a) $\frac{2}{4}$, $\frac{3}{6}$

   b) $\frac{4}{6}$, $\frac{8}{12}$

   c) $\frac{2}{10}$, $\frac{3}{15}$

   d) $\frac{2}{8}$, $\frac{3}{12}$

   e) $\frac{6}{8}$, $\frac{3}{4}$

### Exercise 19: Number - Fractions (including decimals)

1  $\frac{35}{100}$, $\frac{36}{100}$, $\frac{39}{100}$, $\frac{40}{100}$, $\frac{41}{100}$, $\frac{42}{100}$, $\frac{44}{100}$, $\frac{45}{100}$

2 a) $\frac{46}{100}$ or equivalent

   b) $\frac{71}{100}$    c) $\frac{69}{100}$

3 a) $\frac{8}{10} = \frac{80}{100}$    b) $\frac{3}{10} = \frac{30}{100}$

   c) $\frac{5}{10} = \frac{50}{100}$    d) $\frac{7}{10} = \frac{70}{100}$

4 a) 0·05    b) 0·28    c) 0·67    d) 0·80

5 a) 0·03    b) 0·08    c) 0·06    d) 0·01

### Exercise 20: Number - Fractions (including decimals)

Q3–6: Award 2 marks per question for the correct answer. If the answer is incorrect, award 1 mark for identifying the correct calculation(s).

1 a) 4    b) 9    c) 12

   d) 26    e) 16    f) 14

2 a) 24    b) 57    c) 36

   d) 70    e) 105    f) 50

3  £8

4  £198

5  £180

6  £150

### Exercise 21: Number - Fractions (including decimals)

1 a) $\frac{4}{5}$    b) $\frac{5}{7}$    c) $\frac{12}{9}$    d) $\frac{16}{12}$

2 a) $\frac{4}{10}$    b) $\frac{1}{11}$    c) $\frac{1}{5}$    d) $\frac{2}{8}$

3 a) $\frac{3}{11}$    b) $\frac{4}{6}$    c) $\frac{7}{8}$    d) $\frac{7}{10}$

4 a) $\frac{6}{10}$    b) $\frac{3}{5}$    c) $\frac{5}{7}$    d) $\frac{2}{12}$

5 a) $\frac{3}{5}$    b) $\frac{7}{10}$    c) $\frac{6}{7}$    d) $\frac{7}{12}$

### Exercise 22: Number - Fractions (including decimals)

1 a) $\frac{26}{100} = 0·26$    b) $\frac{77}{100} = 0·77$

   c) $\frac{12}{100} = 0·12$    d) $\frac{59}{100} = 0·59$

   e) $\frac{91}{100} = 0·91$

---

2 a) 0·3    b) 0·44    c) 0·91

   d) 0·7    e) 0·52

3 a) $\frac{9}{10}$ or equivalent

   b) $\frac{71}{100}$

   c) $\frac{38}{100}$ or equivalent

   d) $\frac{5}{10}$ or equivalent

   e) $\frac{12}{100}$ or equivalent

4

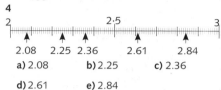

   a) 2.08    b) 2.25    c) 2.36

   d) 2.61    e) 2.84

### Exercise 23: Number - Fractions (including decimals)

1 a) $\frac{3}{4}$    b) $\frac{1}{4}$    c) $\frac{1}{2}$

2 a) 0·25    b) 0·5    c) 0·75

3  0·75 —— 3/4 —— 75/100

   0·5 —— 1/2 —— 50/100

   0·25 ——1/4 —— 25/100

4

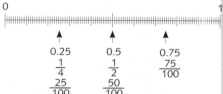

### Exercise 24: Number - Fractions (including decimals)

1 a) 0·6    b) 0·2    c) 1·3

   d) 0·9    e) 5·8    f) 2·5

2 a) 0·05    b) 0·12    c) 0·34

   d) 0·07    e) 0·61    f) 0·89

3 a) 0·8; 8 circled    b) 5·2; 2 circled

4 a) 9·6; 9 circled    b) 0·2; 0 circled

5 a) 0·78; 8 circled    b) 0·03; 3 circled

6 a) 0·04; 0 circled    b) 0·49; 4 circled

### Exercise 25: Fractions (including decimals)

1 a) 1    b) 1    c) 2

   d) 12    e) 8    f) 24

   g) 62    h) 85

2  Any two numbers from 3·5 to 4·49

3  Any two numbers from 45·5 to 46·49

4  For each question part: Award 1 mark for identifying which two whole numbers the decimal lies between. Award 1 mark for identifying which whole number the decimal rounds to.

   a) 7, 8; 8 circled

   b) 16, 17; 16 circled

   c) 39, 40; 40 circled

   d) 73, 74; 73 circled

## Exercise 26: Number – Fractions (including decimals)

**1 a)** Any number between 5·5 and 6·5

**b)** Any number between 18·7 and 19·1

**c)** Any number between 2·47 and 2·53

**d)** Any number between 36·27 and 36·34

**2 a)** 45·8 < 48·5

**b)** 12·27 > 12·07

**c)** 37·14 < 37·18

**d)** 71·52 < 71·55

**3 a)** 4·1, 4·2, 4·5, 4·9, 5·1, 5·2, 5·4, 5·9

**b)** 7·44, 7·48, 7·84, 7·88, 8·44, 8·48, 8·84, 8·88

**c)** 10·1, 10·2, 10·3, 10·5, 10·6, 10·7, 10·8, 10·9

**d)** 45·03, 45·07, 45·17, 45·33, 45·37, 45·71, 45·73, 45·77

**4 a)** 7·5 **b)** 12·43

**5 a)** 58·59 **b)** 26·9

**6 a)** 81·66 **b)** 3·43

**7 a)** 19·86 **b)** 60·07

## Exercise 27: Number – Fractions (including decimals)

Q1–3: Award 2 marks per question for the correct answer. If the answer is incorrect, award 1 mark for identifying the correct calculation(s).

**1 a)** £94.70 **b)** £44.60

**2** 1·80 metres

**3** £900.00

**4 a)** 200 ml **b)** 300 ml

## Exercise 28: Measurement

**1 a)** 4200 m **b)** 1600 m

**c)** 5800 m **d)** 84 100 m

**2 a)** 5·6 km **b)** 8·3 km

**c)** 12·5 km **d)** 7·1 km

**3 a)** 600 cm **b)** 1900 cm

**c)** 370 cm **d)** 500 cm

**4 a)** 0·7 m **b)** 0·6 m

**c)** 4·5 m **d)** 0·2 m

**5 a)** 4700 g **b)** 5100 g

**c)** 12 900 g **d)** 24 600 g

**6 a)** 6·8 kg **b)** 1·9 kg

**c)** 2·4 kg **d)** 5·6 kg

**7 a)** 1900 ml **b)** 3700 ml

**c)** 2500 ml **d)** 12 300 ml

**8 a)** 3·8 *l* **b)** 5·4 *l*

**c)** 1·6 *l* **d)** 2·9 *l*

**9 a)** 270 min **b)** 4 h

**c)** 72 h **d)** 5 days

**e)** 28 days **f)** 6 weeks

**g)** 4 h and 10 min **h)** 2 days and 12 h

## Exercise 29: Measurement

**1** A = 22 cm   B = 12 cm   C = 20 cm

**2 a)** 12 cm **b)** 14 cm **c)** 16 cm

**3 a)** 12 m **b)** 28 m **c)** 18 m

**4** A rectangle drawn with a perimeter of 20 cm, for example: 4 × 6 rectangle; 3 × 7 rectangle; 2 × 8 rectangle; 1 × 10 rectangle.

## Exercise 30: Measurement

**1** A = 9 cm² B = 20 cm² C = 24 cm²

D = 14 cm² E = 16 cm² F = 21 cm²

G = 16 cm² H = 15 cm² I = 16 cm²

**2** J = 15 cm²

## Exercise 31: Measurement

Q5–9: Award 2 marks per question for the correct answer. If the answer is incorrect, award 1 mark for identifying the correct calculation(s).

**1** A 4·4 kg   B 3·2 kg

C 3·6 kg   D 4·8 kg

**2** Scale A < Scale D     Scale C > Scale B

**3** A 700 ml   B 400 ml

C 800 ml   D 1 *l*

**4** Jug C > Jug A     Jug B < Jug D

**5** £24.30

**6** 14p

**7** 2·6 m

**8** 240 ml

## Exercise 32: Measurement

**1 a)**  **b)**

**c)** **d)**

**2 a)** 2:41 **b)** 10:38 **c)** 4:26 **d)** 6:05

**3 a)**  **b)**

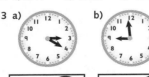

**c)**  **d)**

**4 a)** 06:24 **b)** 23:40

**c)** 21:06 **d)** 01:21

**5 a)** 02:25 **b)** 16:45

**c)** 07:13 **d)** 20:42

## Exercise 33: Measurement

**1** 50

**2** 10:17

**3** £45

**4** Approximately 3 hours

**5** 11:26 a.m.

**6**

|  | Start | Finish |
|---|---|---|
| Screening 1 | 11:20 | 13:05 |
| Screening 2 | 17:05 | 18:50 |

**7** 9 hours and 27 minutes

**8** 8 years and 7 months

**9 a)** 45 minutes

**b)** 1 hour and 30 minutes

## Exercise 34: Properties of shapes

**1**

| equilateral triangle | isosceles triangle | scalene triangle |
|---|---|---|
| B, E | A, C, G, H | D, F, I |

**2**

| square | rectangle | parallelogram |
|---|---|---|
| G | C, E | D, I |
| rhombus | trapezium | kite |
| A, J | F, K | B, H |

**3**

|  | square | rectangle | parallelogram | rhombus | trapezium | kite |
|---|---|---|---|---|---|---|
| opposite angles equal | ✓ | ✓ | ✓ | ✓ | ✗ | ✓ |
| opposite sides equal | ✓ | ✓ | ✓ | ✓ | ✗ | ✗ |
| adjacent sides equal | ✓ | ✗ | ✗ | ✓ | ✗ | ✗ |
| at least one pair of opposite sides parallel | ✓ | ✓ | ✓ | ✓ | ✓ | ✗ |
| at least one pair of perpendicular sides | ✓ | ✓ | ✗ | ✗ | ✗ | ✗ |

## Exercise 35: Geometry – Properties of shapes

**1** Acute angles labelled 'a' (4)

Obtuse angles labelled 'o' (4)

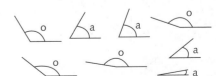

**2** Acute angles labelled 'a' (3)

Obtuse angles labelled 'o' (5)

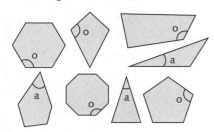

**3 a)** C, B, A, D    **b)** C, D, B, A    **c)** A, C, B, D

**4** B, E, F, A, D, C

### Exercise 36: Properties of shapes
**1**

|  | shapes |
|---|---|
| no lines of symmetry | J, L, M |
| 1 line of symmetry | F, K |
| more than 1 line of symmetry | A, B, C, D, E, G, H, I, N |

**2** Any **one** of the dotted lines of symmetry for each shape

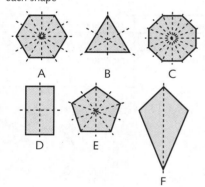

### Exercise 37: Geometry - Properties of shapes

**1 a)**

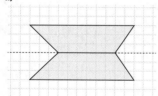

**b)**

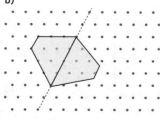

**c)**

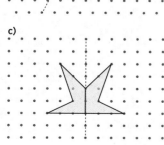

**d)**

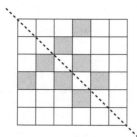

**2 a)**

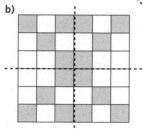

**b)**

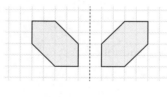

**3 a)**

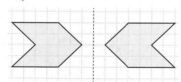

**b)**

**c)**

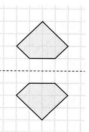

**d)**

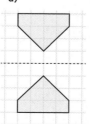

### Exercise 38: Geometry - Position and direction

**1 a)** A (2, 6)    **b)** B (4, 1)

   **c)** C (7, 9)    **d)** D (10, 2)

The following points correctly plotted:

E (5, 7)       F (9, 8)

G (3, 4)       H (8, 5)

**2** The following points circled: (6, 6), (3, 4)

**3** B (9, 3)

### Exercise 39: Geometry - Position and direction

**1**

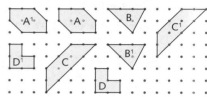

**2 a)** 5 dots to the right.

   **b)** 6 dots to the left and 1 dot down.

**3**

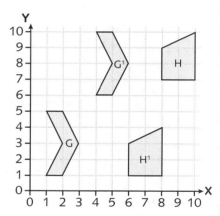

**4 a)** 4 squares to the left.

   **b)** 5 squares to the right and 3 squares up.

### Exercise 40: Geometry - Position and direction

**1** (0, 5)   (3, 9)   (3, 7)   (7, 7)   (7, 9)
(10,5)   (7, 1)   (7, 3)   (3, 3)   (3, 1)
(0, 5)
Award 1 mark each for plotting points A to F correctly.
Award 1 mark for joining the points to draw the hexagon.
Award 1 mark for naming the polygon.

**2**

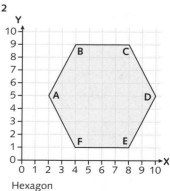

Hexagon

**3 a)**

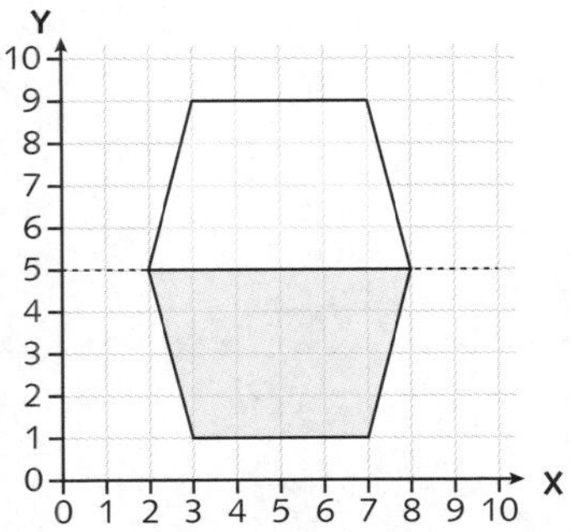


**b)** Hexagon

**c)** (3, 1) (2, 5) (3, 9) (7,9) (8, 5) (7, 1) (3,1)

## Exercise 41: Statistics

**1** Books borrowed from the library in one week

**Key:** 📖 **= 10 books**

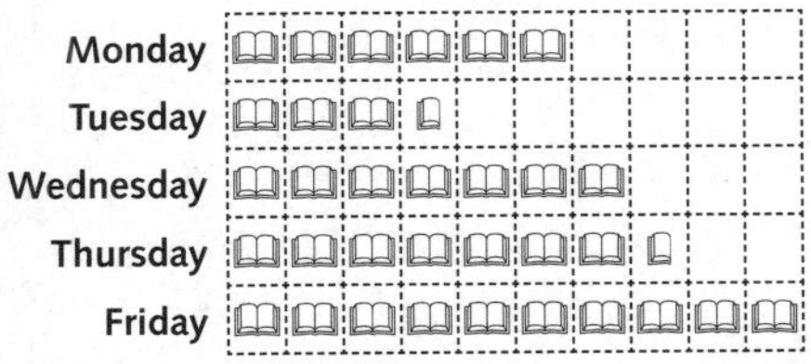


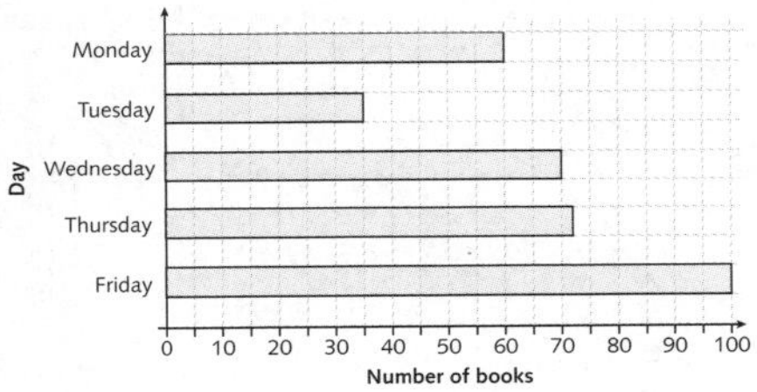


**2 a)** 15

**b)** Wednesday

**c)** 340

**d) i)** Friday

**ii)** 100

**iii)** Answers will vary

**3**

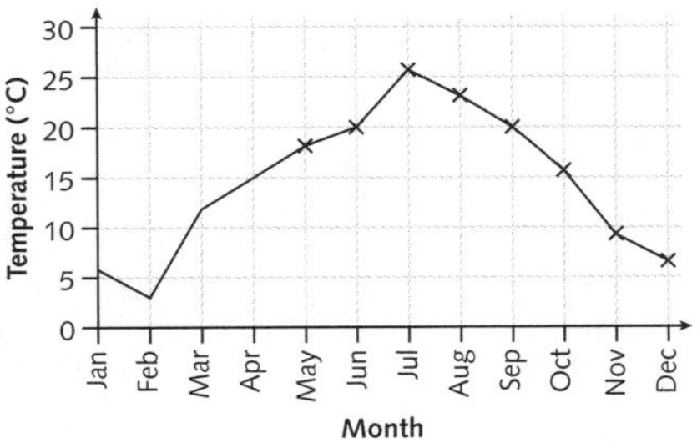


**4 a)** 15 °C

**b)** 3 °C

**c)** 6

**d)** 19 °C

**e) i)** February and March

**ii)** 9 °C

## Exercise 42: Statistics

**1 a)** Europe **b)** 9

**c)** 3 **d)** South America

**e)** 39

**2 a)** 17 **b)** 14

**c)** Jacket potato **d)** 65

**e)** Answers will vary

**3 a)** 31 **b)** 12 **c)** 33

**d) i)** 10

**ii)** 12

**4 a)** 650 m

**b)** 15 minutes

**c)** 10 minutes

**d)** 40 minutes

**e)** 38 minutes

**1**  Write the numbers shown by the Base 10 material.

a)

b)

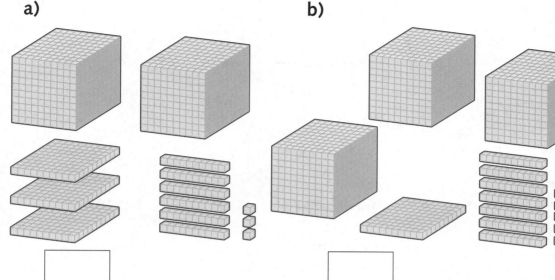

◻

◻

**1**
2 marks

**2**  Write the numbers.

a) ⟋500⟍ ⟋4000⟍ ⟋2⟍ ⟋80⟍   b) ⟋50⟍ ⟋7000⟍ ⟋9⟍ ⟋800⟍

◻

◻

**2**
2 marks

**3**  Fill in the missing numbers.

a) $2000 + 900 + \boxed{\phantom{000}} + 7 = 2967$

b) $6000 + \boxed{\phantom{000}} + 30 + 8 = 6538$

**3**
2 marks

**4**  Order each set of numbers, smallest to largest.

a) 5687, 5896, 5678, 5866, 5750

◻ , ◻ , ◻ , ◻ , ◻

b) 4376, 4358, 4367, 4369, 4354

◻ , ◻ , ◻ , ◻ , ◻

**4**
2 marks

**5**  Write the number that is

   1000 less   1000 more          1000 less   1000 more
a) ◻  6457  ◻          b) ◻  8793  ◻

**5**
2 marks

**1**

a) $400 + 56 =$ ☐

b) $310 + 75 =$ ☐

c) $564 + 70 =$ ☐

d) $570 + 358 =$ ☐

e) $650 + 62 =$ ☐

f) $440 + 285 =$ ☐

 1

6 marks

**2**

a) $456 - 200 =$ ☐

b) $703 - 280 =$ ☐

c) $679 - 90 =$ ☐

d) $825 - 350 =$ ☐

e) $478 - 260 =$ ☐

f) $756 - 300 =$ ☐

 2

6 marks

**3**

a) At Dover, 348 cars and 180 trucks board a ferry for France. How many vehicles is this altogether?

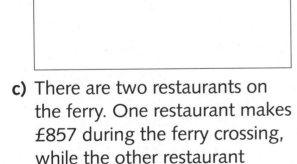

b) On the ferry there are a total of 920 people. If 50 of these are crew, how many passengers are there?

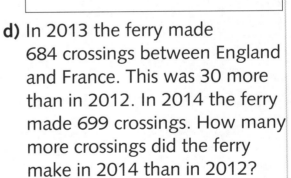

c) There are two restaurants on the ferry. One restaurant makes £857 during the ferry crossing, while the other restaurant makes £160 less than this. How much money do the two restaurants make altogether during the ferry crossing?

d) In 2013 the ferry made 684 crossings between England and France. This was 30 more than in 2012. In 2014 the ferry made 699 crossings. How many more crossings did the ferry make in 2014 than in 2012?

 3

8 marks

Name: _____  Date: _____

**1**  Use a mirror to test each of these shapes for symmetry.

     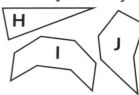 

Write the letters of the 2-D shapes that have:

**a)** no lines of symmetry

**b)** 1 line of symmetry

**c)** more than 1 line of symmetry

**1**
3 marks

**2**  Reflect each of these shapes.

**a)** 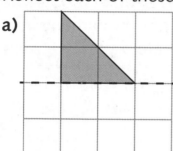  **b)** 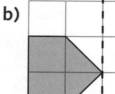 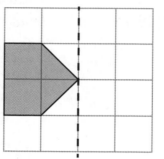  **c)**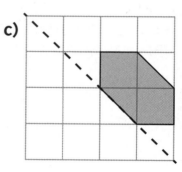

**2**
3 marks

**3**  Draw the reflected image of the dots.

**a)** 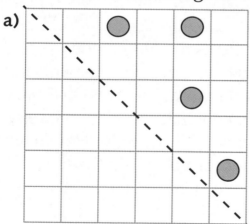  **b)**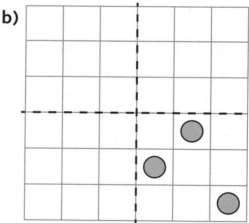

**3**
2 marks

**4**  Reflect each of these shapes.

**a)** 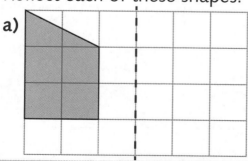  **b)**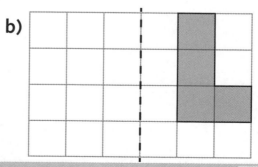

**4**
2 marks

Total: _____ out of 10   Mastery: NYA  A  A&E

**1**
a) $6 \times 9 = \boxed{\phantom{00}}$   b) $10 \times 9 = \boxed{\phantom{00}}$   c) $3 \times 9 = \boxed{\phantom{00}}$

d) $9 \times 9 = \boxed{\phantom{00}}$   e) $2 \times 9 = \boxed{\phantom{00}}$   f) $12 \times 9 = \boxed{\phantom{00}}$

**1**
6 marks

**2**
a) $27 \div 9 = \boxed{\phantom{00}}$   b) $36 \div 9 = \boxed{\phantom{00}}$   c) $63 \div 9 = \boxed{\phantom{00}}$

d) $45 \div 9 = \boxed{\phantom{00}}$   e) $72 \div 9 = \boxed{\phantom{00}}$   f) $108 \div 9 = \boxed{\phantom{00}}$

**2**
6 marks

**3**
a) $54 \div \boxed{\phantom{00}} = 9$   b) $9 \times \boxed{\phantom{00}} = 45$   c) $\boxed{\phantom{00}} \div 9 = 9$

d) $\boxed{\phantom{00}} \times 9 = 99$   e) $36 = 9 \times \boxed{\phantom{00}}$   f) $2 = \boxed{\phantom{00}} \div 9$

**3**
6 marks

**4**
a) $5 \times 6 = \boxed{\phantom{00}}$   b) $2 \times 6 = \boxed{\phantom{00}}$   c) $8 \times 6 = \boxed{\phantom{00}}$

d) $11 \times 6 = \boxed{\phantom{00}}$   e) $7 \times 6 = \boxed{\phantom{00}}$   f) $4 \times 6 = \boxed{\phantom{00}}$

**4**
6 marks

**5**
a) $18 \div 6 = \boxed{\phantom{00}}$   b) $36 \div 6 = \boxed{\phantom{00}}$   c) $54 \div 6 = \boxed{\phantom{00}}$

d) $72 \div 6 = \boxed{\phantom{00}}$   e) $24 \div 6 = \boxed{\phantom{00}}$   f) $60 \div 6 = \boxed{\phantom{00}}$

**5**
6 marks

**6**
a) $36 \div \boxed{\phantom{00}} = 6$   b) $6 \times \boxed{\phantom{00}} = 48$   c) $\boxed{\phantom{00}} \div 6 = 4$

d) $\boxed{\phantom{00}} \times 6 = 54$   e) $3 = \boxed{\phantom{00}} \div 6$   f) $66 = 6 \times \boxed{\phantom{00}}$

**6**
6 marks

**7**
a) $30 \times 6 = \boxed{\phantom{00}}$       b) $80 \times 6 = \boxed{\phantom{00}}$

c) $70 \times 9 = \boxed{\phantom{00}}$       d) $40 \times 9 = \boxed{\phantom{00}}$

**7**
4 marks

**1** Colour half of each circle. Then complete the fraction that is equivalent to a half.

You will need:
· coloured pencil

a)
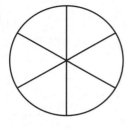

$\frac{1}{2} = \frac{\Box}{6}$

b)
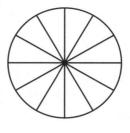

$\frac{1}{2} = \frac{\Box}{12}$

1
2 marks

**2** Colour one quarter of each circle. Then complete the fraction that is equivalent to a quarter.

a)
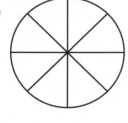

$\frac{1}{4} = \frac{\Box}{8}$

b)

$\frac{1}{4} = \frac{\Box}{12}$

2
2 marks

**3** Fill in the missing numbers to show the equivalent fractions.

a) $\frac{1}{2} = \frac{2}{\Box} = \frac{3}{\Box} = \frac{\Box}{8} = \frac{5}{\Box} = \frac{6}{\Box}$

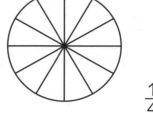

b) $\frac{1}{4} = \frac{2}{\Box} = \frac{3}{\Box} = \frac{\Box}{16} = \frac{5}{\Box} = \frac{6}{\Box}$

3
2 marks

**4** Work out these non-unit fractions. Show all your working.

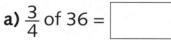

a) $\frac{3}{4}$ of 36 = ☐

b) $\frac{2}{3}$ of 27 = ☐

c) $\frac{5}{8}$ of 48 = ☐

d) $\frac{4}{9}$ of 72 = ☐

4
4 marks

**1**

**a)** Translate the shape 4 dots to the right.

**b)** Translate the shape 3 dots up.

You will need:
· ruler

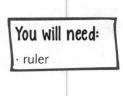

**1**
2 marks

**2**

**a)** Translate the shape 4 squares to the right and 3 squares up.

**b)** Translate the shape 3 squares to the left and 4 squares down.

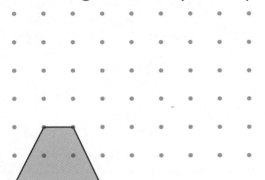

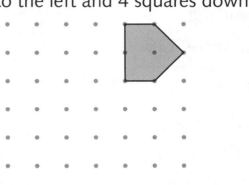

**2**
2 marks

**3**

**a)** Write the coordinates of point A. [ ]

**b)** Write the coordinates of point B. [ ]

Plot these points on the grid:
**C** (4, 5)
**D** (3, 2)

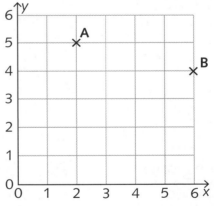

**3**
4 marks

**4**

**a)** Translate the shape 3 squares to the left and 2 squares up.

**b)** Translate the shape 3 squares to the right and 4 squares down.

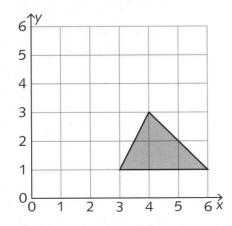

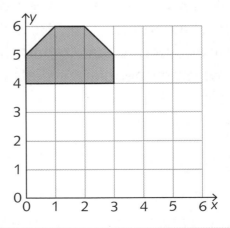

**4**
2 marks

**1** Complete each number chain.

a) 540 → [ ] → [ ] → [ ] → [ ] → [ ]
+ 8, + 200, + 60, + 7, + 20

b) 270 → [ ] → [ ] → [ ] → [ ] → [ ]
+ 34, + 300, + 8, + 45, + 120

1
2 marks

**2** Estimate the answer to each calculation and write it in the bubble. Then use a written method to work out the answer. Show all your working.

a) 456 + 238

b) 145 + 483

c) 268 + 574

d) 435 + 387

2
12 marks

**3**

a) During one weekend 544 people went to an ice skating rink. 236 went on Saturday and the rest on Sunday. How many people went on Sunday?

b) Of the 544 visitors to the skating rink, 368 people hired skates. The rest had their own skates. How many people had their own skates?

c) Tickets to the skating rink cost £17 for children and £23 for adults. What is the total cost for 2 adults and 3 children?

3
6 marks



Total: out of 20 Mastery: NYA A A&E

**1** Write the decimal equivalent for each fraction.

a) $\frac{1}{10}$ = ☐

b) $\frac{4}{10}$ = ☐

c) $\frac{6}{10}$ = ☐

**1**
3 marks

**2** Write each decimal as a fraction.

a) 0·7 = ☐

b) 0·3 = ☐

c) 0·9 = ☐

**2**
3 marks

**3** Order each set of decimals, smallest to largest.

a) 4·5, 4·2, 4·7, 4·4, 4·6  ☐ , ☐ , ☐ , ☐ , ☐

b) 8·8, 8·3, 8·9, 8·5, 8·1  ☐ , ☐ , ☐ , ☐ , ☐

**3**
2 marks

**4** Use the < or > sign to make each statement correct.

a) 4·6 ☐ 5·4    b) 8·7 ☐ 7·8    c) 1·4 ☐ 1·9    d) 2·5 ☐ 2·7

**4**
4 marks

**5** Round each of these decimals to the nearest whole number.

a) 3·7 ☐

b) 2·3 ☐

c) 4·6 ☐

**5**
3 marks

**6** Write the missing decimals on the number line.

7    7·1            ☐        7·6        ☐        8

**6**
2 marks

**7** Write the decimals that are one tenth smaller and one tenth larger.

|  |  | One tenth smaller | One tenth larger |
|---|---|---|---|
| a) | 6·5 |  |  |
| b) | 2·8 |  |  |
| c) | 1·2 |  |  |

**7**
3 marks

**1** Write each mass in kilograms.

**a)** 6400 g = ⬜  **b)** 3800 g = ⬜  **c)** 5200 g = ⬜

1
3 marks

**2** Write each mass in grams.

**a)** 2·3 kg = ⬜  **b)** 1·9 kg = ⬜  **c)** 4·5 kg = ⬜

2
3 marks

**3** Write the mass shown on each set of weighing scales.
Then round each mass to the nearest kilogram.

**a)**   **b)**   **c)**

⬜  ⬜  ⬜

Rounded = ⬜  Rounded = ⬜  Rounded = ⬜

3
6 marks

**4** Using the fewest number of standard weights needed, balance each of the following. You can use each weight more than once.

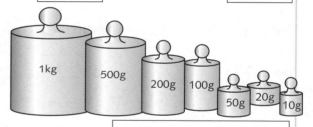

**a)** 850 g = ⬜  **b)** 1320 g = ⬜

**c)** 1·9 g = ⬜  **d)** 2·7 g = ⬜

4
4 marks

**5** A bag of 10 oranges weighs 2·5 kg and a bag of 10 apples weighs 2 kg.

**a)** What is the mass in grams of 1 orange? ⬜

**b)** What is the mass in grams of 1 apple? ⬜

**c)** What is the total mass of a bag of oranges and a bag of apples? ⬜

**d)** What is the total mass of 15 oranges? ⬜

5
4 marks

**1**
a) $4^2 =$ ☐   b) $7^2 =$ ☐   c) $12^2 =$ ☐

d) $5^2 =$ ☐   e) $8^2 =$ ☐   f) $9^2 =$ ☐

**1** 6 marks

**2**
a) $4 \times 7 =$ ☐   b) $6 \times 7 =$ ☐   c) $8 \times 7 =$ ☐

d) $9 \times 7 =$ ☐   e) $7 \times 7 =$ ☐   f) $5 \times 7 =$ ☐

**2** 6 marks

**3**
a) $70 \div 7 =$ ☐   b) $21 \div 7 =$ ☐   c) $84 \div 7 =$ ☐

d) $14 \div 7 =$ ☐   e) $77 \div 7 =$ ☐   f) $42 \div 7 =$ ☐

**3** 6 marks

**4**
a) $3 \times 11 =$ ☐   b) $7 \times 11 =$ ☐   c) $8 \times 11 =$ ☐

d) $11 \times 11 =$ ☐   e) $9 \times 11 =$ ☐   f) $6 \times 11 =$ ☐

**4** 6 marks

**5**
a) $110 \div 11 =$ ☐   b) $66 \div 11 =$ ☐   c) $44 \div 11 =$ ☐

d) $55 \div 11 =$ ☐   e) $132 \div 11 =$ ☐   f) $99 \div 11 =$ ☐

**5** 6 marks

**6**
a) $2 \times 12 =$ ☐   b) $11 \times 12 =$ ☐   c) $7 \times 12 =$ ☐

d) $8 \times 12 =$ ☐   e) $9 \times 12 =$ ☐   f) $3 \times 12 =$ ☐

**6** 6 marks

**7**
a) $72 \div 12 =$ ☐   b) $144 \div 12 =$ ☐   c) $60 \div 12 =$ ☐

d) $36 \div 12 =$ ☐   e) $48 \div 12 =$ ☐   f) $84 \div 12 =$ ☐

**7** 6 marks

**8**
a) $28 \div$ ☐ $= 4$   b) $7 \times$ ☐ $= 21$

c) ☐ $\times 12 = 48$   d) $44 = 11 \times$ ☐

e) ☐ $\div 7 = 6$   f) $2 =$ ☐ $\div 11$

g) $12 \times$ ☐ $= 72$   h) $11 = 132 \div$ ☐

**8** 8 marks

Questions 1, 2 and 3:

Listen carefully. Your teacher will tell you which method to use to answer each of these calculations. Circle that method. Estimate the answer to each calculation and write it in the cloud. Then work out the answer. Show all your working.

**1** $68 \times 7$

Partitioning

Grid method

Expanded method

Formal method

**1**
3 marks

**2** $84 \times 6$

Partitioning

Grid method

Expanded method

Formal method

**2**
3 marks

**3** $53 \times 9$

Partitioning

Grid method

Expanded method

Formal method

**3**
3 marks

**4** $6 \times 8 \times 5 =$ [  ]

**4**
1 mark

**1**  **a)** 3 hours = [ ] minutes        **b)** 6 days = [ ] hours

   **c)** 4 weeks = [ ] days        **d)** 50 days = [ ] weeks and [ ] day(s)

   **e)** 60 hours = [ ] days and [ ] hours

1
5 marks

**2**  Write the 12-hour digital time to match these times.

   **a)** 18 minutes past 3    **b)** 19 minutes to 7    **c)** 6 minutes to 12

   [ : ]                [ : ]                [ : ]

2
3 marks

**3**  Write the time shown on each of these 12-hour digital clocks in words.

   **a)** 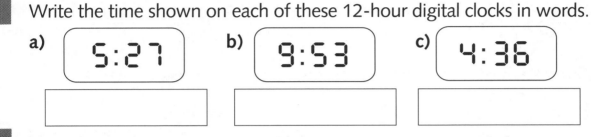  5:27    **b)** 9:53    **c)** 4:36

   [ ]                [ ]                [ ]

3
3 marks

**4**  Write the 24-hour digital time to match these a.m. times.

   **a)**                **b)**                **c)**

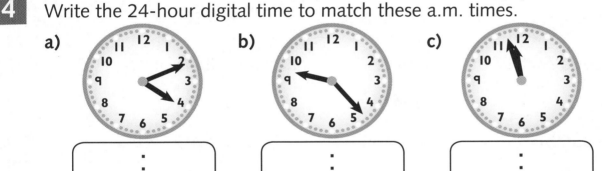

   [ : ]                [ : ]                [ : ]

4
3 marks

**5**  Write the 24-hour digital time to match these p.m. times.

   **a)**                **b)**                **c)**

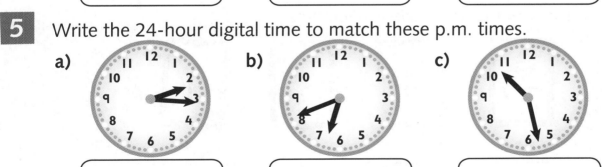

   [ : ]                [ : ]                [ : ]

5
3 marks

**6**  Write the 12-hour a.m. or p.m. time to match these 24-hour digital times.

   **a)** 22:32        **b)** 19:48        **c)** 08:13

   [ ] ○ a.m.     [ ] ○ a.m.     [ ] ○ a.m.
       ○ p.m.          ○ p.m.          ○ p.m.

6
3 marks

**1** Order each set of numbers, smallest to largest.

a) 6879, 6987, 6789, 6897, 6978

☐ , ☐ , ☐ , ☐ , ☐

b) 5236, 5256, 5506, 5258, 5238

☐ , ☐ , ☐ , ☐ , ☐

**1**
2 marks

**2** Use the < or > sign to make each statement correct.

a) 687 ☐ 678                    b) 1856 ☐ 1586

c) 2587 ☐ 2857                  d) 5078 ☐ 5088

**2**
4 marks

**3** Round each of these numbers to the nearest multiple of 10.

a) 56 = ☐          b) 72 = ☐          c) 143 = ☐

d) 557 = ☐         e) 1458 = ☐        f) 2205 = ☐

**3**
6 marks

**4** Round each of these numbers to the nearest multiple of 100.

a) 576 = ☐         b) 839 = ☐         c) 308 = ☐

d) 3569 = ☐        e) 2485 = ☐        f) 4712 = ☐

**4**
6 marks

**5** Write these numbers on the number line.

−3   4   −5   1

|   |   |   |   |   |   |   |   |   |   |
                    0

**5**
1 mark

**6** Write the missing numbers.

− 12, − 11, ☐ , ☐ , − 8, ☐ , ☐ , − 5, ☐ , − 3, ☐ , ☐ , 0, ☐ , ☐

**6**
1 mark

Name: ______________________ Date: ____________

**1** Complete each number chain.

a) 720 → [ ] → [ ] → [ ] → [ ] → [ ]
– 60, – 200, – 5, – 40, – 8

b) 680 → [ ] → [ ] → [ ] → [ ] → [ ]
– 9, – 40, – 300, – 6, – 90

1 — 2 marks

**2** Estimate the answer to each calculation and write it in the bubble. Then use a written method to work out the answer. Show all your working.

a) 578 – 284

b) 793 – 356

c) 4657 – 1288

d) 6519 – 2873

2 — 12 marks

**3**

a) Simon buys a used car for £879. Before he can drive it, he has to spend £365 on repairs. How much does the car cost Simon altogether?

b) Simon has £798 saved in one bank account and £784 in another account. He uses £925 of these savings to help buy the car. How much is left in Simon's bank accounts?

c) There were two cars that Simon was interested in buying. The car that Simon eventually bought cost £879. The other car was £186 more expensive. What was the cost of the other car?

3 — 6 marks



Total: ____ out of 20 Mastery: NYA A A&E

**1** Label each acute angle 'a' and each obtuse angle 'o'.

You will need:
· right-angle tester
· ruler

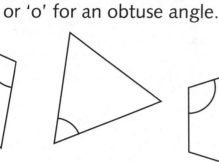

1
6 marks

**2** Label the marked angle in each shape as 'a' for an acute angle or 'o' for an obtuse angle.

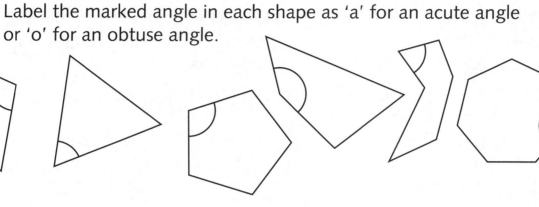

2
6 marks

**3** Order each set of the angles, smallest to largest.

a)

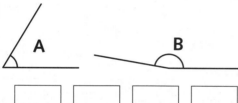
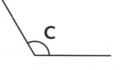

[ ] [ ] [ ] [ ]

b)

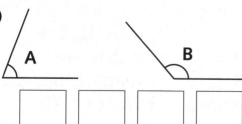

[ ] [ ] [ ] [ ]

3
2 marks

**4** Mark each shape with an 'R' if it is a regular shape or an 'I' if it is an irregular shape.

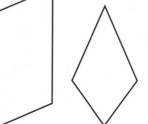
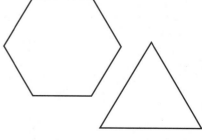

4
6 marks

Name: ______________________ Date: ____________

## 1

Continue each sequence.

**a)** 1000, 2000, 3000, ☐, ☐, ☐, ☐, ☐, ☐

**b)** 25, 50, 75, ☐, ☐, ☐, ☐, ☐, ☐

**c)** 100, 200, 300, ☐, ☐, ☐, ☐, ☐, ☐

**d)** 50, 100, 150, ☐, ☐, ☐, ☐, ☐, ☐

1
4 marks

## 2

Estimate the answer to each calculation and write it in the bubble. Then use the formal written method to work out the answer. Show all your working.

**a)** 76 × 4

**b)** 68 × 7

**c)** 54 × 8

**d)** 93 × 6

2
12 marks

## 3

**a)** A copy of *The Life of Parin* costs £9. A bookshop buys 35 copies. How much does this cost them altogether?

**b)** A bookshop sells 10 copies of *Olive and Co* for a total of £120. What is the difference in price between a copy of *The Life of Parin* and a copy of *Olive and Co*?

3
4 mark



Total: ____ out of 20 Mastery: NYA A A&E

**1** Write the fractions on the number lines.

a)

6 [ ] [ ] [ ] 7

b)

10 [ ] [ ] [ ] [ ] 11 [ ] [ ] [ ] 12

**1**
2 marks

**2** Write the missing hundredths.

a) $\frac{45}{100}$, $\frac{46}{100}$, [ ], [ ], [ ], $\frac{50}{100}$, [ ], [ ],

b) $\frac{82}{100}$, [ ], [ ], $\frac{85}{100}$, [ ], [ ], $\frac{88}{100}$, [ ]

**2**
2 marks

**3** What fraction of each grid is shaded?

a) 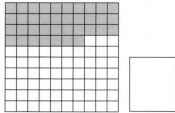 [ ]

b) 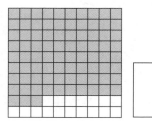 [ ]

**3**
2 marks

**4** Work out these tenths. Show your working.

a) $\frac{7}{10}$ of 40 = [ ]    b) $\frac{3}{10}$ of 300 = [ ]    c) $\frac{9}{10}$ of 120 = [ ]

**4**
6 marks

**5** Work out these hundredths. Show your working.

a) $\frac{8}{100}$ of 300 = [ ]    b) $\frac{28}{100}$ of 800 = [ ]    c) $\frac{62}{100}$ of 500 = [ ]

**5**
6 marks

**6** Next month during their annual sale, Electronics Nation is going to sell the television for two-thirds of the normal price. What will be the price of the television during the sale?

**6**
2 marks

Total: [ ] out of 20   Mastery: NYA  A  A&E

**1** Write each distance in metres.

**a)** 4·7 km = [ ] m     **b)** 11·8 km = [ ] m

**2** Write each distance in kilometres.

**a)** 6300 m = [ ] km     **b)** 12 500 m = [ ] km

**3** Write these lengths as metres using decimals.

**a)** 230 cm = [ ] m     **b)** 400 mm = [ ] m

**4** **a)** 600 mm = [ ] cm = [ ] m

**b)** [ ] mm = 40 cm = [ ] m

**c)** [ ] mm = [ ] cm = 5 m

**d)** [ ] mm = [ ] cm = 1·8 m

**5** Round each length to the nearest centimetre and to the nearest 10 cm.

A        B            C        D

12 13 14 15 16 17 18 19 20 21 22 23 24 25 26 27

18 17 16 15 14 13 12 11 10 9 8 7 6 5 4 3

A = [ ] to the nearest centimetre.     A = [ ] to the nearest 10 cm.

B = [ ] to the nearest centimetre.     B = [ ] to the nearest 10 cm.

C = [ ] to the nearest centimetre.     C = [ ] to the nearest 10 cm.

D = [ ] to the nearest centimetre.     D = [ ] to the nearest 10 cm.

**6** Use points A, B, C and D in Question 5 to work out these distances.

**a)** What is the approximate distance between Point A and Point C? [ ]

**b)** What is the approximate distance from Point B to Point D and back to Point C? [ ]

**1**

**a)** 478 + 80 = ☐

**b)** 687 + 6 = ☐

**c)** 786 + 600 = ☐

**d)** 576 + 150 = ☐

**e)** 287 + 340 = ☐

**f)** 398 + 820 = ☐

**g)** 2168 + 480 = ☐

**h)** 1628 + 650 = ☐

**i)** 3691 + 540 = ☐

**1**
9 marks

**2**

**a)** 1452 − 7 = ☐

**b)** 1237 − 300 = ☐

**c)** 1816 − 40 = ☐

**d)** 1759 − 280 = ☐

**e)** 1546 − 190 = ☐

**f)** 1434 − 620 = ☐

**g)** 1288 − 350 = ☐

**h)** 2269 − 990 = ☐

**i)** 2175 − 540 = ☐

**2**
9 marks

**3** Estimate the answer to each calculation and write it in the bubble. Then use a written method to work out the answer. Show all your working.

**a)** 3457 + 2538

**b)** 2674 + 5187

**c)** 1538 + 6275

**d)** 5768 + 3684

**3**
12 marks

**1** Estimate the answer to each calculation and write it in the bubble. Then use a written method to work out the answer. Show all your working.

**a)** 4869 – 1683

**b)** 5857 – 2379

**c)** 4426 – 1819

**d)** 6256 – 4578

**1**

12 marks

**2** **a)** Jamie, Naomi and Leo are playing Jonah's Quest. Jamie has 1546 points. Naomi has 772 more points than Jamie. Leo has 286 fewer points than Naomi.
**i)** How many points does Naomi have?
**ii)** How many points does Leo have?

**i)** [ ]     **ii)** [ ]

**b)** To reach Level 3 of Jonah's Quest you need 2750 points. Jamie currently has 1546 points. How many more points does Jamie need to reach Level 3?

**c)** To reach Level 3 of Jonah's Quest you need 2750 points. You need another 1550 points to reach Level 4. How many points do you need altogether to reach Level 4?

**d)** The highest score that Jamie has reached on Jonah's Quest is 4235. Naomi's best score is 986 more than this. Leo's top score is 357 fewer than Jamie's top score.
**i)** What is Naomi's top score?
**ii)** What is Leo's top score?

**i)** [ ]     **ii)** [ ]

**2**

8 marks

**1**   Use the data in the pictogram and the bar chart to complete each diagram.

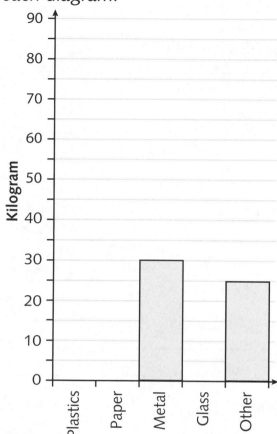

Key: =  10 kg

| Materials | | | | | | | | | |
|---|---|---|---|---|---|---|---|---|---|
| Plastics | ♻ | ♻ | ♻ | ♻ | | | | | |
| Paper | ♻ | ♻ | ♻ | ♻ | ♻ | ♻ | ♻ | ♻ | ♻ |
| Metal | | | | | | | | | |
| Glass | ♻ | ♻ | ♻ | ♻ | ♻ | | | | |
| Other | | | | | | | | | |

**1**

5 marks

**2**   Use the data in the pictogram and bar chart to answer these questions.

**a)** How much more glass than metal was recycled? ☐

**b)** What is the total weight of non-paper material that the school recycled? ☐

**c)** What is the difference in weight between the material the school recycled the most of and the material they recycled the least of? ☐

**d)** The weight of which two other materials combined was the same as the weight of paper? ☐

**e)** The school were aiming to recycle 200 kg of material during the term.

  **i)** Did the school reach their target? ☐

  **ii)** If not, by how many kilograms were the school short of their target? If so, by how many kilograms did the school beat their target? ☐

**2**

6 marks

**3**  Use the data in the table to complete the line graph.
The first four months are shown on the graph.

Average daytime temperatures in Hyderabad, India (°C)

| Jan | Feb | Mar | Apr | May | Jun | Jul | Aug | Sep | Oct | Nov | Dec |
|-----|-----|-----|-----|-----|-----|-----|-----|-----|-----|-----|-----|
| 29 | 32 | 35 | 38 | 39 | 34 | 31 | 30 | 30 | 31 | 29 | 28 |

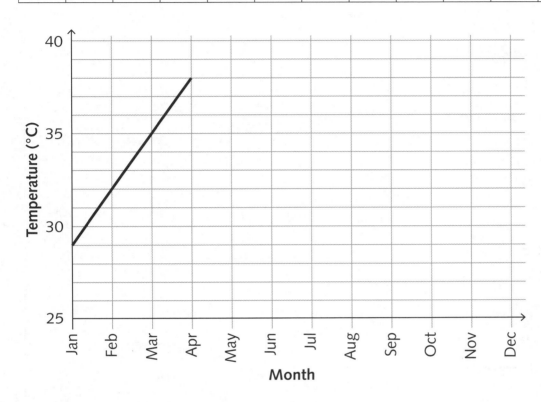

**3**
3 marks

**4**  Use the data above to answer the questions.

**a)** What is the average daytime temperature in June?

**b)** What is the average daytime temperature for the hottest month?

**c)** Which two months have an average daytime temperature of 29°C?  ⬚ and ⬚

**d)** What is the difference in temperature between the coldest and the hottest months?

**e) i)** Which two consecutive months show the greatest change in temperature?  ⬚ and ⬚

**ii)** By how many degrees does the temperature change between these two months?

**4**
6 marks

Questions 1 and 2:

Listen carefully. Your teacher will tell you which method to use to answer each of these calculations. Circle that method. Estimate the answer to each calculation and write it in the cloud. Then work out the answer. Show all your working.

**1**  524 × 3

Partitioning

Grid method

Expanded method

Formal method

1

3 marks

**2**  869 × 6

Partitioning

Grid method

Expanded method

Formal method

2

3 marks

**3**

THE SPIDER'S REVENGE
Adult TICKETS: £8
Child TICKETS: £5

**a)** Yesterday, the cinema sold a total of 847 child tickets for all four screenings of *The Spider's Revenge*. How much is this altogether?

**b)** At the 2 o'clock screening of *The Spider's Revenge*, the cinema sold 74 adult tickets and 263 child tickets. How much money did the cinema take altogether?

3

4 marks

**1** Write the decimal equivalent for each fraction.

**a)** $\frac{1}{100}$ = [    ]　　　　**b)** $\frac{8}{100}$ = [    ]　　　　**c)** $\frac{56}{100}$ = [    ]

1
3 marks

**2** Write each decimal as a fraction.

**a)** 0·05 = [  ]　　　**b)** 0·86 = [  ]　　　**c)** 0·49 = [  ]

2
3 marks

**3** Order each set of decimals, smallest to largest.

**a)** 2·45, 2·36, 2·47, 2·24, 2·63　　[  ] , [  ] , [  ] , [  ] , [  ]

**b)** 5·08, 5·81, 5·09, 5·85, 5·58　　[  ] , [  ] , [  ] , [  ] , [  ]

3
2 marks

**4** Use the < or > sign to make each statement correct.

**a)** 2·56 [  ] 3·56　　　　　　**b)** 4·05 [  ] 4·25

**c)** 6·74 [  ] 6·73　　　　　　**d)** 2·55 [  ] 2·49

4
4 marks

**5** Divide each of these numbers by 10.

**a)** 8 [    ]　　　　　　**b)** 65 [    ]

**c)** 15 [    ]　　　　　**d)** 82 [    ]

5
4 marks

**6** Divide each of these numbers by 100.

**a)** 3 [    ]　　　　　　**b)** 18 [    ]

**c)** 75 [    ]　　　　　**d)** 52 [    ]

6
4 marks

　　　　Total: [  ] out of 20　Mastery: NYA　A　A&E

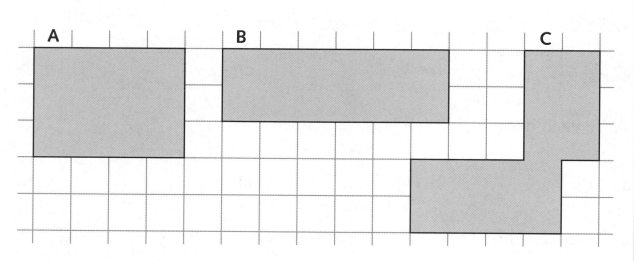

**1** Find the perimeter of Shapes A to C.

A = [      ]          B = [        ]          C = [        ]

1
3 marks

**2** Find the area of Shapes A to C.

A = [      ]          B = [        ]          C = [        ]

2
3 marks

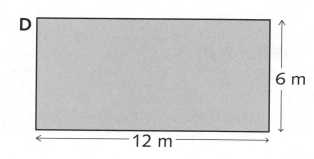

6 m

12 m

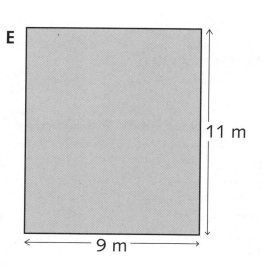

11 m

9 m

**3** Calculate the perimeter of Shapes D and E.

D = [        ]                    E = [        ]

3
2 marks

**4** Calculate the area of Shapes D and E.

D = [        ]                    E = [        ]

4
2 marks

**1**  Order each set of numbers, smallest to largest.

a) 5768, 5668, 5786, 5686, 5666

[  ] , [  ] , [  ] , [  ] , [  ]

b) 8067, 8076, 8061, 8016, 8071

[  ] , [  ] , [  ] , [  ] , [  ]

**1**
2 marks

**2**  Use the < or > sign to make each statement correct.

a) 4289 [  ] 4298     b) 3345 [  ] 3343     c) 2008 [  ] 2080

**2**
3 marks

**3**  Round each of these numbers to the nearest multiple of 10.

a) 68 [  ]          b) 42 [  ]          c) 759 [  ]

d) 428 [  ]         e) 4758 [  ]        f) 3724 [  ]

**3**
6 marks

**4**  Round each of these numbers to the nearest multiple of 100.

a) 869 [  ]         b) 542 [  ]         c) 671 [  ]

d) 5378 [  ]        e) 3562 [  ]        f) 4717 [  ]

**4**
6 marks

**5**  Round each of these numbers to the nearest multiple of 1000.

a) 2846 [  ]        b) 1538 [  ]        c) 3485 [  ]

**5**
3 marks

**6**  a) Count back 5 from 0. [  ]     b) Count back 3 from −2. [  ]

c) Count on 4 from −7. [  ]          d) Count on 2 from −5. [  ]

**6**
4 marks

**7**  Write each of these numbers in Roman numerals.

a) 87 = [  ]        b) 142 = [  ]       c) 34 = [  ]

**7**
3 marks

**8**  Write each of these numbers in Hindu-Arabic numerals.

a) LXII = [  ]      b) CXXV = [  ]      c) XVII = [  ]

**8**
3 marks

**1** Estimate the answer to each calculation and write it in the bubble. Then use a written method to work out the answer. Show all your working.

**a)** 2856 + 3488

**b)** 5867 + 475

**c)** 4324 − 1756

**d)** 3564 − 876

**e)** £34.67 + £43.16

**f)** £23.88 + £48.57

**1**
18 marks

**2** Order these amounts of money, from smallest to largest.

**a)** £56.07, £46.70, £56.70, £47.60, £47.07

☐ , ☐ , ☐ , ☐ , ☐

**b)** £28.46, £28.65, £29.64, £26.65, £29.45

☐ , ☐ , ☐ , ☐ , ☐

**2**
2 marks

**1** Label each triangle.

E Equilateral triangle

I Isosceles triangle

S Scalene triangle

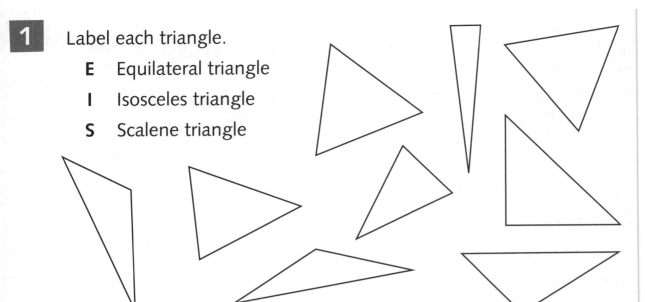

1

9 marks

**2** Label each quadrilateral.

S Square

Re Rectangle

P Parallelogram

Rh Rhombus

T Trapezium

K Kite

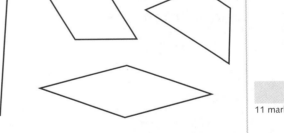

2

11 marks

**3** Complete the table. Write ✓ for yes and ✗ for no.

| Quadrilateral | Opposite sides equal | Opposite sides parallel | Opposite angles equal | All sides equal | Four right angles |
|---|---|---|---|---|---|
| square | | | | | |
| rectangle | | | | | |
| parallelogram | | | | | |
| rhombus | | | | | |

3

20 marks

Total: ____ out of 40    Mastery: NYA   A   A&E

Questions 1 and 2:
Listen carefully. Your teacher will tell you which method to use to answer each of these calculations. Circle that method.
Estimate the answer to each calculation and write it in the cloud. Then work out the answer. Show all your working.

**1**    536 × 4

Partitioning

Grid method

Expanded method

Formal method

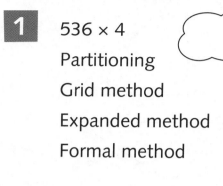

**1**
3 marks

**2**    482 × 6

Partitioning

Grid method

Expanded method

Formal method

**2**
3 marks

**3**

£162

£328

**a)** How much change would you receive from £1000 if you bought six dining chairs?

**b)** What is the total cost of one dining table and four dining chairs?

**3**
4 marks

**1** Write the numerator or denominator to show pairs of equivalent fractions.

a) $\frac{1}{2} = \frac{\boxed{\phantom{0}}}{6}$     b) $\frac{1}{5} = \frac{3}{\boxed{\phantom{0}}}$     c) $\frac{1}{\boxed{\phantom{0}}} = \frac{4}{12}$   d) $\frac{1}{7} = \frac{2}{\boxed{\phantom{0}}}$     **1**
4 marks

**2** Simplify each fraction.

a) $\frac{5}{25} = \boxed{\phantom{0}}$     b) $\frac{3}{21} = \boxed{\phantom{0}}$     c) $\frac{8}{12} = \boxed{\phantom{0}}$     d) $\frac{6}{14} = \boxed{\phantom{0}}$     **2**
4 marks

**3** a) $\frac{2}{7} + \frac{4}{7} = \boxed{\phantom{0}}$     b) $\frac{5}{12} + \frac{3}{12} = \boxed{\phantom{0}}$

c) $\frac{3}{8} + \frac{2}{8} = \boxed{\phantom{0}}$     d) $\frac{7}{11} + \frac{1}{11} = \boxed{\phantom{0}}$     **3**
4 marks

**4** a) $\frac{7}{9} - \frac{2}{9} = \boxed{\phantom{0}}$     b) $\frac{10}{12} - \frac{4}{12} = \boxed{\phantom{0}}$

c) $\frac{12}{15} - \frac{8}{15} = \boxed{\phantom{0}}$     d) $\frac{7}{8} - \frac{6}{8} = \boxed{\phantom{0}}$     **4**
4 marks

**5** a) 3 children share 1 pizza. What fraction of the pizza does each child receive?

b) 2 children share 3 apples. What fraction of the apples does each child receive?

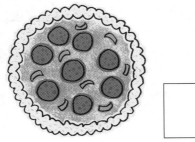   $\boxed{\phantom{0}}$

   $\boxed{\phantom{0}}$

c) 5 children share 3 bars of chocolate. What fraction of the chocolates does each child receive?

d) 4 children share 2 bottles of juice. How many millilitres of juice does each child receive?

   $\boxed{\phantom{0}}$

600 ml   600 ml
$\boxed{\phantom{0}}$     **5**
4 marks

**1** Write these amounts in litres.

**a)** 1600 ml = ☐　　　　　　**b)** 2600 ml = ☐

**c)** 3480 ml = ☐　　　　　　**d)** 15 750 ml = ☐

1<br>4 marks

**2** Write these amounts in millilitres.

**a)** 2·56 *l* = ☐　　　　**b)** 3·04 *l* = ☐

**c)** 8·29 *l* = ☐　　　　**d)** 6·38 *l* = ☐

2<br>4 marks

**3** For each measuring jug, write **(i)** the volume of liquid in millilitres. Then **(ii)** round each volume to the nearest 100 ml.

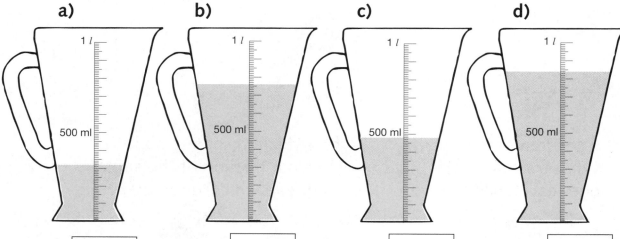

**a)**　　　　**b)**　　　　**c)**　　　　**d)**

**i =** ☐　　**i =** ☐　　**i =** ☐　　**i =** ☐

**ii =** ☐　　**ii =** ☐　　**ii =** ☐　　**ii =** ☐

3<br>8 marks

**4** Complete the table.

| Number of people | Orange concentrate | Water | Total |
|---|---|---|---|
| 1 | 50 ml | 250 ml | ml |
| 2 | ml | ml | ml |
| 4 | ml | *l* | *l* |
| 6 | ml | *l* | *l* |

4<br>4 marks

**1** Estimate the answer to each calculation and write it in the bubble.
Then use a written method to work out the answer.
Show all your working.

**a)** 4756 + 2675

**b)** 3886 + 1578

**c)** 8504 – 3827

**d)** 7715 – 4869

**e)** £72.87 – £34.29

**f)** £53.02 – £38.56

**1**
18 marks

**2** Order these amounts of money, smallest to largest.
**a)** £22.02, £22.20, £20.02, £22.22, £20.20

[ ] , [ ] , [ ] , [ ] , [ ]

**b)** £13.24, £14.23, £13.42, £12.34, £14.32

[ ] , [ ] , [ ] , [ ] , [ ]

**2**
2 marks

Name: _____ Date: _____

**1** Write the decimal equivalent for each fraction.

a) $\frac{7}{10}$ = ☐   b) $\frac{8}{100}$ = ☐   c) $\frac{59}{100}$ = ☐

**1**
3 marks

**2** Write each decimal as a fraction.

a) 0·02 = ☐   b) 0·9 = ☐   c) 0·34 = ☐

**2**
3 marks

**3** Order each set of decimals, smallest to largest.

a) 3·52, 3·24, 3·42, 3·45, 3·25

☐ , ☐ , ☐ , ☐ , ☐

b) 15·41, 15·14, 15·44, 15·11, 15·01

☐ , ☐ , ☐ , ☐ , ☐

**3**
2 marks

**4** Use the < or > sign to make each statement correct.

a) 12·43 ☐ 12·53   b) 18·62 ☐ 18·26   c) 15·03 ☐ 15·3

**4**
3 marks

**5** Round each of these decimals to the nearest whole number.

a) 5·8 ☐   b) 11·4 ☐   c) 9·5 ☐

**5**
3 marks

**6** a) 3 ÷ 10 = ☐   b) 18 ÷ 10 = ☐   c) 95 ÷ 10 = ☐

**6**
3 marks

**7** a) 52 ÷ 100 = ☐   b) 7 ÷ 100 = ☐   c) 12 ÷ 100 = ☐

**7**
3 marks

Year 4 | Unit 11 | Week 2: Decimals          Total: ☐ out of 20   Mastery: NYA   A   A&E

You will need:
• ruler

**1**   **a)** Write the coordinates of point A.

[ ]

**b)** Write the coordinates of point B.

[ ]

Plot these points on the grid:
**C** (4, 1)   **D** (6, 4)   **E** (5, 2)

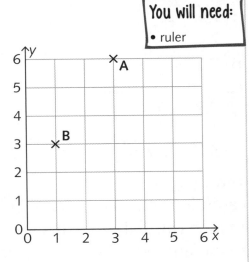

**1**

5 marks

**2**   The coordinates are joined to make a star. Write the coordinates in order.

(3, 6) → ( [ ] , [ ] ) → ( [ ] , [ ] )

→ ( [ ] , [ ] ) → ( [ ] , [ ] ) → ( [ ] , [ ] )

→ ( [ ] , [ ] ) → ( [ ] , [ ] ) → (3, 6)

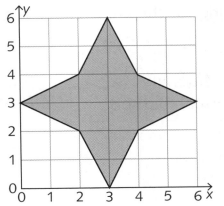

**2**

7 marks

**3**   Plot these points on the grid.
**A** (1, 3)      **B** (3, 6)
**C** (6, 5)      **D** (6, 1)
**E** (3, 0)
Then join the points to make a
2-D shape.
Join **A** to **B**, **B** to **C**, **C** to **D**, **D** to **E**
and **E** to **A**.

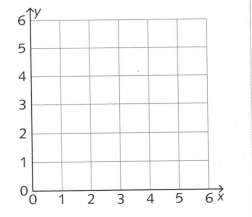

**3**

6 marks

**4**   **a)** Reflect this shape in the dotted line
of symmetry.
**b)** Name the whole shape.

[ ]

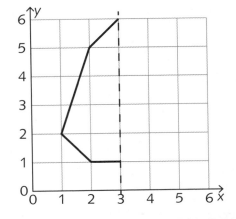

**4**

2 marks

Total: [ ] out of 20   Mastery: NYA   A   A&E

**1**   a) 54 ÷ 6 = ☐

b) 540 ÷ 6 = ☐

**2**   a) 32 ÷ 4 = ☐

b) 3200 ÷ 4 = ☐

**3**   a) 350 ÷ 7 = ☐

b) 3500 ÷ 7 = ☐

**4**   a) 72 ÷ 9 = ☐

b) 7200 ÷ 9 = ☐

**1**
2 marks

**2**
2 marks

**3**
2 marks

**4**
2 marks

## Questions 5–8

Listen carefully. Your teacher will tell you which method to use to answer each of these calculations. Circle that method.

Estimate the answer to each calculation and write it in the cloud.

Then work out the answer. Show all your working.

**5**   84 ÷ 3

Partitioning
Formal method

**6**   96 ÷ 4

Partitioning
Formal method

**5**
3 marks

**6**
3 marks

**7**   296 ÷ 8

Partitioning
Exapanded method
Formal method

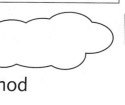

**8**   522 ÷ 6

Partitioning
Exapanded method
Formal method

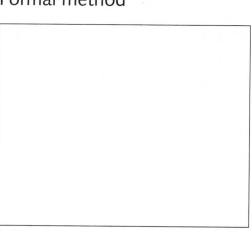

**7**
3 marks

**8**
3 marks

Year 4 | Unit 12 | Week 1: Multiplication and division          Total: ☐ out of 20   Mastery: NYA   A   A&E

## Questions 1 and 2

Listen carefully. Your teacher will tell you which method to use to answer each of these calculations. Circle that method.

Estimate the answer to each calculation and write it in the cloud.

Then work out the answer. Show all your working.

**1** $581 \div 7$

Partitioning

Expanded method

Formal method

**1**
3 marks

**2** $603 \div 9$

Partitioning

Expanded method

Formal method

**2**
3 marks

**3** Tubs of chocolate ice cream are packed into boxes of 8. How many tubs are there in 46 boxes?

**4** Tubs of vanilla ice cream are packed into boxes of 6. How many boxes are needed for 312 tubs?

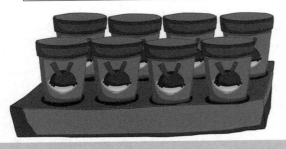

**3**
2 marks

**4**
2 marks

Total: ____ out of 10  Mastery: NYA  A  A&E

**1** Use the data in the pictogram to complete the bar chart.

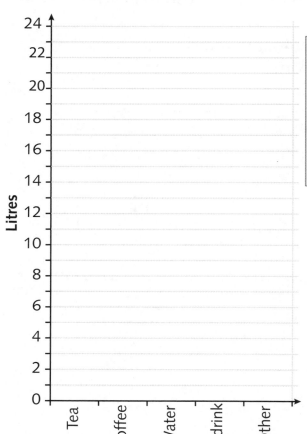

**1**

4 marks

**2** Use the data above to answer these questions.

7 litres of soft drink were consumed during the week.

a) Show this on the pictogram.    b) Show this on the bar chart.

c) 17 litres of which drink were consumed during the week?

d) How many more litres of water than soft drink were consumed during the week?

e) How many litres of the two most popular drinks were consumed during the week?

f) What might be some of the 'other' drinks that were consumed during the week? Suggest at least two.

**2**

6 marks

**3** Use the data in the table to complete the time graph.

**Morning courier delivery times**

| Time | 9:00 | 9:30 | 10:00 | 10:30 | 11:00 | 11:30 | 12:00 |
|---|---|---|---|---|---|---|---|
| Distance from depot (miles) | 0 | 3 | 6 | 9 | 5 | 2 | 0 |
| Location | Depot | Berry Street | Junction Street | Kinghorne Street | Osborne Street | Bridge Road | Depot |

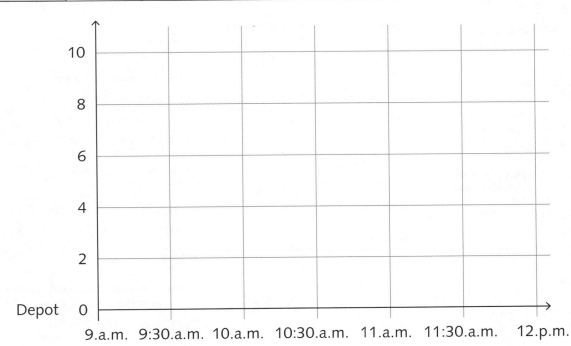

**3**

5 marks

**4** Use the data above to answer the questions.

a) Where was the courier at 10:15?

b) How many deliveries did the courier make between 9:45 and 11:15?

c) How far from the depot was the courier at 11:00?

d) How many miles did the courier travel between 9:00 and 10:30?

e) Between which two locations did the courier have to travel the greatest distance?

_____ and _____

**4**

5 marks

# Year 4 End-of-unit Tests — Answers and marking commentary

## Unit 1

### Week 1: Number - Number and place value

**1 a)** 2363  **b)** 3175

**2 a)** 4582  **b)** 7859

**3 a)** 60  **b)** 500

**4 a)** 5678, 5687, 5750, 5866, 5896
**b)** 4354, 4358, 4367, 4369, 4376

**5 a)** 5457, 7457  **b)** 7793, 9793

### Week 2: Number - Addition and subtraction

**1 a)** 456  **b)** 385  **c)** 634
**d)** 928  **e)** 712  **f)** 725

**2 a)** 256  **b)** 423  **c)** 589
**d)** 475  **e)** 218  **f)** 456

**3** Award 2 marks per question for the correct answer. If the answer is incorrect, award 1 mark for identifying the correct calculation(s).

**a)** 528 vehicles  **b)** 870 passengers
**c)** £1554  **d)** 45 more crossings

### Week 3: Geometry - Properties of shapes

**1 a)** D, F, J
**b)** A, C, H, K, I
**c)** B, E, G

**2 a)** 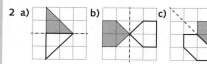 **b)** **c)**

**3 a)** 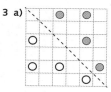 **b)**

**4 a)** 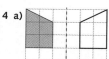 **b)**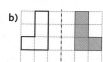

## Unit 2

### Week 1: Number - Multiplication and division, including Number and place value

**1 a)** 54  **b)** 90  **c)** 27
**d)** 81  **e)** 18  **f)** 108

**2 a)** 3  **b)** 4  **c)** 7
**d)** 5  **e)** 8  **f)** 12

**3 a)** 6  **b)** 5  **c)** 81
**d)** 11  **e)** 4  **f)** 18

**4 a)** 30  **b)** 12  **c)** 48
**d)** 66  **e)** 42  **f)** 24

**5 a)** 3  **b)** 6  **c)** 9
**d)** 12  **e)** 4  **f)** 10

**6 a)** 6  **b)** 8  **c)** 24
**d)** 9  **e)** 18  **f)** 11

**7 a)** 180  **b)** 480  **c)** 630  **d)** 360

### Week 2: Number - Fractions

**1 a)** Three sectors coloured; $\frac{1}{2} = \frac{3}{6}$
**b)** Six sectors coloured; $\frac{1}{2} = \frac{6}{12}$

**2 a)** Two sectors coloured; $\frac{1}{4} = \frac{2}{8}$
**b)** Three sectors coloured; $\frac{1}{4} = \frac{3}{12}$

**3 a)** $\frac{1}{2} = \frac{2}{4} = \frac{3}{6} = \frac{4}{8} = \frac{5}{10} = \frac{6}{12}$
**b)** $\frac{1}{4} = \frac{2}{8} = \frac{3}{12} = \frac{4}{16} = \frac{5}{20} = \frac{6}{24}$

**4 a)** 27  **b)** 18  **c)** 30  **d)** 32

### Week 3: Geometry - Position and direction

**1 a)** 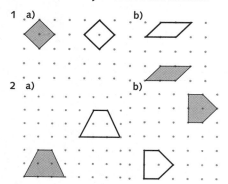 **b)**

**2 a)** **b)**

**3 a)** A(2, 5)
**b)** B(6, 4)
**c)** Point C plotted at (4, 5)
Point D plotted at (3, 2)

**4**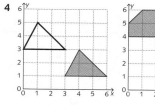

## Unit 3

### Week 1: Number - Addition and subtraction

**1 a)** 540, 548, 748, 808, 815, 835
**b)** 270, 304, 604, 612, 657, 777

**2** Award 1 mark per question for making a reasonable estimate.
Award 1 mark per question for using an effective, efficient and appropriate method.
Award 1 mark per question for calculating the correct answer.

**a)** Estimates will vary; 694
**b)** Estimates will vary; 628
**c)** Estimates will vary; 842
**d)** Estimates will vary; 822

**3** Award 2 marks per question for the correct answer. If the answer is incorrect, award 1 mark for identifying the correct calculation(s).

**a)** 308 people
**b)** 176 people
**c)** £97

### Week 2: Number - Decimals

**1 a)** 0·1  **b)** 0·4  **c)** 0·6

**2 a)** $\frac{7}{10}$  **b)** $\frac{3}{10}$  **c)** $\frac{9}{10}$

**3 a)** 4·2, 4·4, 4·5, 4·6, 4·7
**b)** 8·1, 8·3, 8·5, 8·8, 8·9

**4 a)** 4·6 < 5·4  **b)** 8·7 > 7·8
**c)** 1·4 < 1·9  **d)** 2·5 < 2·7

**5 a)** 4  **b)** 2  **c)** 5

**6 a)**

**7 a)** 6·4, 6·6  **b)** 2·7, 2·9
**c)** 1·1, 1·3

### Week 3: Measurement (mass)

**1 a)** 6·4 kg  **b)** 3·8 kg  **c)** 5·2 kg

**2 a)** 2300 g  **b)** 1900 g  **c)** 4500 g

**3 a)** 3·75 kg, 4 kg  **b)** 2·3 kg, 2 kg
**c)** 6·5 kg, 7 kg

**4 a)** 500 g + 200 g + 100 g + 50 g
**b)** 1 kg + 200 g + 100 g + 20 g
**c)** 1 kg + 500 g + 200 g + 200 g
**d)** 1 kg + 1 kg + 500 g + 200 g

**5 a)** 250 g  **b)** 200 g  **c)** 4·5 kg  **d)** 3·75 kg

## Unit 4

### Week 1: Number - Multiplication and division, including Number and place value

**1 a)** 16  **b)** 49  **c)** 144
**d)** 25  **e)** 64  **f)** 81

**2 a)** 28  **b)** 42  **c)** 56
**d)** 63  **e)** 49  **f)** 35

**3 a)** 10  **b)** 3  **c)** 12
**d)** 2  **e)** 11  **f)** 6

**4 a)** 33  **b)** 77  **c)** 88
**d)** 121  **e)** 99  **f)** 66

**5 a)** 10  **b)** 6  **c)** 4
**d)** 5  **e)** 12  **f)** 9

**6 a)** 24  **b)** 132  **c)** 84
**d)** 96  **e)** 108  **f)** 36

**7 a)** 6  **b)** 12  **c)** 5
**d)** 3  **e)** 4  **f)** 7

**8 a)** 7  **b)** 3  **c)** 4  **d)** 4
**e)** 42  **f)** 22  **g)** 6  **h)** 12

### Week 2: Number - Multiplication and division

Q1–3: For each question, tell the pupil(s) which method you want them to use: partitioning, the grid method, the expanded written method or the formal written method.
Award 1 mark per question for making a reasonable estimate.
Award 1 mark per question for using the method effectively and appropriately.
Award 1 mark per question for calculating the correct answer.

1 476

2 504

3 477

4 240

### Week 3: Measurement (time)

1 a) 180 minutes    b) 144 hours
   c) 28 days    d) 7 weeks 1 day
   e) 2 days 12 hours

2 a) 3:18    b) 6:41    c) 11:54

3 a) 27 minutes past 5
   b) 7 minutes to 10
   c) 24 minutes to 5

4 a) 04:11    b) 09:23    c) 11:57

5 a) 14:16    b) 18:41    c) 22:28

6 a) 10:32 p.m.    b) 7:48 p.m.    c) 8:13 a.m.

## Unit 5

### Week 1: Number - Number and place value

1 a) 6789, 6879, 6897, 6978, 6987
   b) 5236, 5238, 5256, 5258, 5506

2 a) 687 > 678    b) 1856 > 1586
   c) 2587 < 2857    d) 5078 < 5088

3 a) 60    b) 70    c) 140
   d) 560    e) 1460    f) 2210

4 a) 600    b) 800    c) 300
   d) 3600    e) 2500    f) 4700

5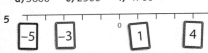

6 −10, −9, −7, −6, −4, −2, −1, 1, 2

### Week 2: Number - Addition and subtraction

1 a) 720, 660, 460, 455, 415, 407
   b) 680, 671, 631, 331, 325, 235

2 Award 1 mark per question for making a reasonable estimate.
Award 1 mark per question for using an effective, efficient and appropriate method.
Award 1 mark per question for calculating the correct answer.

   a) 294    b) 437    c) 3369    d) 9392

3 Award 2 marks per question for the correct answer. If the answer is incorrect, award 1 mark for identifying the correct calculation(s).

   a) £1244    b) £657    c) £1065

### Week 3: Geometry - Properties of shapes

1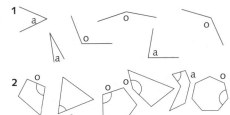

2

3 a) A, D, C, B      b) D, A, B, C

4 Rhombus, regular hexagon and equilateral triangle marked 'R'
Trapezium, parallelogram and kite marked 'I'

## Unit 6

### Week 1: Number - Multiplication and division, including Number and place value

1 a) 4000, 5000, 6000, 7000, 8000, 9000
   b) 100, 125, 150, 175, 200, 225
   c) 400, 500, 600, 700, 800, 900
   d) 200, 250, 300, 350, 400, 450

2 Award 1 mark per question for making a reasonable estimate.
Award 1 mark per question for using an effective, efficient and appropriate method.
Award 1 mark per question for calculating the correct answer.

   a) 304    b) 476    c) 432    d) 558

3 Award 2 marks per question for the correct answer. If the answer is incorrect, award 1 mark for identifying the correct calculation(s).

   a) £315    b) £3

### Week 2: Number - Fractions

1 a)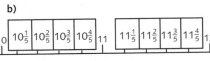

   b)

2 a) $\frac{47}{100}$, $\frac{48}{100}$, $\frac{49}{100}$, $\frac{51}{100}$, $\frac{52}{100}$
   b) $\frac{83}{100}$, $\frac{84}{100}$, $\frac{86}{100}$, $\frac{87}{100}$, $\frac{89}{100}$

3 a) $\frac{37}{100}$    b) $\frac{83}{100}$

Q4–6: Award 2 marks per question for the correct answer. If the answer is incorrect, award 1 mark for identifying the correct calculation(s).

4 a) 28    b) 90    c) 108

5 a) 24    b) 224    c) 310

6 £432

### Week 3: Measurement (length)

1 a) 4700 m    b) 11800 m

2 a) 6·3 km    b) 12·5 km

3 a) 2·3 m    b) 0·4 m

4 a) 600 mm = 60 cm = 0·6 m
   b) 400 mm = 40 cm = 0·4 m
   c) 5000 mm = 500 cm = 5 m
   d) 1800 mm = 180 cm = 1·8 m

5 A = 14 cm    A = 10 cm
   B = 17 cm    B = 20 cm
   C = 22 cm    C = 20 cm
   D = 26 cm    D = 30 cm

6 a) 8 cm    b) 13 cm

## Unit 7

### Week 1: Number - Addition and subtraction

1 a) 558    b) 693    c) 1386
   d) 726    e) 627    f) 1218
   g) 2648    h) 2278    i) 4231

2 a) 1445    b) 937    c) 1776
   d) 1479    e) 1356    f) 814
   g) 938    h) 1279    i) 1635

3 Award 1 mark per question for making a reasonable estimate.
Award 1 mark per question for using an effective, efficient and appropriate method.
Award 1 mark per question for calculating the correct answer.

   a) 5995    b) 7861    c) 7813    d) 9452

### Week 2: Number - Addition and subtraction

1 Award 1 mark per question for making a reasonable estimate.
Award 1 mark per question for using an effective, efficient and appropriate method.
Award 1 mark per question for calculating the correct answer.

   a) 3186    b) 3478    c) 2607    d) 1678

2 Award 2 marks per question for the correct answer. If the answer is incorrect, award 1 mark for identifying the correct calculation(s).

   a) i) 2318 points    ii) 2032 points
   b) 1204 more points    c) 4300 points
   d) i) 5221 points    ii) 3878 points

### Week 3: Statistics

1 Key: ♻ = 10 kg

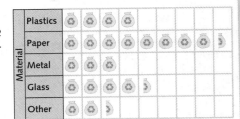

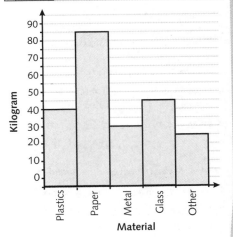

**2 a)** 15 kg   **b)** 140 kg   **c)** 60 kg
   **d)** Plastics and glass
   **e)** Award 1 mark for each question.
   **i)** Yes
   **ii)** They beat their target by 25 kg

**3** Award 3 marks if the graph is
   completely correct.
   Award 2 marks if the graph is
   partially correct.
   Award 1 mark if the pupil has made an
   acceptable attempt to complete the graph and
   shows some understanding of line graphs.

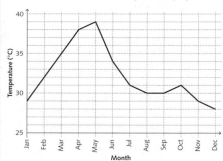

**4 a)** 34 °C   **b)** 39 °C
   **c)** January and November
   **d)** 11 °C   **e) i)** May and June
                      **ii)** 5 °C

## Unit 8

### Week 1: Number - Multiplication and division

Q1–2: For each question, tell the pupil(s) which
method you want them to use: partitioning, the
grid method, the expanded written method or
the formal written method.

Award 1 mark per question for making a
reasonable estimate.
Award 1 mark per question for using the
method effectively and appropriately.
Award 1 mark per question for calculating the
correct answer.

**1** 1572

**2** 5214

**3** Award 2 marks per question for the
   correct answer. If the answer is incorrect,
   award 1 mark for identifying the correct
   calculation(s).

   **a)** £4235   **b)** £1907

### Week 2: Number - Decimals

**1 a)** 0·01   **b)** 0·08   **c)** 0·56

**2 a)** $\frac{5}{100}$   **b)** $\frac{86}{100}$   **c)** $\frac{49}{100}$

**3 a)** 2·24, 2·36, 2·45, 2·47, 2·63
   **b)** 5·08, 5·09, 5·58, 5·81, 5·85

**4 a)** 2·56 < 3·56   **b)** 4·05 < 4·25
   **c)** 6·74 > 6·73   **d)** 2·55 > 2·49

**5 a)** 0·8   **b)** 6·5   **c)** 1·5   **d)** 8·2

**6 a)** 0·03   **b)** 0·18   **c)** 0·75   **d)** 0·52

### Week 3: Measurement (perimeter and area)

**1** A = 14 cm   B = 16 cm   C = 20 cm

**2** A = 12 cm²   B = 12 cm²   C = 14 cm²

**3** D = 36 m   E = 40 m

**4** D = 72 m²   E = 99 m²

## Unit 9

### Week 1: Number - Number and place value

**1 a)** 5666, 5668, 5686, 5768, 5786
   **b)** 8016, 8061, 8067, 8071, 8076

**2 a)** 4289 < 4298
   **b)** 3345 > 3343
   **c)** 2008 < 2080

**3 a)** 70   **b)** 40   **c)** 760
   **d)** 430   **e)** 4760   **f)** 3720

**4 a)** 900   **b)** 500   **c)** 700
   **d)** 5400   **e)** 3600   **f)** 4700

**5 a)** 3000   **b)** 2000   **c)** 3000

**6 a)** −5   **b)** −5   **c)** −3   **d)** −3

**7 a)** LXXXVII **b)** CXLII   **c)** XXXIV

**8 a)** 62   **b)** 125   **c)** 17

### Week 2: Number - Addition and subtraction, including Measurement (money)

**1** Award 1 mark per question for making a
   reasonable estimate.
   Award 1 mark per question for using an
   effective, efficient and appropriate method.
   Award 1 mark per question for calculating
   the correct answer.

   **a)** 6344   **b)** 6342   **c)** 2568
   **d)** 2688   **e)** £77.83   **f)** £72.45

**2 a)** £46.70, £47.07, £47.60, £56.07, £56.70
   **b)** £26.65, £28.46, £28.65, £29.45, £29.64

### Week 3: Geometry - Properties of shapes

**1** Both equilateral triangles labelled 'E'
   Four isosceles triangles labelled 'I'
   Three scalene triangles labelled 'S'

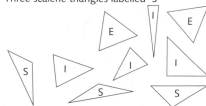

**2** The square labelled 'S'
   Two rectangles labelled 'R'
   Two parallelograms labelled 'P'
   Two rhombuses labelled 'Rh'
   Two trapeziums labelled 'T'
   Two kites labelled 'K'

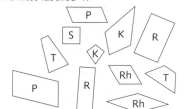

**3**

| Quadrilateral | Opposite sides equal | Opposite sides parallel | Opposite angles equal | All sides equal | Four right angles |
|---|---|---|---|---|---|
| square | ✓ | ✓ | ✓ | ✓ | ✓ |
| rectangle | ✓ | ✓ | ✓ | ✗ | ✓ |
| parallelogram | ✓ | ✓ | ✗ | ✗ | ✗ |
| rhombus | ✓ | ✓ | ✗ | ✓ | ✗ |

## Unit 10

### Week 1: Number - Multiplication and division

Q1–2: For each question, tell the pupil(s) which
method you want them to use: partitioning, the
grid method, the expanded written method or
the formal written method.
Award 1 mark per question for making a
reasonable estimate.
Award 1 mark per question for using the
method effectively and appropriately.
Award 1 mark per question for calculating the
correct answer.

**1** 2144

**2** 2892

**3** Award 2 marks per question for the
   correct answer. If the answer is incorrect,
   award 1 mark for identifying the correct
   calculation(s).

   **a)** £28   **b)** £976

### Week 2: Number - Fractions

**1 a)** $\frac{3}{6}$   **b)** $\frac{3}{15}$   **c)** $\frac{1}{3}$   **d)** $\frac{2}{14}$

**2 a)** $\frac{1}{5}$   **b)** $\frac{1}{7}$   **c)** $\frac{2}{3}$   **d)** $\frac{3}{7}$

**3 a)** $\frac{6}{7}$   **b)** $\frac{8}{12}$   **c)** $\frac{5}{8}$   **d)** $\frac{8}{11}$

**4 a)** $\frac{5}{9}$   **b)** $\frac{6}{12}$   **c)** $\frac{4}{15}$   **d)** $\frac{1}{8}$

**5 a)** $\frac{1}{3}$   **b)** $\frac{3}{2}$ or $1\frac{1}{2}$ **c)** $\frac{3}{5}$   **d)** 300 ml

### Week 3: Measurement (volume and capacity)

**1 a)** 1·6 *l*   **b)** 2·6 *l*   **c)** 3·48 *l*   **d)** 15·75 *l*

**2 a)** 2560 ml   **b)** 3040 ml
   **c)** 8290 ml   **d)** 6380 ml

**3 a)** 320 ml; 300 ml   **b)** 760 ml; 800 ml
   **c)** 480 ml; 500 ml   **d)** 840 ml; 800 ml

**4** 1 mark for each correct row of the table.

| Number of people | Orange concentrate | Water | Total |
|---|---|---|---|
| 1 | 50 ml | 250 ml | 300 ml |
| 2 | 100 ml | 500 ml | 600 ml |
| 4 | 200 ml | 1 *l* | 1·2 *l* |
| 6 | 300 ml | 1·5 *l* | 1·8 *l* |

## Unit 11

### Week 1: Number - Addition and subtraction, including Measurement (money)

**1** Award 1 mark per question for making a
   reasonable estimate.
   Award 1 mark per question for using an
   effective, efficient and appropriate method.
   Award 1 mark per question for calculating
   the correct answer.

   **a)** 7431   **b)** 5464   **c)** 4677
   **d)** 2846   **e)** £38.58   **f)** £14.46

**2 a)** £20·02, £20·20, £22·02, £22·20, £22·22
   **b)** £12.34, £13.24, £13.42, £14.23, £14.32

**Week 2: Number - Decimals**

1 a) 0·7    b) 0·08    c) 0·59

2 a) $\frac{2}{100}$    b) $\frac{9}{10}$    c) $\frac{34}{100}$

3 a) 3·24, 3·25, 3·42, 3·45, 3·52
  b) 15·01, 15·11, 15·14, 15·41, 15·44

4 a) 12·43 < 12·53
  b) 18·62 > 18·26
  c) 15·03 < 15·3

5 a) 6    b) 11    c) 10

6 a) 0·3    b) 1·8    c) 9·5

7 a) 0·52    b) 0·07    c) 0·12

**Week 3: Geometry - Position and direction**

1 a) (3, 6)    b) (1, 3)

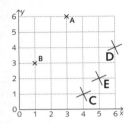

2 (3, 6), (4, 4), (6, 3), (4, 2), (3, 0), (2, 2), (0, 3), (2, 4), (3, 6)

3 Award 1 mark each for plotting points A to E correctly.
  Award 1 mark for joining the points to draw the pentagon.

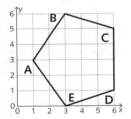

4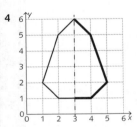

  b) Irregular heptagon

## Unit 12

**Week 1: Number - Multiplication and division**
Q5–6: For each question, tell the pupil(s) which method you want them to use: partitioning or the formal written method.

Q7–8: For each question, tell the pupil(s) which method you want them to use: partitioning, the expanded written method or the formal written method.

Q5–8: Award 1 mark per question for making a reasonable estimate.
Award 1 mark per question for using the method effectively and appropriately.
Award 1 mark per question for calculating the

correct answer.

1 a) 9    b) 90

2 a) 8    b) 800

3 a) 50    b) 500

4 a) 8    b) 800

5 28

6 24

7 37

8 87

**Week 2: Number - Multiplication and division**
Q1–2: For each question, tell the pupil(s) which method you want them to use: partitioning, the expanded written method or the formal written method.
Award 1 mark per question for making a reasonable estimate.
Award 1 mark per question for using the method effectively and appropriately.
Award 1 mark per question for calculating the correct answer.

1 83

2 67

Q3 and 4: Award 2 marks per question for the correct answer. If the answer is incorrect, award 1 mark for identifying the correct calculation(s).

3 368 tubs

4 52 boxes

**Week 3: Statistics**

1

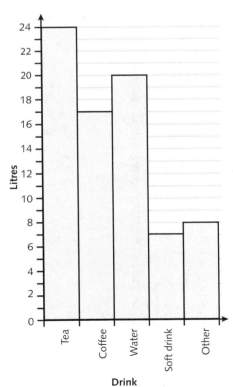

2   a)

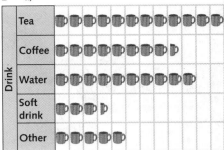

Key:  = 2 litres

  b) Bar as shown on bar chart
  c) Coffee
  d) 13 *l*
  e) 44 *l*
  f) Answers will vary

3 Award 1 mark for the correct labelling on the time graph of each of the five deliveries.

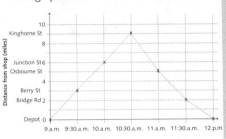

4 a) Between Junction Street and Kinghorne Street
  b) 3 deliveries
  c) 5 miles
  d) 9 miles
  e) Kinghorne Street and Osborne Street

# My record sheet

Year 4

Unit 1

Name: _____

Date: _____

Week 3 — Properties of shapes

| | Start of the week | End of the week |
|---|---|---|
| • I can identify horizontal, vertical and diagonal lines of symmetry in polygons | 😀 😐 😟 | 😀 😐 😟 |
| • I can identify shapes with more than one line of symmetry | 😀 😐 😟 | 😀 😐 😟 |
| • I can reflect shapes in one and two lines of symmetry in different orientations | 😀 😐 😟 | 😀 😐 😟 |
| • I can reflect shapes in vertical lines of symmetry to make a repeating pattern | 😀 😐 😟 | 😀 😐 😟 |

# Week 2 — Addition and subtraction

| | Start of the week | End of the week |
|---|---|---|
| • I can add a 3-digit number and 10s | 🙂 😐 ☹️ | 🙂 😐 ☹️ |
| • I can subtract a 3-digit number and 10s | 🙂 😐 ☹️ | 🙂 😐 ☹️ |
| • I can add a 3-digit number and 100s | 🙂 😐 ☹️ | 🙂 😐 ☹️ |
| • I can subtract a 3-digit number and 100s | 🙂 😐 ☹️ | 🙂 😐 ☹️ |
| • I can choose an appropriate mental method | 🙂 😐 ☹️ | 🙂 😐 ☹️ |
| • I can solve word problems by recognising the operation needed, writing the calculation and working out the answer | 🙂 😐 ☹️ | 🙂 😐 ☹️ |

# Week 1 — Number and place value

| | Start of the week | End of the week |
|---|---|---|
| • I can read and write numbers to 10000 | 🙂 😐 ☹️ | 🙂 😐 ☹️ |
| • I can identify the value of each digit in a 4-digit number | 🙂 😐 ☹️ | 🙂 😐 ☹️ |
| • I can split a number into 1000s, 100s, 10s and 1s | 🙂 😐 ☹️ | 🙂 😐 ☹️ |
| • I can use place value to compare and order a set of numbers to 10000 | 🙂 😐 ☹️ | 🙂 😐 ☹️ |
| • I can find 1000 more or less than a given number | 🙂 😐 ☹️ | 🙂 😐 ☹️ |

# My record sheet

## Year 4
## Unit 2

Name: _____

Date: _____

**Week 3 — Position and direction**

| | Start of the week | End of the week |
|---|---|---|
| • I can use coordinates to describe the position of a point on a grid in the first quadrant | 😊 😐 ☹ | 😊 😐 ☹ |
| • I can use coordinates to plot specific points on a grid in the first quadrant | 😊 😐 ☹ | 😊 😐 ☹ |
| • I can translate a 2-D shape a given number of units to the left/right and up/down on a coordinate grid in the first quadrant | 😊 😐 ☹ | 😊 😐 ☹ |

# Week 2 — Fractions

| | Start of the week | End of the week |
|---|---|---|
| • I can recognise and show, using diagrams, families of common equivalent fractions | ☺ 😐 ☹ | ☺ 😐 ☹ |
| • I can find a non-unit fraction of a number by dividing the number by the fraction's denominator and multiplying the answer by the fraction's numerator | ☺ 😐 ☹ | ☺ 😐 ☹ |

# Week 1 — Multiplication and division, including Number and place value

| | Start of the week | End of the week |
|---|---|---|
| • I can recognise the multiples of 6 and 9 | ☺ 😐 ☹ | ☺ 😐 ☹ |
| • I know the multiplication and division facts for the 6 multiplication table | ☺ 😐 ☹ | ☺ 😐 ☹ |
| • I know the multiplication and division facts for the 9 multiplication table | ☺ 😐 ☹ | ☺ 😐 ☹ |
| • I can describe the relationship between two multiplication facts such as 7 × 6 and 6 × 7 | ☺ 😐 ☹ | ☺ 😐 ☹ |

# My record sheet

### Year 4
### Unit 3

Name: _____

Date: _____

## Week 3 — Measurement (mass)

| | Start of the week | End of the week |
|---|---|---|
| • I can use decimal notation to tenths to record mass in kilograms | ☺ 😐 ☹ | ☺ 😐 ☹ |
| • I can convert from larger to smaller units of mass using multiplication | ☺ 😐 ☹ | ☺ 😐 ☹ |
| • I can estimate, compare and round numbers on scales to the nearest kilogram and to the nearest 100 g | ☺ 😐 ☹ | ☺ 😐 ☹ |
| • I can calculate different measures | ☺ 😐 ☹ | ☺ 😐 ☹ |

| | Start of the week | End of the week |
|---|---|---|
| • I recognise the link between fractions and decimals | 😊 😐 🙁 | 😊 😐 🙁 |
| • I can recognise and write decimal equivalents for tenths | 😊 😐 🙁 | 😊 😐 🙁 |
| • I can compare and order decimals with one decimal place | 😊 😐 🙁 | 😊 😐 🙁 |
| • I can round decimals with one decimal place to the nearest whole number | 😊 😐 🙁 | 😊 😐 🙁 |

| | Start of the week | End of the week |
|---|---|---|
| • I can add mentally, counting on in 100s, 10s and 1s depending on the calculation | 😊 😐 🙁 | 😊 😐 🙁 |
| • I can use jottings to support mental calculations when necessary | 😊 😐 🙁 | 😊 😐 🙁 |
| • I can estimate the answer to a calculation | 😊 😐 🙁 | 😊 😐 🙁 |
| • I can use the formal written method to add 3-digit numbers | 😊 😐 🙁 | 😊 😐 🙁 |
| • I can solve word problems by recognising the operation needed, writing the calculation and working out the answer | 😊 😐 🙁 | 😊 😐 🙁 |

# My record sheet

## Year 4
## Unit 4

Name: _____

Date: _____

## Week 3 – Measurement (time)

| | Start of the week | End of the week |
|---|---|---|
| • I can convert between different units of time | ☺ 😐 ☹ | ☺ 😐 ☹ |
| • I can read, write and convert time between analogue and digital 12-hour clocks | ☺ 😐 ☹ | ☺ 😐 ☹ |
| • I can read, write and convert time between analogue and digital 24-hour clocks | ☺ 😐 ☹ | ☺ 😐 ☹ |

## Week 2 — Multiplication and division

| | Start of the week | End of the week |
|---|---|---|
| • I can estimate the answer to a calculation | 😀 😐 😞 | 😀 😐 😞 |
| • I can use a written method to calculate multiplication of TO × O | 😀 😐 😞 | 😀 😐 😞 |
| • I can multiply together three 1-digit numbers | 😀 😐 😞 | 😀 😐 😞 |

## Week 1 — Multiplication and division, including Number and place value

| | Start of the week | End of the week |
|---|---|---|
| • I can recall squares of numbers to 12 × 12 | 😀 😐 😞 | 😀 😐 😞 |
| • I can recognise the multiples of 7, 11 and 12 | 😀 😐 😞 | 😀 😐 😞 |
| • I know the multiplication and division facts for the 7 multiplication table | 😀 😐 😞 | 😀 😐 😞 |
| • I know the multiplication and division facts for the 11 multiplication table | 😀 😐 😞 | 😀 😐 😞 |
| • I know the multiplication and division facts for the 12 multiplication table | 😀 😐 😞 | 😀 😐 😞 |
| • I can find factors of numbers to multiples up to 12 × 12 | 😀 😐 😞 | 😀 😐 😞 |

# My record sheet

## Year 4
## Unit 5

Name: _____

Date: _____

**Week 3 — Properties of shapes**

|  | Start of the week | End of the week |
|---|---|---|
| • I can identify, name and define acute and obtuse angles | 🙂 😐 🙁 | 🙂 😐 🙁 |
| • I can identify acute and obtuse angles in 2-D shapes | 🙂 😐 🙁 | 🙂 😐 🙁 |
| • I can compare and order angles up to two right angles by size | 🙂 😐 🙁 | 🙂 😐 🙁 |
| • I can identify if a polygon is regular or irregular by comparing sides and angles | 🙂 😐 🙁 | 🙂 😐 🙁 |

## Week 1 — Number and place value

| | Start of the week | End of the week |
|---|---|---|
| • I can read and write numbers to 10 000 | 😊 😐 ☹ | 😊 😐 ☹ |
| • I can identify the value of each digit in a 4-digit number | 😊 😐 ☹ | 😊 😐 ☹ |
| • I can split a number into 1000s, 100s, 10s and 1s | 😊 😐 ☹ | 😊 😐 ☹ |
| • I can use place value to compare and order a set of numbers to 10 000 | 😊 😐 ☹ | 😊 😐 ☹ |
| • I can round a number to the nearest 10 or 100 | 😊 😐 ☹ | 😊 😐 ☹ |
| • I can count backwards through zero to include negative numbers | 😊 😐 ☹ | 😊 😐 ☹ |

## Week 2 — Addition and subtraction

| | Start of the week | End of the week |
|---|---|---|
| • I can subtract mentally, counting back in 100s, 10s and 1s depending on the calculation | 😊 😐 ☹ | 😊 😐 ☹ |
| • I can use jottings to support mental calculations when necessary | 😊 😐 ☹ | 😊 😐 ☹ |
| • I can estimate the answer to a calculation | 😊 😐 ☹ | 😊 😐 ☹ |
| • I can use the formal written method to subtract 3-digit and 4-digit numbers | 😊 😐 ☹ | 😊 😐 ☹ |
| • I can use the inverse operation to check the answer to a calculation | 😊 😐 ☹ | 😊 😐 ☹ |
| • I can solve word problems by recognising the operation needed, writing the calculation and working out the answer | 😊 😐 ☹ | 😊 😐 ☹ |

# My record sheet

## Year 4
## Unit 6

Name: _____

Date: _____

Week 3 — Measurement (length)

| | Start of the week | End of the week |
|---|---|---|
| • I can convert between kilometres and metres, including decimal notation to tenths | 😊 😐 😞 | 😊 😐 😞 |
| • I can convert between metres and centimetres, including decimal notation to tenths | 😊 😐 😞 | 😊 😐 😞 |
| • I can convert between metres and millimetres | 😊 😐 😞 | 😊 😐 😞 |
| • I can convert between centimetres and millimetres | 😊 😐 😞 | 😊 😐 😞 |
| • I can round numbers on measuring tapes to the nearest 10 cm and 100 cm | 😊 😐 😞 | 😊 😐 😞 |

## Week 2 – Fractions

| | Start of the week | End of the week |
|---|---|---|
| I can use a number line to order fractions | ☺ 😐 ☹ | ☺ 😐 ☹ |
| I can count up and down in hundredths | ☺ 😐 ☹ | ☺ 😐 ☹ |
| I can recognise that hundredths arise when dividing a whole number by 100 and dividing tenths by 10 | ☺ 😐 ☹ | ☺ 😐 ☹ |
| I can use place value to find $\frac{1}{10}$ or $\frac{1}{100}$ of a number, then multiply the answer by the numerator | ☺ 😐 ☹ | ☺ 😐 ☹ |
| I can solve problems involving fractions | ☺ 😐 ☹ | ☺ 😐 ☹ |

## Week 1 – Multiplication and division, including Number and place value

| | Start of the week | End of the week |
|---|---|---|
| I can recognise the multiples of 25, 100 and 1000 | ☺ 😐 ☹ | ☺ 😐 ☹ |
| I can estimate the answer to a calculation | ☺ 😐 ☹ | ☺ 😐 ☹ |
| I can use a written method to calculate multiplication of TO × O | ☺ 😐 ☹ | ☺ 😐 ☹ |
| I can use the most efficient method to calculate multiplication of TO × O | ☺ 😐 ☹ | ☺ 😐 ☹ |
| I can solve word problems by recognising the operation needed, writing the calculation and working out the answer | ☺ 😐 ☹ | ☺ 😐 ☹ |

# My record sheet

## Year 4
## Unit 7

Name: _____

Date: _____

### Week 3 — Statistics

| | Start of the week | End of the week |
|---|---|---|
| • I can use a table and tally chart to record data | ☺ ☺ ☹ | ☺ ☺ ☹ |
| • I can interpret the data in a table and tally chart | ☺ ☺ ☹ | ☺ ☺ ☹ |
| • I can present data in a scaled pictogram | ☺ ☺ ☹ | ☺ ☺ ☹ |
| • I can interpret the data in a scaled pictogram | ☺ ☺ ☹ | ☺ ☺ ☹ |
| • I can present data in a scaled bar chart | ☺ ☺ ☹ | ☺ ☺ ☹ |
| • I can interpret the data in a scaled bar chart | ☺ ☺ ☹ | ☺ ☺ ☹ |
| • I can present data in a simple time graph | ☺ ☺ ☹ | ☺ ☺ ☹ |
| • I can interpret the data in a simple time graph | ☺ ☺ ☹ | ☺ ☺ ☹ |

## Week 2 — Addition and subtraction

| | Start of the week | End of the week |
|---|---|---|
| • I can estimate the answer to a calculation | 😊 😐 🙁 | 😊 😐 🙁 |
| • I can use the formal written method to add 4-digit numbers | 😊 😐 🙁 | 😊 😐 🙁 |
| • I can use the formal written method to subtract 4-digit numbers | 😊 😐 🙁 | 😊 😐 🙁 |
| • I can use the inverse operation to check the answer to a calculation | 😊 😐 🙁 | 😊 😐 🙁 |
| • I can solve word problems by recognising the operation needed, writing the calculation and working out the answer | 😊 😐 🙁 | 😊 😐 🙁 |

## Week 1 — Addition and subtraction

| | Start of the week | End of the week |
|---|---|---|
| • I can add mentally, counting on in 100s, 10s and 1s depending on the calculation | 😊 😐 🙁 | 😊 😐 🙁 |
| • I can subtract mentally, counting back in 100s, 10s and 1s depending on the calculation | 😊 😐 🙁 | 😊 😐 🙁 |
| • I can use jottings to support mental calculations when necessary | 😊 😐 🙁 | 😊 😐 🙁 |
| • I can estimate the answer to a calculation | 😊 😐 🙁 | 😊 😐 🙁 |
| • I can use the formal written method to add 4-digit numbers | 😊 😐 🙁 | 😊 😐 🙁 |

# My record sheet

## Year 4
## Unit 8

Name: _____

Date: _____

**Week 3 — Measurement (perimeter and area)**

| | Start of the week | End of the week |
|---|---|---|
| • I can measure and calculate the perimeter of a rectangle using the rule P = 2(a + b) | 😊 😐 🙁 | 😊 😐 🙁 |
| • I can find the area of a rectangle and other shapes by counting squares | 😊 😐 🙁 | 😊 😐 🙁 |
| • I can use multiplication to calculate the area of a rectangle in square centimetres | 😊 😐 🙁 | 😊 😐 🙁 |

## Week 2 — Decimals

| | Start of the week | End of the week |
|---|---|---|
| I recognise the link between fractions and decimals | 😊 😐 🙁 | 😊 😐 🙁 |
| I can recognise and write decimal equivalents for hundredths | 😊 😐 🙁 | 😊 😐 🙁 |
| I can compare and order decimals with 2 decimal places | 😊 😐 🙁 | 😊 😐 🙁 |
| I can divide a 1-digit or a 2-digit number by 10 or 100 and understand the effect | 😊 😐 🙁 | 😊 😐 🙁 |

## Week 1 — Multiplication and division

| | Start of the week | End of the week |
|---|---|---|
| I can estimate the answer to a calculation | 😊 😐 🙁 | 😊 😐 🙁 |
| I can use a written method to calculate multiplication of HTO × O | 😊 😐 🙁 | 😊 😐 🙁 |
| I can solve word problems by recognising the operation needed, writing the calculation and working out the answer | 😊 😐 🙁 | 😊 😐 🙁 |

# My record sheet

## Year 4
## Unit 9

Name: _____

Date: _____

## Week 3 — Properties of shapes

| | Start of the week | End of the week |
|---|---|---|
| • I can use properties and sizes to classify equilateral, isosceles and scalene triangles | 😀 🙂 ☹️ | 😀 🙂 ☹️ |
| • I can use properties and sizes to classify named quadrilaterals: square, rectangle, parallelogram, rhombus, trapezium and kite | 😀 🙂 ☹️ | 😀 🙂 ☹️ |
| • I can use properties and sizes to classify irregular quadrilaterals | 😀 🙂 ☹️ | 😀 🙂 ☹️ |

| | Start of the week | End of the week |
|---|---|---|
| • I can read and write numbers to 10 000 | 🙂 😐 🙁 | 🙂 😐 🙁 |
| • I can identify the value of each digit in a 4-digit number | 🙂 😐 🙁 | 🙂 😐 🙁 |
| • I can use place value to compare and order a set of numbers to 10 000 | 🙂 😐 🙁 | 🙂 😐 🙁 |
| • I can round a number to the nearest 10, 100 or 1000 | 🙂 😐 🙁 | 🙂 😐 🙁 |
| • I can count backwards through zero to include negative numbers | 🙂 😐 🙁 | 🙂 😐 🙁 |
| • I can read and write Roman numerals to 100 | 🙂 😐 🙁 | 🙂 😐 🙁 |

| | Start of the week | End of the week |
|---|---|---|
| • I can estimate the answer to a calculation | 🙂 😐 🙁 | 🙂 😐 🙁 |
| • I can use the formal written method to add 3-digit and 4-digit numbers | 🙂 😐 🙁 | 🙂 😐 🙁 |
| • I can use the formal written method to subtract 3-digit and 4-digit numbers | 🙂 😐 🙁 | 🙂 😐 🙁 |
| • I can use the inverse operation to check the answer to a calculation | 🙂 😐 🙁 | 🙂 😐 🙁 |
| • I can compare and order amounts of money in pounds and pence | 🙂 😐 🙁 | 🙂 😐 🙁 |
| • I can add amounts of money in pounds and pence mentally and using the formal written method | 🙂 😐 🙁 | 🙂 😐 🙁 |
| • I can solve problems and reason mathematically | 🙂 😐 🙁 | 🙂 😐 🙁 |

# My record sheet

## Year 4
## Unit 10

Name: _____

Date: _____

---

Week 3 — Measurement (volume and capacity)

| | Start of the week | End of the week |
|---|---|---|
| • I can use the relationship between litres and millilitres to record capacity using decimals | ☺ ☺ ☹ | ☺ ☺ ☹ |
| • I can use multiplication to convert between litres and millilitres | ☺ ☺ ☹ | ☺ ☺ ☹ |
| • I can find the value of each interval on a scale and use this to give approximate values of readings between divisions | ☺ ☺ ☹ | ☺ ☺ ☹ |
| • I can calculate capacities in litres and in millilitres using decimals to 2 places | ☺ ☺ ☹ | ☺ ☺ ☹ |

## Week 2 — Fractions

| | Start of the week | End of the week |
|---|---|---|
| • I can recognise equivalent fractions | | |
| • I can simplify a fraction | | |
| • I can add fractions with the same denominator | | |
| • I can subtract fractions with the same denominator | | |
| • I know if a fraction is more or less than one whole | | |
| • I can solve problems involving fractions | | |

## Week 1 — Multiplication and division

| | Start of the week | End of the week |
|---|---|---|
| • I can estimate the answer to a calculation | | |
| • I can use a written method to calculate multiplication of HTO × O | | |
| • I can use the most efficient method to calculate multiplication of HTO × O | | |
| • I can solve word problems by recognising the operation needed, writing the calculation and working out the answer | | |

Year 4 Unit 10

# My record sheet

### Year 4
### Unit 11

Name: _____

Date: _____

---

**Week 3 — Position and direction**

| | Start of the week | End of the week |
|---|---|---|
| • I can use coordinates to describe the position of a point on a grid in the first quadrant | 😀 😐 ☹️ | 😀 😐 ☹️ |
| • I can use coordinates to plot specific points and join them to make a 2-D shape | 😀 😐 ☹️ | 😀 😐 ☹️ |

## Week 1 — Addition and subtraction, including Measurement (money)

| | Start of the week | End of the week |
|---|---|---|
| I can estimate the answer to a calculation | 😊 😐 😟 | 😊 😐 😟 |
| I can use the formal written method to add 3-digit and 4-digit numbers | 😊 😐 😟 | 😊 😐 😟 |
| I can use the formal written method to subtract 3-digit and 4-digit numbers | 😊 😐 😟 | 😊 😐 😟 |
| I can use the inverse operation to check the answer to a calculation | 😊 😐 😟 | 😊 😐 😟 |
| I can compare and order amounts of money in pounds and pence | 😊 😐 😟 | 😊 😐 😟 |
| I can subtract amounts of money in pounds and pence mentally and using the formal written method | 😊 😐 😟 | 😊 😐 😟 |
| I can solve problems and reason mathematically | 😊 😐 😟 | 😊 😐 😟 |

## Week 2 — Decimals

| | Start of the week | End of the week |
|---|---|---|
| I recognise the link between fractions and decimals | 😊 😐 😟 | 😊 😐 😟 |
| I can recognise and write decimal equivalents for any number of tenths or hundredths | 😊 😐 😟 | 😊 😐 😟 |
| I can compare and order decimals with 2 decimal places | 😊 😐 😟 | 😊 😐 😟 |
| I can round decimals with 1 decimal place to the nearest whole number | 😊 😐 😟 | 😊 😐 😟 |
| I can divide a 1-digit or a 2-digit number by 10 or 100 and understand the effect | 😊 😐 😟 | 😊 😐 😟 |
| I can solve measurement problems, including money, involving decimals to 2 places | 😊 😐 😟 | 😊 😐 😟 |

# My record sheet

Year 4

Unit 12

Name: _____

Date: _____

## Week 3 — Statistics

| | Start of the week | End of the week |
|---|---|---|
| • I can use a table and tally chart to record data | 🙂 😐 🙁 | 🙂 😐 🙁 |
| • I can interpret the data in a table and tally chart | 🙂 😐 🙁 | 🙂 😐 🙁 |
| • I can present data in a scaled pictogram | 🙂 😐 🙁 | 🙂 😐 🙁 |
| • I can interpret the data in a scaled pictogram | 🙂 😐 🙁 | 🙂 😐 🙁 |
| • I can present data in a scaled bar chart | 🙂 😐 🙁 | 🙂 😐 🙁 |
| • I can interpret the data in a scaled bar chart | 🙂 😐 🙁 | 🙂 😐 🙁 |
| • I can present data in a simple time graph | 🙂 😐 🙁 | 🙂 😐 🙁 |
| • I can interpret the data in a simple time graph | 🙂 😐 🙁 | 🙂 😐 🙁 |

## Week 1 — Multiplication and division

| | Start of the week | End of the week |
|---|---|---|
| • I can estimate the answer to a calculation | ☺ 😐 ☹ | ☺ 😐 ☹ |
| • I can use a mental method to partition and calculate division of TO ÷ O | ☺ 😐 ☹ | ☺ 😐 ☹ |
| • I can use a written method to calculate division of TO ÷ O | ☺ 😐 ☹ | ☺ 😐 ☹ |
| • I can use a mental method to partition and calculate division of HTO ÷ O | ☺ 😐 ☹ | ☺ 😐 ☹ |
| • I can use a written method to calculate division of HTO ÷ O | ☺ 😐 ☹ | ☺ 😐 ☹ |

## Week 2 — Multiplication and division

| | Start of the week | End of the week |
|---|---|---|
| • I can estimate the answer to a calculation | ☺ 😐 ☹ | ☺ 😐 ☹ |
| • I can use a written method to calculate division of HTO ÷ O | ☺ 😐 ☹ | ☺ 😐 ☹ |
| • I can use the most efficient method to calculate division of HTO ÷ O | ☺ 😐 ☹ | ☺ 😐 ☹ |
| • I can solve word problems by recognising the operation needed, writing the calculation and working out the answer | ☺ 😐 ☹ | ☺ 😐 ☹ |

# Year 4 Whole-class National Curriculum attainment targets

## Number – Number and place value

Class: _____

Year: _____

### Level of mastery key:
**NYA** Not yet achieved
**A** Achieved
**A&E** Achieved and exceeded

| Names | count in multiples of 6, 7, 9, 25 and 1000 | find 1000 more or less than a given number | count backwards through zero to include negative numbers | recognise the place value of each digit in a four-digit number (thousands, hundreds, tens, and ones) | order and compare numbers beyond 1000 | identify, represent and estimate numbers using different representations | round any number to the nearest 10, 100 or 1000 | solve number and practical problems that involve all of the above and with increasingly large positive numbers | read Roman numerals to 100 (I to C) and know that over time, the numeral system changed to include the concept of zero and place value | Overall level of mastery in this Domain |
|---|---|---|---|---|---|---|---|---|---|---|
| | | | | | | | | | | |
| | | | | | | | | | | |
| | | | | | | | | | | |
| | | | | | | | | | | |
| | | | | | | | | | | |
| | | | | | | | | | | |
| | | | | | | | | | | |
| | | | | | | | | | | |
| | | | | | | | | | | |
| | | | | | | | | | | |
| | | | | | | | | | | |
| | | | | | | | | | | |
| | | | | | | | | | | |
| | | | | | | | | | | |
| | | | | | | | | | | |
| | | | | | | | | | | |
| | | | | | | | | | | |
| | | | | | | | | | | |
| | | | | | | | | | | |
| | | | | | | | | | | |
| | | | | | | | | | | |
| | | | | | | | | | | |
| | | | | | | | | | | |
| | | | | | | | | | | |
| | | | | | | | | | | |
| | | | | | | | | | | |
| | | | | | | | | | | |
| | | | | | | | | | | |
| | | | | | | | | | | |

# Year 4 Whole-class National Curriculum attainment targets

## Number – Addition and subtraction

Class: _____

Year: _____

**Level of mastery key:**

**NYA**  Not yet achieved

**A**  Achieved

**A&E**  Achieved and exceeded

| Names | add and subtract numbers with up to 4 digits using the formal written methods of columnar addition and subtraction where appropriate | estimate and use inverse operations to check answers to a calculation | solve addition and subtraction two-step problems in contexts, deciding which operations and methods to use and why | Overall level of mastery in this Domain |
|---|---|---|---|---|
| | | | | |
| | | | | |
| | | | | |
| | | | | |
| | | | | |
| | | | | |
| | | | | |
| | | | | |
| | | | | |
| | | | | |
| | | | | |
| | | | | |
| | | | | |
| | | | | |
| | | | | |
| | | | | |
| | | | | |
| | | | | |
| | | | | |
| | | | | |
| | | | | |
| | | | | |
| | | | | |

# Year 4 Whole-class National Curriculum attainment targets

## Number – Multiplication and division

Class: _____

Year: _____

**Level of mastery key:**

**NYA** Not yet achieved

**A** Achieved

**A&E** Achieved and exceeded

| Names | recall multiplication and division facts for multiplication tables up to 12 × 12 | use place value, known and derived facts to multiply and divide mentally, including: multiplying by 0 and 1; dividing by 1; multiplying together three numbers | recognise and use factor pairs and commutativity in mental calculations | multiply two-digit and three-digit numbers by a one-digit number using formal written layout | solve problems involving multiplying and adding, including using the distributive law to multiply two digit numbers by one digit, integer scaling problems and harder correspondence problems such as n objects are connected to m objects | Overall level of mastery in this Domain |
|---|---|---|---|---|---|---|
| | | | | | | |
| | | | | | | |
| | | | | | | |
| | | | | | | |
| | | | | | | |
| | | | | | | |
| | | | | | | |
| | | | | | | |
| | | | | | | |
| | | | | | | |
| | | | | | | |
| | | | | | | |
| | | | | | | |
| | | | | | | |
| | | | | | | |
| | | | | | | |
| | | | | | | |
| | | | | | | |
| | | | | | | |
| | | | | | | |
| | | | | | | |
| | | | | | | |

## Number – Fractions (and decimals)

Class: _____

Year: _____

**Level of mastery key:**

**NYA**    Not yet achieved

**A**       Achieved

**A&E**    Achieved and exceeded

| Names | recognise and show, using diagrams, families of common equivalent fractions | count up and down in hundredths; recognise that hundredths arise when dividing an object by one hundred and dividing tenths by ten | solve problems involving increasingly harder fractions to calculate quantities, and fractions to divide quantities, including non-unit fractions where the answer is a whole number | add and subtract fractions with the same denominator | recognise and write decimal equivalents of any number of tenths or hundredths | recognise and write decimal equivalents to $\frac{1}{4}, \frac{1}{2}, \frac{3}{4}$ | find the effect of dividing a one- or two-digit number by 10 and 100, identifying the value of the digits in the answer as ones, tenths and hundredths | round decimals with one decimal place to the nearest whole number | compare numbers with the same number of decimal places up to two decimal places | solve simple measure and money problems involving fractions and decimals to two decimal places | Overall level of mastery in this Domain |
|---|---|---|---|---|---|---|---|---|---|---|---|
| | | | | | | | | | | | |
| | | | | | | | | | | | |
| | | | | | | | | | | | |
| | | | | | | | | | | | |
| | | | | | | | | | | | |
| | | | | | | | | | | | |
| | | | | | | | | | | | |
| | | | | | | | | | | | |
| | | | | | | | | | | | |
| | | | | | | | | | | | |
| | | | | | | | | | | | |
| | | | | | | | | | | | |
| | | | | | | | | | | | |
| | | | | | | | | | | | |
| | | | | | | | | | | | |
| | | | | | | | | | | | |
| | | | | | | | | | | | |
| | | | | | | | | | | | |
| | | | | | | | | | | | |
| | | | | | | | | | | | |
| | | | | | | | | | | | |
| | | | | | | | | | | | |
| | | | | | | | | | | | |
| | | | | | | | | | | | |
| | | | | | | | | | | | |
| | | | | | | | | | | | |
| | | | | | | | | | | | |
| | | | | | | | | | | | |
| | | | | | | | | | | | |

# Year 4 Whole-class National Curriculum attainment targets

## Measurement

Class: _____

Year: _____

### Level of mastery key:

**NYA**  Not yet achieved

**A**  Achieved

**A&E**  Achieved and exceeded

| Names | convert between different units of measure [for example, kilometre to metre; hour to minute] | measure and calculate the perimeter of a rectilinear figure (including squares) in centimetres and metres | find the area of rectilinear shapes by counting squares | estimate, compare and calculate different measures, including money in pounds and pence | read, write and convert time between analogue and digital 12- and 24-hour clocks | solve problems involving converting from hours to minutes; minutes to seconds; years to months; weeks to days | Overall level of mastery in this Domain |
|---|---|---|---|---|---|---|---|
| | | | | | | | |
| | | | | | | | |
| | | | | | | | |
| | | | | | | | |
| | | | | | | | |
| | | | | | | | |
| | | | | | | | |
| | | | | | | | |
| | | | | | | | |
| | | | | | | | |
| | | | | | | | |
| | | | | | | | |
| | | | | | | | |
| | | | | | | | |
| | | | | | | | |
| | | | | | | | |
| | | | | | | | |
| | | | | | | | |
| | | | | | | | |
| | | | | | | | |
| | | | | | | | |
| | | | | | | | |
| | | | | | | | |
| | | | | | | | |
| | | | | | | | |
| | | | | | | | |

# Year 4 Whole-class National Curriculum attainment targets

## Geometry – Properties of shapes

Class: _____

Year: _____

Level of mastery key:

**NYA** Not yet achieved

**A** Achieved

**A&E** Achieved and exceeded

| Names | compare and classify geometric shapes, including quadrilaterals and triangles, based on their properties and sizes | identify acute and obtuse angles and compare and order angles up to two right angles by size | identify lines of symmetry in 2-D shapes presented in different orientations | complete a simple symmetric figure with respect to a specific line of symmetry | Overall level of mastery in this Domain |
|---|---|---|---|---|---|
| | | | | | |
| | | | | | |
| | | | | | |
| | | | | | |
| | | | | | |
| | | | | | |
| | | | | | |
| | | | | | |
| | | | | | |
| | | | | | |
| | | | | | |
| | | | | | |
| | | | | | |
| | | | | | |
| | | | | | |
| | | | | | |
| | | | | | |
| | | | | | |
| | | | | | |
| | | | | | |
| | | | | | |
| | | | | | |
| | | | | | |
| | | | | | |
| | | | | | |
| | | | | | |
| | | | | | |
| | | | | | |
| | | | | | |
| | | | | | |

# Year 4 Whole-class National Curriculum attainment targets

## Geometry – Position and direction

Class: _____

Year: _____

**Level of mastery key:**

**NYA** Not yet achieved

**A** Achieved

**A&E** Achieved and exceeded

| Names | describe positions on a 2-D grid as coordinates in the first quadrant | describe movements between positions as translations of a given unit to the left/right and up/down | plot specified points and draw sides to complete a given polygon | Overall level of mastery in this Domain |
|---|---|---|---|---|
| | | | | |
| | | | | |
| | | | | |
| | | | | |
| | | | | |
| | | | | |
| | | | | |
| | | | | |
| | | | | |
| | | | | |
| | | | | |
| | | | | |
| | | | | |
| | | | | |
| | | | | |
| | | | | |
| | | | | |
| | | | | |
| | | | | |
| | | | | |
| | | | | |
| | | | | |
| | | | | |
| | | | | |
| | | | | |
| | | | | |
| | | | | |
| | | | | |
| | | | | |
| | | | | |
| | | | | |

# Year 4 Whole-class National Curriculum attainment targets

## Statistics

**Level of mastery key:**

**NYA** Not yet achieved

**A** Achieved

**A&E** Achieved and exceeded

| Names | interpret and present discrete and continuous data using appropriate graphical methods, including bar charts and time graphs | solve comparison, sum and difference problems using information presented in bar charts, pictograms, tables and other graphs | Overall level of mastery in this Domain |
|---|---|---|---|
| | | | |
| | | | |
| | | | |
| | | | |
| | | | |
| | | | |
| | | | |
| | | | |
| | | | |
| | | | |
| | | | |
| | | | |
| | | | |
| | | | |
| | | | |
| | | | |
| | | | |
| | | | |
| | | | |
| | | | |
| | | | |
| | | | |
| | | | |

# Year 4 Whole-class Domains (View 1)

Class: _____

Year: _____

## Level of mastery key:

**NYA**  Not yet achieved

**A**  Achieved

**A&E**  Achieved and exceeded

| Names | Year 4 National Curriculum Programme of Study Domains | | | | | | | |
|---|---|---|---|---|---|---|---|---|
| | Number – Number and place value | Number – Addition and subtraction | Number – Multiplication and division | Number – Fractions (including decimals) | Measurement | Geometry – Properties of shapes | Geometry – Position and direction | Statistics |
| | | | | | | | | |
| | | | | | | | | |
| | | | | | | | | |
| | | | | | | | | |
| | | | | | | | | |
| | | | | | | | | |
| | | | | | | | | |
| | | | | | | | | |
| | | | | | | | | |
| | | | | | | | | |
| | | | | | | | | |
| | | | | | | | | |
| | | | | | | | | |
| | | | | | | | | |
| | | | | | | | | |
| | | | | | | | | |
| | | | | | | | | |
| | | | | | | | | |
| | | | | | | | | |
| | | | | | | | | |
| | | | | | | | | |
| | | | | | | | | |
| | | | | | | | | |
| | | | | | | | | |
| | | | | | | | | |
| | | | | | | | | |
| | | | | | | | | |
| | | | | | | | | |

# Year 4 Whole-class Domains (View 2)   Class: _____   Year: _____

## Number – Number and place value
- count in multiples of 6, 7, 9, 25 and 1000
- find 1000 more or less than a given number
- count backwards through zero to include negative numbers
- recognise the place value of each digit in a four-digit number (thousands, hundreds, tens, and ones)
- order and compare numbers beyond 1000
- identify, represent and estimate numbers using different representations
- round any number to the nearest 10, 100 or 1000
- solve number and practical problems that involve all of the above and with increasingly large positive numbers
- read Roman numerals to 100 (I to C) and know that over time, the numeral system changed to include the concept of zero and place value

| NYA | A | A&E |
| --- | --- | --- |
|  |  |  |

## Number – Addition and subtraction
- add and subtract numbers with up to 4 digits using the formal written methods of columnar addition and subtraction where appropriate
- estimate and use inverse operations to check answers to a calculation
- solve addition and subtraction two-step problems in contexts, deciding which operations and methods to use and why

| NYA | A | A&E |
| --- | --- | --- |
|  |  |  |

## Number – Multiplication and division
- recall multiplication and division facts for multiplication tables up to 12 × 12
- use place value, known and derived facts to multiply and divide mentally, including: multiplying by 0 and 1; dividing by 1; multiplying together three numbers
- recognise and use factor pairs and commutativity in mental calculations
- multiply two-digit and three-digit numbers by a one-digit number using formal written layout
- solve problems involving multiplying and adding, including using the distributive law to multiply two digit numbers by one digit, integer scaling problems and harder correspondence problems such as n objects are connected to m objects

| NYA | A | A&E |
| --- | --- | --- |
|  |  |  |

## Number – Fractions (including decimals)
- recognise and show, using diagrams, families of common equivalent fractions
- count up and down in hundredths; recognise that hundredths arise when dividing an object by one hundred and dividing tenths by ten
- solve problems involving increasingly harder fractions to calculate quantities, and fractions to divide quantities, including non-unit fractions where the answer is a whole number
- add and subtract fractions with the same denominator
- recognise and write decimal equivalents of any number of tenths or hundredths
- recognise and write decimal equivalents to $\frac{1}{4}$, $\frac{1}{2}$, $\frac{3}{4}$
- find the effect of dividing a one- or two-digit number by 10 and 100, identifying the value of the digits in the answer as ones, tenths and hundredths
- round decimals with one decimal place to the nearest whole number
- compare numbers with the same number of decimal places up to two decimal places
- solve simple measure and money problems involving fractions and decimals to two decimal places

| NYA | A | A&E |
| --- | --- | --- |
|  |  |  |

## Measurement
- convert between different units of measure [for example, kilometre to metre; hour to minute]
- measure and calculate the perimeter of a rectilinear figure (including squares) in centimetres and metres
- find the area of rectilinear shapes by counting squares
- estimate, compare and calculate different measures, including money in pounds and pence
- read, write and convert time between analogue and digital 12- and 24-hour clocks
- solve problems involving converting from hours to minutes; minutes to seconds; years to months; weeks to days

| NYA | A | A&E |
| --- | --- | --- |
|  |  |  |

## Geometry – Properties of shapes
- compare and classify geometric shapes, including quadrilaterals and triangles, based on their properties and sizes
- identify acute and obtuse angles and compare and order angles up to two right angles by size
- identify lines of symmetry in 2-D shapes presented in different orientations
- complete a simple symmetric figure with respect to a specific line of symmetry

| NYA | A | A&E |
| --- | --- | --- |
|  |  |  |

## Geometry – Position and direction
- describe positions on a 2-D grid as coordinates in the first quadrant
- describe movements between positions as translations of a given unit to the left/right and up/down
- plot specified points and draw sides to complete a given polygon

| NYA | A | A&E |
| --- | --- | --- |
|  |  |  |

## Statistics
- interpret and present discrete and continuous data using appropriate graphical methods, including bar charts and time graphs.
- solve comparison, sum and difference problems using information presented in bar charts, pictograms, tables and other graphs

| NYA | A | A&E |
| --- | --- | --- |
|  |  |  |

**Level of mastery key:** NYA – Not yet achieved     A – Achieved     A&E – Achieved and exceeded

© HarperCollins*Publishers* Ltd. 2015

# Year 4 Individual pupil National Curriculum attainment targets and Domains

Name: _____  Class: _____  Year: _____

| Domain | National Curriculum attainment target | Level of mastery | | |
|---|---|---|---|---|
| | | Not yet achieved | Achieved | Achieved and exceeded |
| Number – Number and place value | Count in multiples of 6, 7, 9, 25 and 1000 | | | |
| | Find 1000 more or less than a given number | | | |
| | Count backwards through zero to include negative numbers | | | |
| | Recognise the place value of each digit in a four-digit number (thousands, hundreds, tens, and ones) | | | |
| | Order and compare numbers beyond 1000 | | | |
| | Identify, represent and estimate numbers using different representations | | | |
| | Round any number to the nearest 10, 100 or 1000 | | | |
| | Solve number and practical problems that involve all of the above and with increasingly large positive numbers | | | |
| | Read Roman numerals to 100 (I to C) and know that over time, the numeral system changed to include the concept of zero and place value | | | |
| Number – Addition and subtraction | Add and subtract numbers with up to 4 digits using the formal written methods of columnar addition and subtraction where appropriate | | | |
| | Estimate and use inverse operations to check answers to a calculation | | | |
| | Solve addition and subtraction two-step problems in contexts, deciding which operations and methods to use and why | | | |
| Number – Multiplication and division | Recall multiplication and division facts for multiplication tables up to 12 × 12 | | | |
| | Use place value, known and derived facts to multiply and divide mentally, including: multiplying by 0 and 1; dividing by 1; multiplying together three numbers | | | |
| | Recognise and use factor pairs and commutativity in mental calculations | | | |
| | Multiply two-digit and three-digit numbers by a one-digit number using formal written layout | | | |
| | Solve problems involving multiplying and adding, including using the distributive law to multiply two digit numbers by one digit, integer scaling problems and harder correspondence problems such as n objects are connected to m objects | | | |

| Domain | National Curriculum attainment target | Level of mastery | | |
|---|---|---|---|---|
| | | Not yet achieved | Achieved | Achieved and exceeded |
| Number – Fractions (and decimals) | Recognise and show, using diagrams, families of common equivalent fractions | | | |
| | Count up and down in hundredths; recognise that hundredths arise when dividing an object by one hundred and dividing tenths by ten | | | |
| | Solve problems involving increasingly harder fractions to calculate quantities, and fractions to divide quantities, including non-unit fractions where the answer is a whole number | | | |
| | Add and subtract fractions with the same denominator | | | |
| | Recognise and write decimal equivalents of any number of tenths or hundredths | | | |
| | Recognise and write decimal equivalents to $\frac{1}{4}$, $\frac{1}{2}$, $\frac{3}{4}$ | | | |
| | Find the effect of dividing a one- or two-digit number by 10 and 100, identifying the value of the digits in the answer as ones, tenths and hundredths | | | |
| | Round decimals with one decimal place to the nearest whole number | | | |
| | Compare numbers with the same number of decimal places up to two decimal places | | | |
| | Solve simple measure and money problems involving fractions and decimals to two decimal places | | | |
| Measurement | Convert between different units of measure [for example, kilometre to metre; hour to minute] | | | |
| | Measure and calculate the perimeter of a rectilinear figure (including squares) in centimetres and metres | | | |
| | Find the area of rectilinear shapes by counting squares | | | |
| | Estimate, compare and calculate different measures, including money in pounds and pence | | | |
| | Read, write and convert time between analogue and digital 12- and 24-hour clocks | | | |
| | Solve problems involving converting from hours to minutes; minutes to seconds; years to months; weeks to days | | | |
| Geometry – Properties of shapes | Compare and classify geometric shapes, including quadrilaterals and triangles, based on their properties and sizes | | | |
| | Identify acute and obtuse angles and compare and order angles up to two right angles by size | | | |
| | Identify lines of symmetry in 2-D shapes presented in different orientations | | | |
| | Complete a simple symmetric figure with respect to a specific line of symmetry | | | |
| Geometry – Position and direction | Describe positions on a 2-D grid as coordinates in the first quadrant | | | |
| | Describe movements between positions as translations of a given unit to the left/right and up/down | | | |
| | Plot specified points and draw sides to complete a given polygon | | | |
| Statistics | Interpret and present discrete and continuous data using appropriate graphical methods, including bar charts and time graphs | | | |
| | Solve comparison, sum and difference problems using information presented in bar charts, pictograms, tables and other graphs | | | |

# Overall level of mastery in each of the National Curriculum Programme of Study Domains

|  |  | Level of mastery | | |
|---|---|---|---|---|
|  |  | Not yet achieved | Achieved | Achieved and exceeded |
| **Domain** | Number – Number and place value |  |  |  |
|  | Number – Addition and subtraction |  |  |  |
|  | Number – Multiplication and division |  |  |  |
|  | Number – Fractions (including decimals) |  |  |  |
|  | Measurement |  |  |  |
|  | Geometry – Properties of shapes |  |  |  |
|  | Geometry – Position and direction |  |  |  |
|  | Statistics |  |  |  |

# Multiples (1)

# Multiples (2)

# Numbers to 10 000

| | | | |
|---|---|---|---|
| 2 | 5 | 7 | 8 |
| 14 | 39 | 65 | 93 |
| 236 | 418 | 702 | 827 |
| 1584 | 2358 | 3725 | 5106 |
| 6249 | 7031 | 8697 | 9413 |

| | | | |
|---|---|---|---|
| 1254 | 1735 | 2483 | 2810 |
| 3169 | 3601 | 3946 | 4072 |
| 4598 | 5327 | 5491 | 6104 |
| 6945 | 7052 | 7589 | 7816 |
| 8370 | 8627 | 9238 | 9763 |

# Symbol cards

Resource 5

| > | > | > | > |
| < | < | < | < |
| = | = | = | = |
| □ | □ | □ | □ |
| ○ | ○ | ○ | ○ |

BUSY ANT MATHS  Assessment Guide 4

© HarperCollins*Publishers* Ltd. 2015

# Gattegno place value chart

| 1000 | 2000 | 3000 | 4000 | 5000 | 6000 | 7000 | 8000 | 9000 |
| 100 | 200 | 300 | 400 | 500 | 600 | 700 | 800 | 900 |
| 10 | 20 | 30 | 40 | 50 | 60 | 70 | 80 | 90 |
| 1 | 2 | 3 | 4 | 5 | 6 | 7 | 8 | 9 |

# Coins and notes

# Number puzzles

Imagine you have 34 beads.
You have to make a four-digit
number on the abacus.
You must use all 34 beads for
each number you make.
How many different four-digit
numbers can you make?
Write them in order, smallest
to largest.

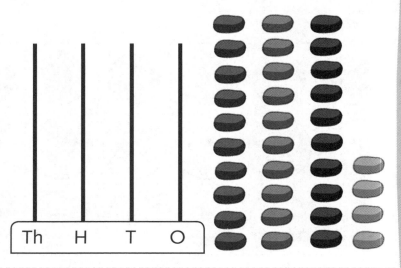

16 000, 8000, 4000, 2000, 1000, ☐, ☐, ☐

26, 21, 23, 18, 20, 15, ☐, ☐, ☐

10, 9, 7, 4, 0, –5, ☐, ☐, ☐

☐458, 84☐7, 7☐56, 645☐, 5☐54, ☐4☐3, 3☐5☐, ☐4☐☐, ☐☐☐☐

**True or false?**

The sum of two
even numbers
equals an
even number.

The sum of an odd
number and an even
number equals an
odd number.

The sum of two odd
numbers equals an
odd number.

The sum of two
consecutive numbers
equals an odd number.

The sum of three
consecutive numbers
equals an odd number.

· The sum of the digits in a
  three-digit number is 24.
· The difference between the
  hundreds digit and the ones
  digit is 2.
· The number is between 700
  and 900.
What is the number?

☐

· The sum of the digits in a four-digit
  number is 14.
· All the digits are less than 6.
· All the digits are different.
· The sum of the thousands and
  hundreds digits equals the ones digit.
· The number is a multiple of 5.
What is the number?

☐

# Roman numerals

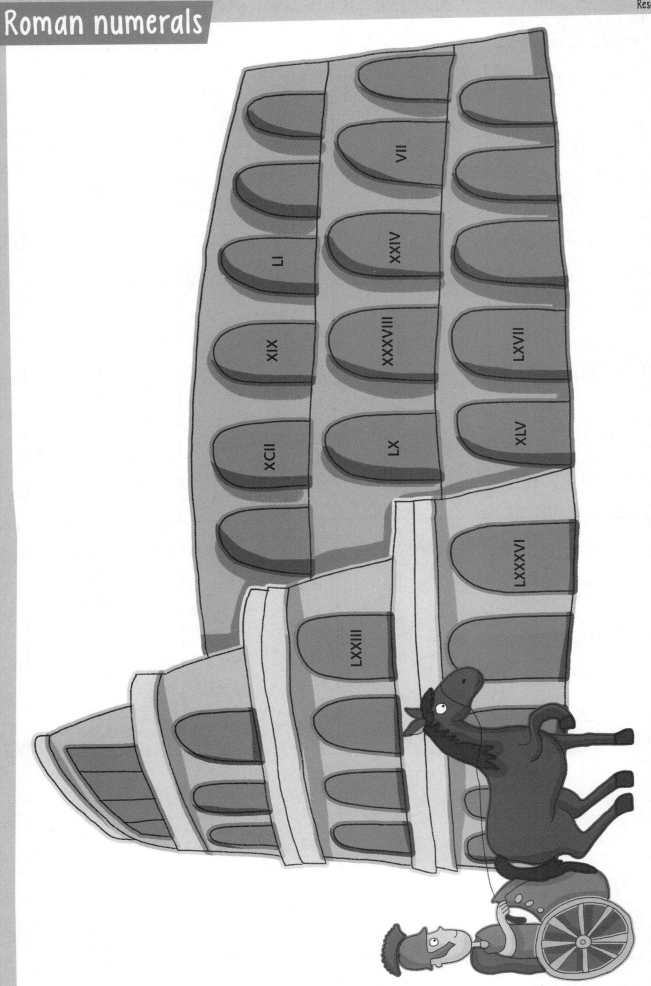

# Estimate, calculate and check

| Estimate | Calculate | Check |
|---|---|---|
| | | |
| | | |

# Word problems

**1** A plane is due to leave at 4:20 p.m. and arrive at 6:10 p.m. It leaves 10 minutes late, but arrives 5 minutes early. How long was the journey?

**2** A 2 kg pack of sausages costs £1.99. A 4 kg pack costs 20p less than two 2 kg packs. What is the price of a 4 kg pack?

**3** 8600 tickets go on sale for a rock concert. Three-quarters of the tickets are sold in just 2 days. How many tickets are sold in 2 days?

**4** A vat of milk holds 80 litres. 100 cartons are filled from a full vat. If each carton holds 500 ml, how many litres are left in the vat?

**5** I am thinking of a number. If you add 47 to this number and then subtract 54, you get 37. What number am I thinking of?

**6** Mrs Herne shares £51 equally among her 6 grandchildren. How much does each grandchild get?

**7** A plane flying north changes direction anticlockwise 90°. In what direction is the plane flying now?

**8** 8 rally cars take part in a race. They each travel 46 km. How far do the 8 cars travel altogether?

**9** Reece is making a bookcase. He cuts a piece of timber 1 m 40 cm long into 4 equal lengths. How many centimetres long is each piece?

**10** At 6:00 p.m. the temperature is 5°C. By 6:00 a.m. the temperature has dropped 7°. What is the temperature at 6:00 a.m.?

**11** A rectangular garden is paved with 1 m square paving stones. The garden is 45 m long and 10 m wide. How many paving stones are used?

**12** A cinema sells 364 tickets at £8 a ticket. How much does the cinema take?

**13** Mrs Young goes shopping with £120 in her purse. She spends £63.20 at the supermarket, £12.60 at the greengrocers, £18.75 at the butchers and £6.45 at the bakers. How much money does she have left in her purse?

**14** Mr Adams is making Christmas cakes. He mixes together 8 kg of wet ingredients and 6 kg of dry ingredients and puts the same amount into 8 cake tins. What is the weight of the ingredients of 1 cake tin?

**15** Better Electrics have a sale on TV and sound bar packages. If you buy a TV costing £684 and a sound bar costing £258 you receive a £75 discount. What is the combined price of a TV and sound bar after the discount?

**16** A waiter is carrying 3 boxes of glasses, each box containing 12 glasses. He drops one of the boxes and breaks one quarter of the glasses in the box. How many glasses does he have left altogether?

**17** A pack of 10 pies costs £26. How much does one pie cost?

**18** There are 12 eggs in a carton, and 12 cartons in a box. How many eggs are there in 8 boxes?

**19** Including the £1 and £2, there are 8 different coins. What is the total of one of each of the 8 coins?

**20** I am thinking of a number. If you multiply this number by 4 and then subtract 10, you get 50. What number am I thinking of?

# Multiples (3)

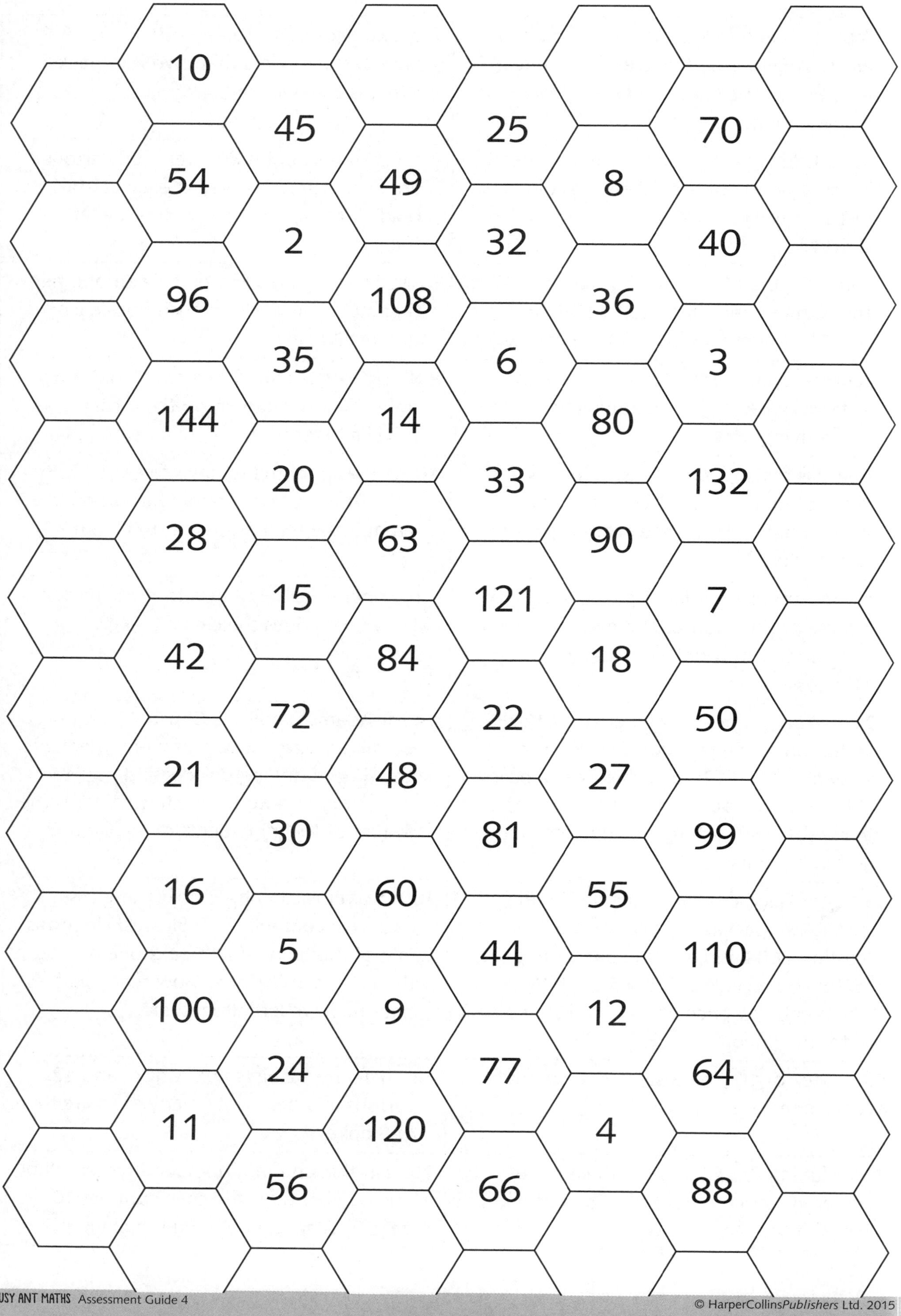

10
45
25
70
54
49
8
2
32
40
96
108
36
35
6
3
144
14
80
20
33
132
28
63
90
15
121
7
42
84
18
72
22
50
21
48
27
30
81
99
16
60
55
5
44
110
100
9
12
24
77
64
11
120
4
56
66
88

# Multiplication and division facts

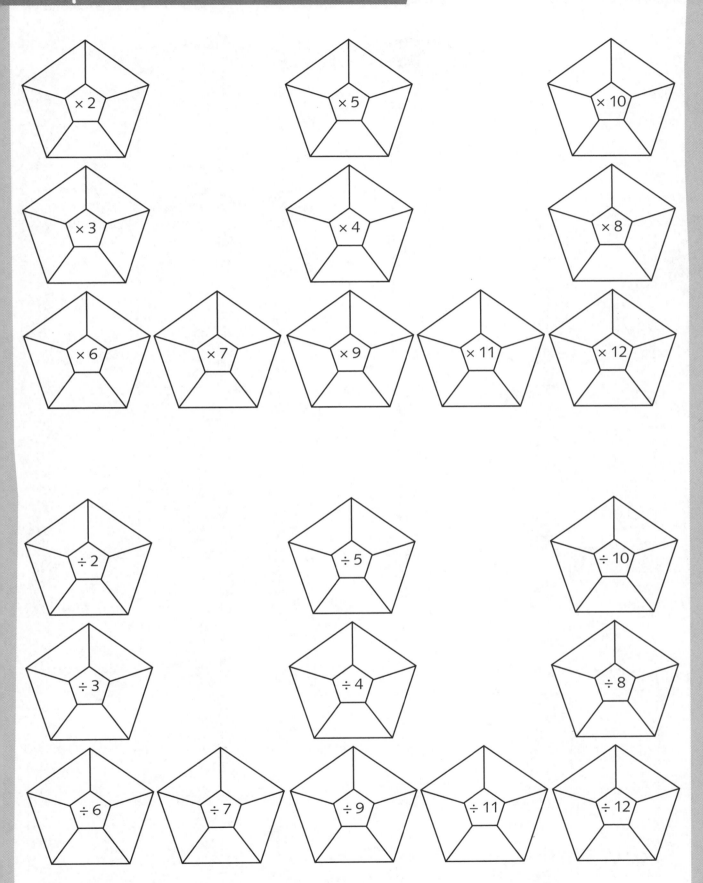

# Multiplying multiples of 10 and 100

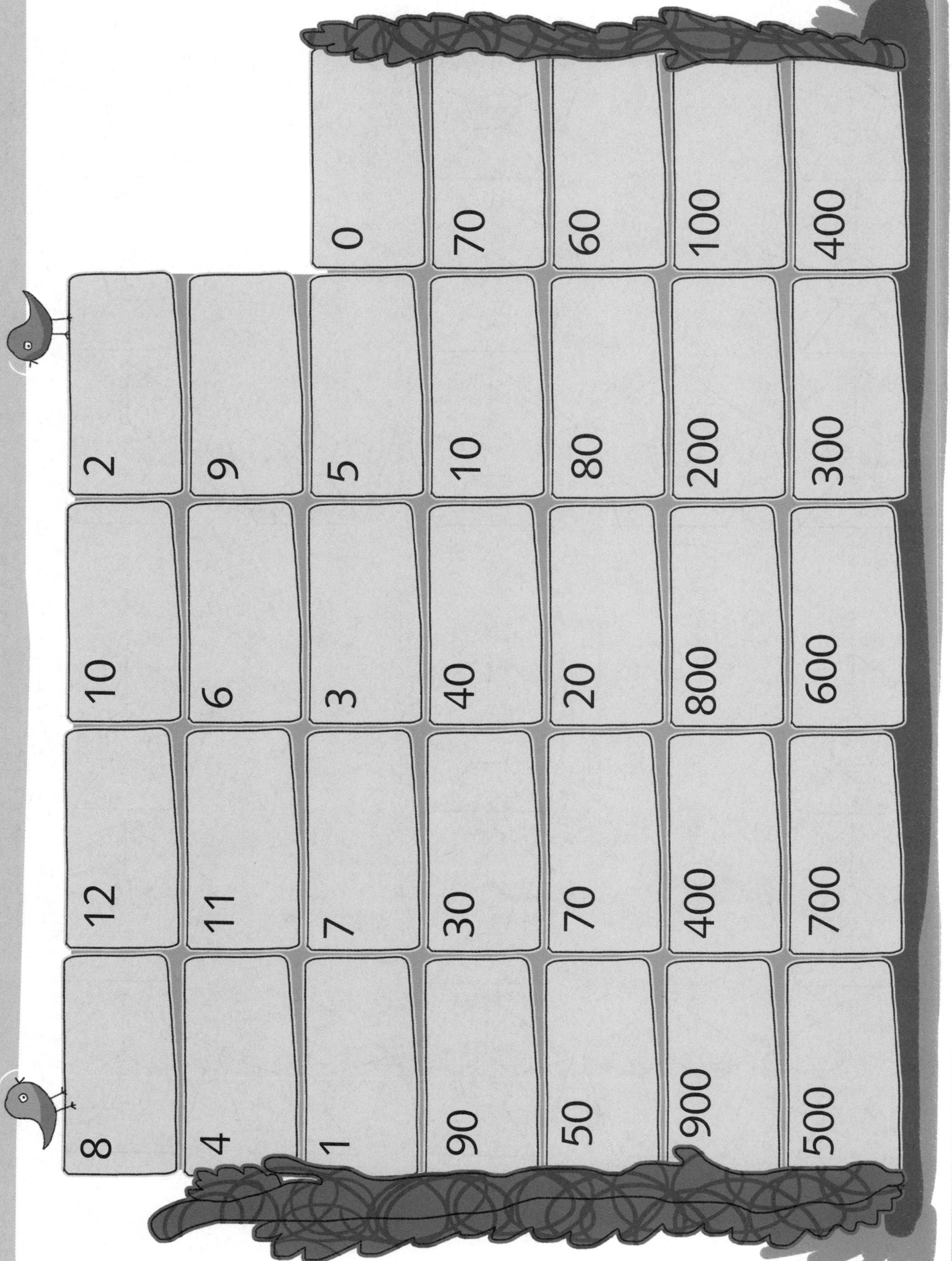

Resource 14

0 · 70 · 60 · 100 · 400

2 · 9 · 5 · 10 · 80 · 200 · 300

10 · 6 · 3 · 40 · 20 · 800 · 600

12 · 11 · 7 · 30 · 70 · 400 · 700

8 · 4 · 1 · 90 · 50 · 900 · 500

BUSY ANT MATHS  Assessment Guide 4

© HarperCollins*Publishers* Ltd. 2015

# Dividing multiples of 10

# Multiplying together three numbers

$3 \times 9 \times 2 =$

$5 \times 8 \times 2 =$

$6 \times 7 \times 5 =$

$3 \times 7 \times 4 =$

$5 \times 9 \times 4 =$

$8 \times 9 \times 7 =$

# Two-digit numbers

| | | | |
|---|---|---|---|
| 12 | 13 | 14 | 18 |
| 20 | 24 | 26 | 27 |
| 32 | 36 | 40 | 45 |
| 48 | 56 | 64 | 72 |
| 80 | 84 | 88 | 96 |

# Mental multiplication

18 × 9 =

24 × 7 =

45 × 8 =

32 × 5 =

# Multiplying two-digit and three-digit numbers

$$76 \times 8 =$$

$$49 \times 3 =$$

$$87 \times 4 =$$

$$368 \times 6 =$$

$$254 \times 9 =$$

$$623 \times 7 =$$

# Equivalent fractions (1)

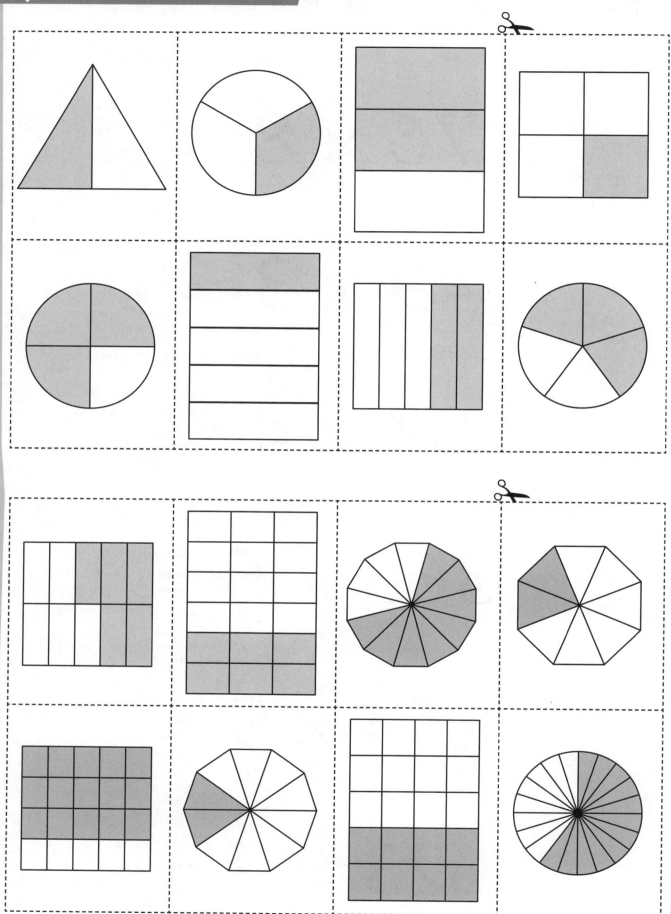

# Equivalent fractions (2)

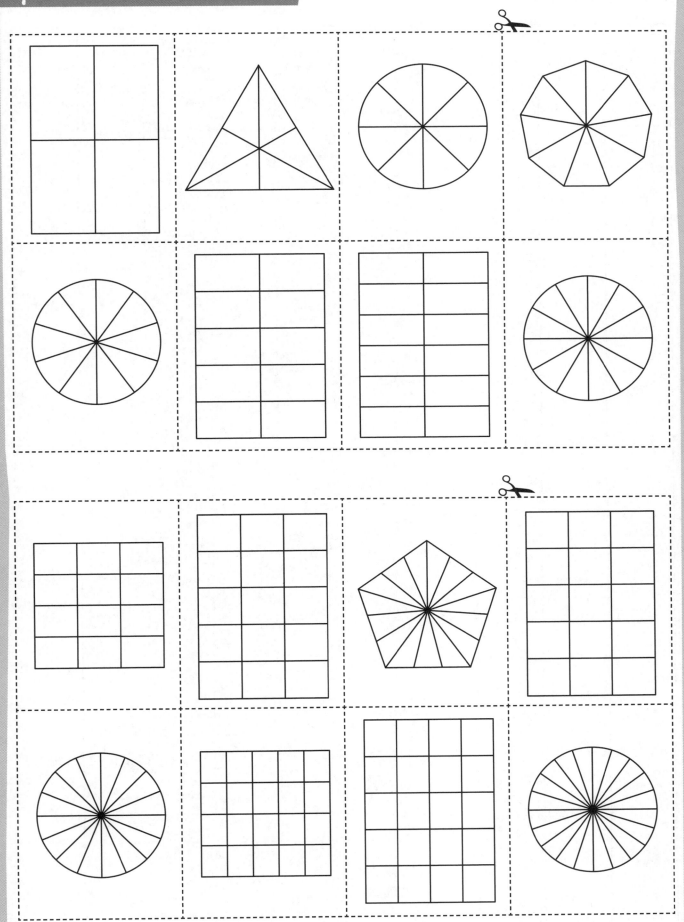

# Fractions wall

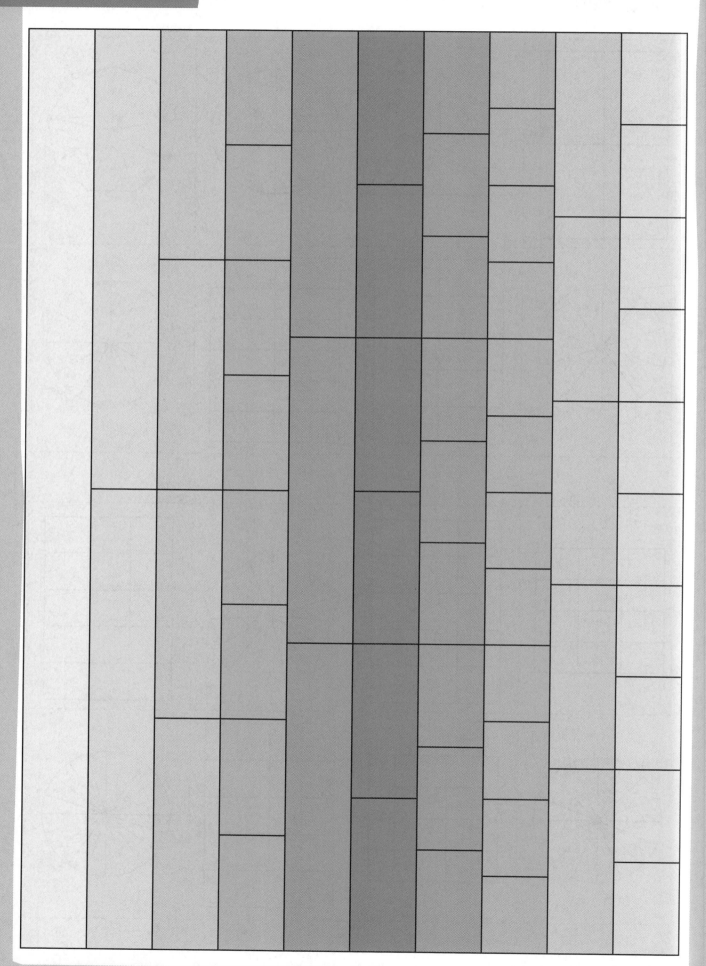

# Equivalent fractions (3)

$\dfrac{1}{2} =$

$\dfrac{1}{3} =$

$\dfrac{2}{3} =$

$\dfrac{1}{4} =$

$\dfrac{3}{4} =$

$\dfrac{1}{5} =$

$\dfrac{2}{5} =$

$\dfrac{3}{5} =$

# Hundredths

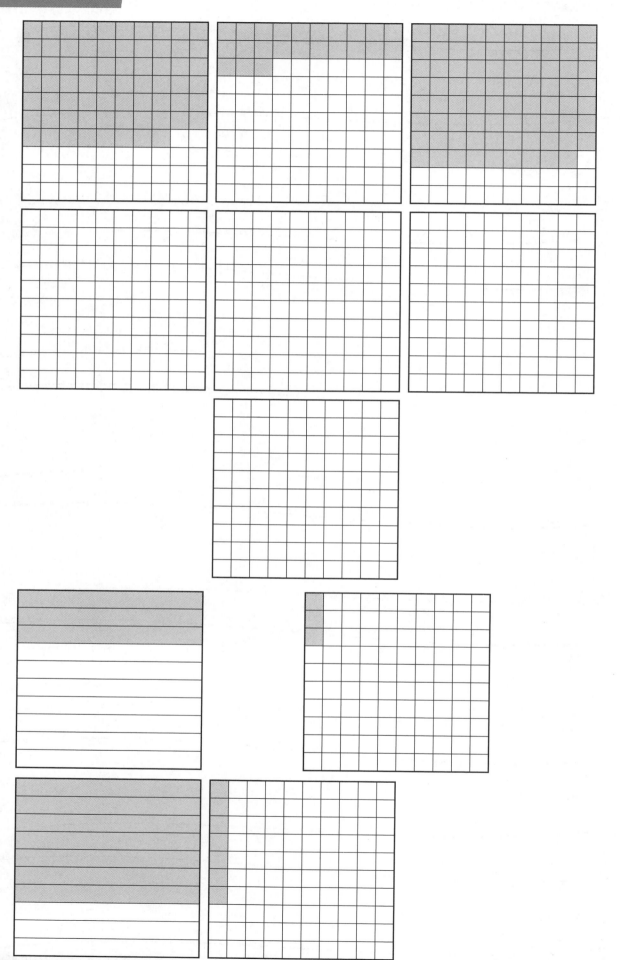

# Fractions of numbers

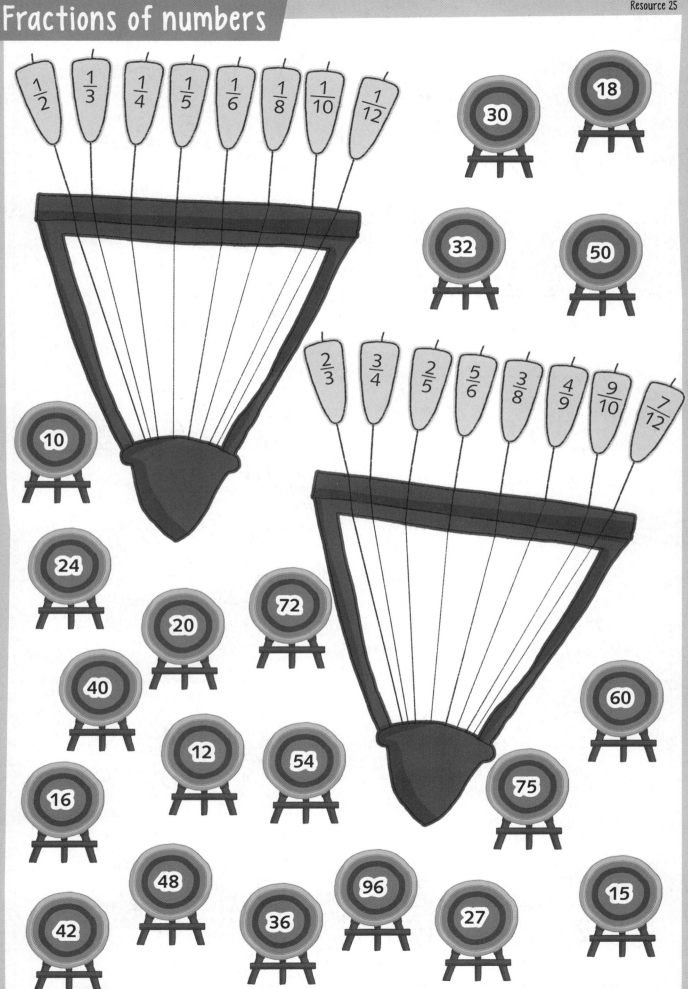

$$\frac{3}{7} + \frac{2}{7} = \frac{\square}{\square}$$

$$\frac{1}{8} + \frac{5}{8} = \frac{\square}{\square}$$

$$\frac{2}{9} + \frac{3}{9} = \frac{\square}{\square}$$

$$\frac{5}{12} + \frac{5}{12} = \frac{\square}{\square}$$

$$\frac{5}{6} + \frac{1}{6} = \frac{\square}{\square}$$

$$\frac{7}{14} + \frac{5}{14} = \frac{\square}{\square}$$

$$\frac{7}{11} + \frac{6}{11} = \frac{\square}{\square}$$

$$\frac{9}{10} + \frac{7}{10} = \frac{\square}{\square}$$

$$\frac{\square}{\square} + \frac{4}{7} = \frac{6}{7}$$

$$\frac{\square}{\square} + \frac{4}{9} = \frac{7}{9}$$

$$\frac{5}{12} + \frac{\square}{\square} = \frac{7}{12}$$

$$\frac{3}{10} + \frac{\square}{\square} = \frac{7}{10}$$

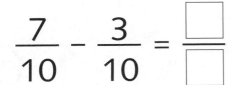

# Subtracting fractions

$$\frac{7}{10} - \frac{3}{10} = \frac{\Box}{\Box} \qquad\qquad \frac{5}{8} - \frac{2}{8} = \frac{\Box}{\Box}$$

$$\frac{5}{7} - \frac{4}{7} = \frac{\Box}{\Box} \qquad\qquad \frac{8}{9} - \frac{2}{9} = \frac{\Box}{\Box}$$

$$\frac{9}{12} - \frac{7}{12} = \frac{\Box}{\Box} \qquad\qquad \frac{11}{15} - \frac{8}{15} = \frac{\Box}{\Box}$$

$$\frac{5}{6} - \frac{1}{6} = \frac{\Box}{\Box} \qquad\qquad \frac{4}{5} - \frac{3}{5} = \frac{\Box}{\Box}$$

$$\frac{\Box}{\Box} - \frac{1}{8} = \frac{5}{8} \qquad\qquad \frac{\Box}{\Box} - \frac{3}{9} = \frac{3}{9}$$

$$\frac{11}{12} - \frac{\Box}{\Box} = \frac{5}{12} \qquad\qquad \frac{9}{10} - \frac{\Box}{\Box} = \frac{3}{10}$$

Resource 27

BUSY ANT MATHS Assessment Guide 4

© HarperCollins*Publishers* Ltd. 2015

# Decimal cards — tenths

| | | | |
|---|---|---|---|
| 0·2 | 0·8 | 1·3 | 1·6 |
| 2·4 | 2·5 | 3·1 | 3·9 |
| 4·7 | 4·9 | 5·4 | 5·8 |
| 6·3 | 6·7 | 7·1 | 7·6 |
| 8·2 | 8·5 | 9·4 | 9·8 |

# Decimal cards — hundredths

| 0·24 | 0·78 | 1·94 | 1·97 |
| 2·43 | 2·46 | 3·01 | 3·65 |
| 4·13 | 4·59 | 5·12 | 5·85 |
| 6·26 | 6·58 | 7·32 | 7·37 |
| 8·06 | 8·79 | 9·81 | 9·63 |

# Fraction and decimal equivalents

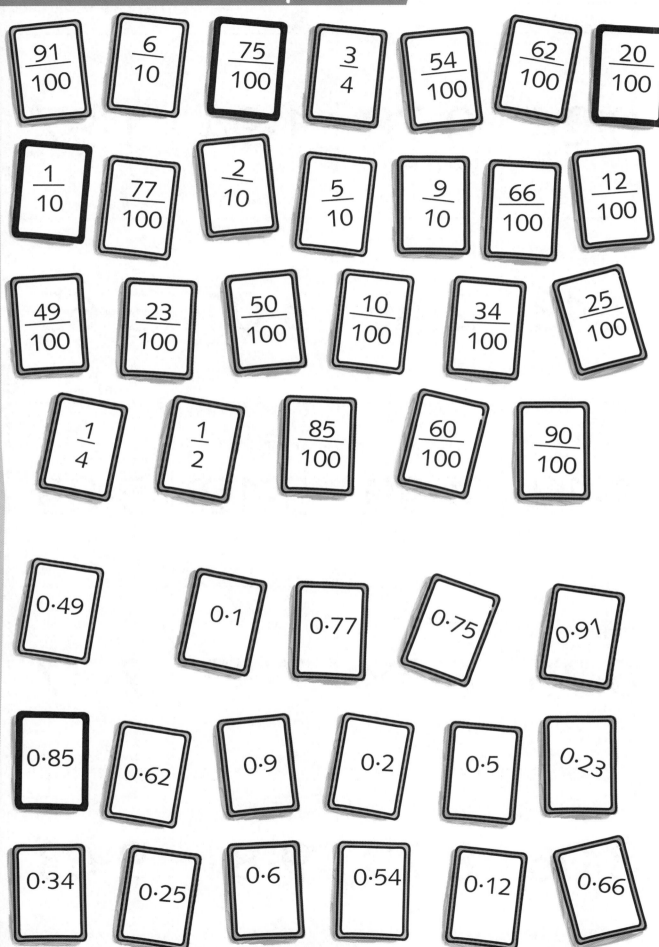

$\frac{91}{100}$   $\frac{6}{10}$   $\frac{75}{100}$   $\frac{3}{4}$   $\frac{54}{100}$   $\frac{62}{100}$   $\frac{20}{100}$

$\frac{1}{10}$   $\frac{77}{100}$   $\frac{2}{10}$   $\frac{5}{10}$   $\frac{9}{10}$   $\frac{66}{100}$   $\frac{12}{100}$

$\frac{49}{100}$   $\frac{23}{100}$   $\frac{50}{100}$   $\frac{10}{100}$   $\frac{34}{100}$   $\frac{25}{100}$

$\frac{1}{4}$   $\frac{1}{2}$   $\frac{85}{100}$   $\frac{60}{100}$   $\frac{90}{100}$

0·49   0·1   0·77   0·75   0·91

0·85   0·62   0·9   0·2   0·5   0·23

0·34   0·25   0·6   0·54   0·12   0·66

# Tenths and hundredths

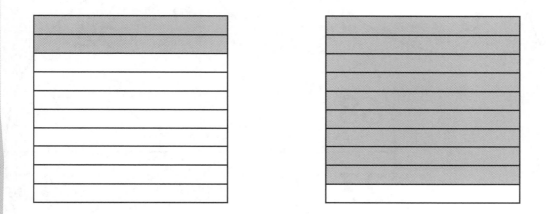

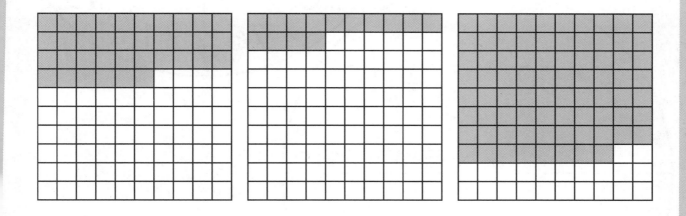

# Dividing by 10 and 100

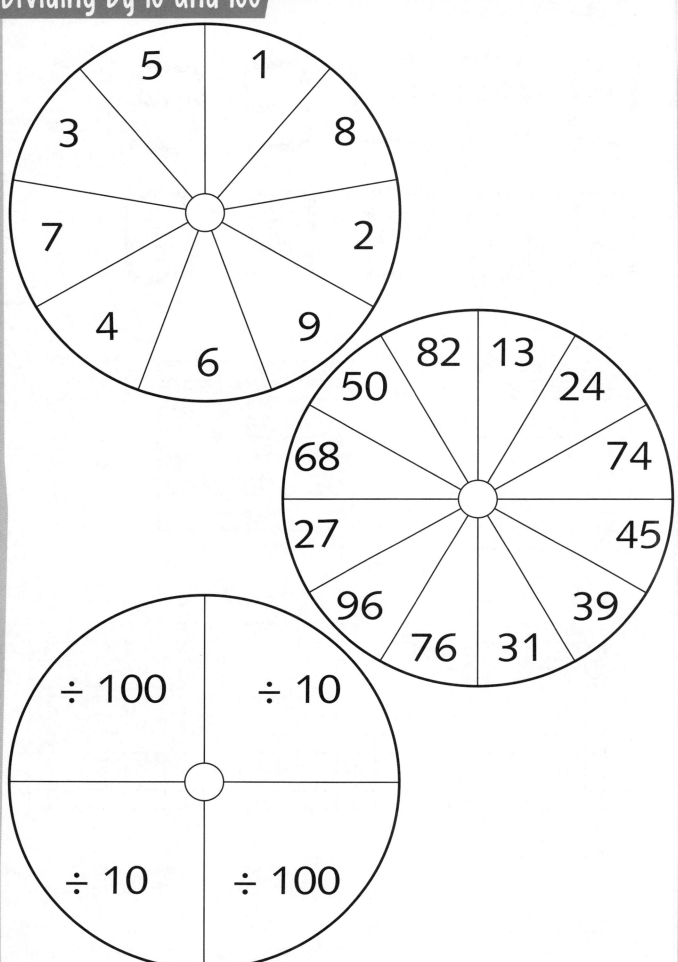

# Fractions and decimals problems

**1.** David earns £600 a week. Each week he saves $\frac{1}{4}$ of his salary. How much does David save each week?

**2.** Simon is 1·5 m tall. Boris is 20 cm shorter than Simon, and Harry is 30 cm taller than Simon. How tall are Boris and Harry?

**3.** Lucy is building a path in her garden. It is 4 m long. The paving stones are the width of the path and 0·2 m long. How many paving stones will Lucy need to build her path?

**4.** Eric has 5 m of wrapping paper to wrap two presents. He uses 2 m of wrapping paper on one present and 1·5 m on the other present. How much wrapping paper does Eric have left?

**5.** Parfum de la Mer is Gillian's favourite perfume. She buys a 50 ml bottle. Each spray of the perfume sprays out 0·5 ml of perfume. If Gillian uses 2 sprays of perfume every day, how many days will the perfume last her?

**6.** A small bottle of shampoo holds 300 ml. A large bottle holds 0·5 litres. How many large bottles of shampoo hold the same as 5 small bottles?

**7.** Yesterday, the Herne family used $1\frac{1}{5}$ litres of milk at breakfast and another 600 ml of milk throughout the rest of the day. At the end of the day, how much milk did they have left from 2 litres of milk?

**8.** Tony the baker buys two 0·5 kg bags of apples and uses 780 g to fill his apple pies. How many grams of apples does Tony have left?

**9.** Francis posted 3 parcels. They weighed 750 g, 1·22 kg and 1·64 kg. What was the total weight of all three parcels in kilograms and grams?

**10.** The mass of Parcel A is 12 kg. The mass of Parcel B is $\frac{1}{4}$ the mass of Parcel A. If the mass of Parcel C is $\frac{3}{4}$ the mass of Parcel A, what is the total mass of the 3 parcels?

**11.** Today, Michael the electrician used $4\frac{3}{10}$ m of brown wire, $7\frac{1}{10}$ m of blue wire and $6\frac{7}{10}$ m of green wire. What is the total length of wire that Michael used today?

**12.** Tom has 16 kg of cement. He uses $\frac{7}{10}$ of it to build a wall. How much cement does he have left?

**13.** Rashid paints his bedroom walls. There are 18 square metres of wall. A 5 litre tin of paint will cover 30 square metres. How many litres of paint does he use?

**14.** Anna goes to the butcher to buy some steaks for dinner. They cost £15 per kilogram. She buys four steaks weighing 1·46 kg in total. How much does she pay for them?

**15.** Humphrey has 8 weeks of summer holidays. He is going to stay with friends for 16 days during the holidays. What fraction of his holidays does he spend with his friends?

**16.** Sorab buys 7 tickets for a concert for £87.50. 3 of his friends can't go, so he returns their tickets and gets a full refund for them. How much refund does he get?

**17.** Tania visits her parents 210 km away. After driving $\frac{2}{5}$ of the way there she stops for a cup of coffee. How many kilometres of her journey has she completed?

**18.** Venetia gets £12 pocket money per week. Last week she spent $\frac{2}{3}$ of it on downloading music. How much money did she spend on music?

**19.** A pack of butter weighs 500 g. A recipe uses 200 g of butter. What fraction of the pack of butter is left?

**20.** Jake is 1 m 40 cm high. His sister Alice is $\frac{9}{10}$ as tall as him. How tall is Alice?

# Relationship between different units of measure (1)

| | | |
|---|---|---|
| 1 kilometre | 1000 metres | 0·1 kilometre |
| 100 metres | 1 metre | 100 centimetres |
| 1000 millimetres | 0·1 metre | 10 centimetres |
| 100 millimetres | 1 centimetre | 10 millimetres |
| 0·1 centimetre | 1 millimetre | 1 kilogram |
| 1000 grams | 0·1 kilogram | 100 grams |

| 0·01 kilogram | 10 grams | 1 litre |
| 1000 millilitres | 0·1 litre | 100 millilitres |
| 0·01 litre | 10 millilitres | 1 year |
| 12 months | 1 week | 7 days |
| 1 day | 24 hours | 1 hour |
| 60 minutes | 1 minute | 60 seconds |

# Convert between different units of measure

5·3 km = ☐ m          5 min = ☐ sec          6·4 *l* = ☐ ml

1·8 m = ☐ mm          10500 g = ☐ kg          8000 mm = ☐ cm

12500 ml = ☐ *l*          20 cm = ☐ m          144 h = ☐ days

3·9 kg = ☐ g          2·6 cm = ☐ mm          4600 m = ☐ km

$6\frac{1}{2}$ h = ☐ min          125 min = ☐ h and ☐ min

8·1 *l* = ☐ ml          880 cm = ☐ m          3200 g = ☐ kg

0·09 kg = ☐ g          2·9 km = ☐ m          7 days = ☐ h

3 mm = ☐ cm          2200 ml = ☐ *l*          46·8 kg = ☐ g

5·2 m = ☐ cm          12·2 kg = ☐ g          0·05 *l* = ☐ ml

15·1 *l* = ☐ ml          6 weeks = ☐ days          7 m = ☐ cm

14 cm = ☐ mm          7700 g = ☐ kg          30 sec = ☐ min

5100 m = ☐ km          80 h = ☐ days and ☐ h

180 min = ☐ h          8500 ml = ☐ *l*          500 mm = ☐ m

BUSY ANT MATHS Assessment Guide 4          © HarperCollins*Publishers* Ltd. 2015

# Rectilinear shapes (1)

□ = 1 square centimetre (cm²)

**1**

**2**

**3**

**4**

**5**

**6**

**7**

**8**

**9**

**10**

# Rectilinear shapes (2)

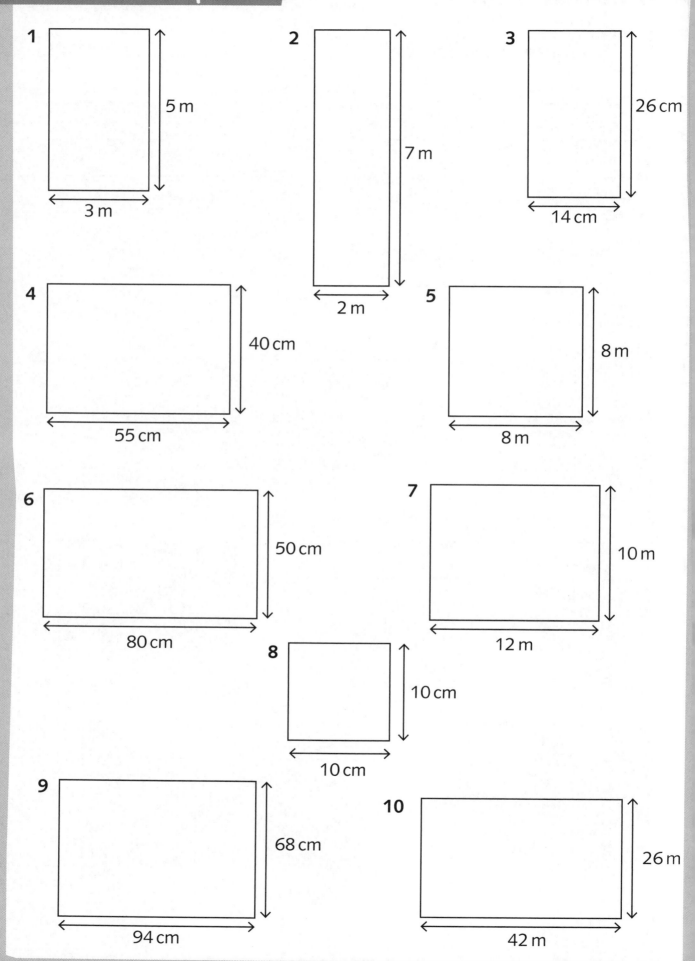

# Length

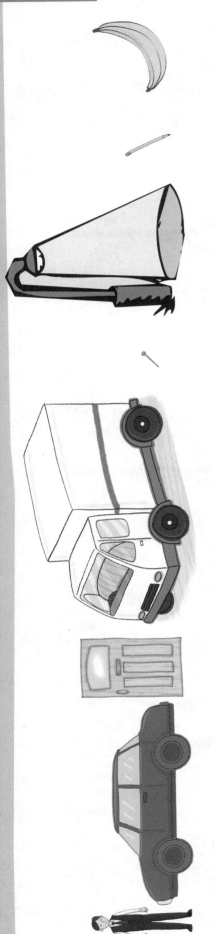

**1** 0cm 1 2 3 4 5 6 7 8 9 10 11 12 13 14 15 16 17 18 19 20 21 22 23 24 25 26 27 28 29 30

**2** 0cm 1 2 3 4 5 6 7 8 9 10 11 12 13 14 15 16 17 18 19 20 21 22 23 24 25 26 27 28 29 30

**3** 0 cm 10 20 30 40 50 60 70 80 90 100

**4** 0 cm 10 20 30 40 50 60 70 80 90 100

**5** 30cm 31 32 33 34 35 36 37 38 39 40 41 42 43 44 45 46 47 48 49 50 51 52 53 54 55 56 57 58 59 60

**6** 70cm 71 72 73 74 75 76 77 78 79 80 81 82 83 84 85 86 87 88 89 90 91 92 93 94 95 96 97 98 99 100

# Mass

**1**

**2**

**3**

**4**

**5**

**6**

# Volume/capacity

**1**

5 l
4 l
3 l
2 l
1 l

**2**

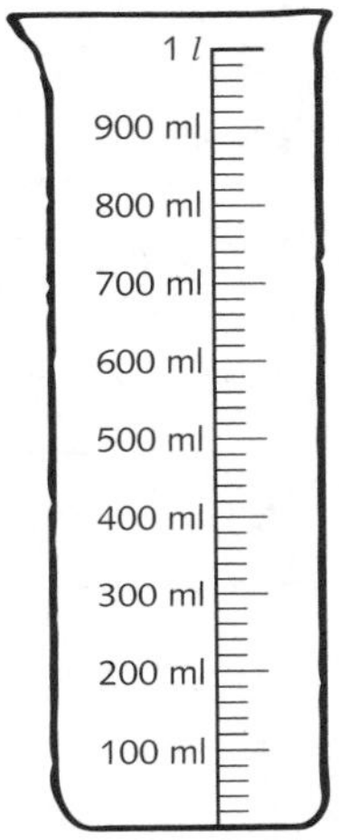

1 l
900 ml
800 ml
700 ml
600 ml
500 ml
400 ml
300 ml
200 ml
100 ml

**3**

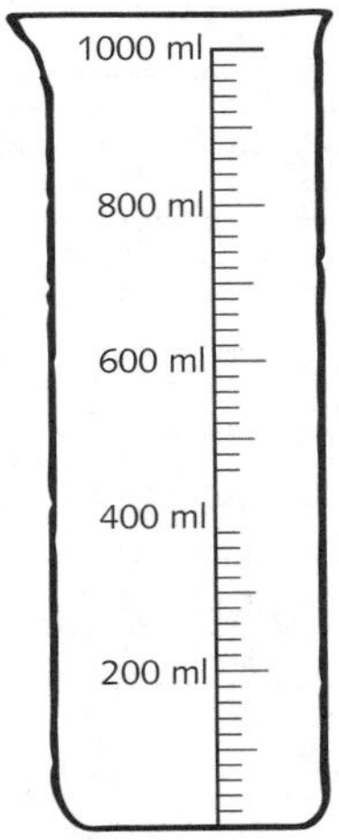

1000 ml
800 ml
600 ml
400 ml
200 ml

**4**

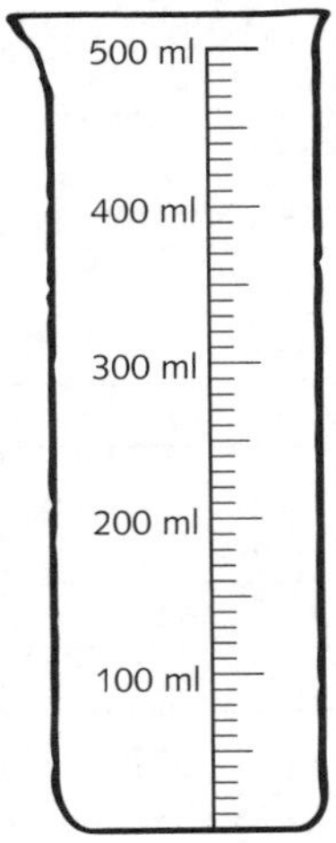

500 ml
400 ml
300 ml
200 ml
100 ml

**5**

2 l
1750 ml
1500 ml
1250 ml
1 l
750 ml
500 ml
250 ml

**6**

1 l
900 ml
800 ml
700 ml
600 ml
500 ml
400 ml
300 ml
200 ml
100 ml
0 l

# Money

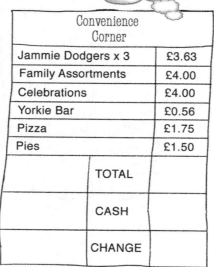

### Middletons

| | |
|---|---|
| Garden Peas | £1.63 |
| Salad | £2.00 |
| Cauliflower | £0.89 |
| Apples | £1.79 |
| Mushrooms | £1.19 |
| Spring Rolls | £1.00 |
| Haddock Portions | £3.99 |
| Toilet Rolls (9 pack) | £5.00 |
| Cornflakes | £1.65 |
| Walnut Bread | £1.45 |
| Onion Rings | £1.04 |
| Peanuts x 3 | £3.75 |
| | TOTAL | |
| | CASH | |
| | CHANGE | |

### Greenway's Store

| | |
|---|---|
| Apples | £1.79 |
| Iceburg Lettuce | £0.49 |
| Tofu | £1.09 |
| Sugar | £0.68 |
| Viennese Biscuits | £1.77 |
| Olive Oil | £1.78 |
| 15 Medium Eggs | £1.35 |
| Malt Vinegar x 2 | £0.46 |
| Boil in the Bag Rice | £1.44 |
| Yoghurt | £0.75 |
| Organic Milk | £0.53 |
| Cotton Wool | £0.54 |
| Cold Cream | £1.61 |
| | TOTAL | |
| | CASH | |
| | CHANGE | |

### Kidl

| | |
|---|---|
| Red Grapes | £1.49 |
| Fun-sized Bananas | £0.87 |
| Chopped Tomatoes x 10 | £1.90 |
| Butter Beans x 3 | £1.20 |
| Mature Cheddar | £2.15 |
| Milk | £1.25 |
| Tuna Chunks | £1.97 |
| Digestives | £0.30 |
| Chips x 4 | £4.24 |
| Medium Noodles | £1.07 |
| | TOTAL | |
| | CASH | |
| | CHANGE | |

### B-Mart

| | |
|---|---|
| Potatoes | £1.75 |
| Summer Fruits | £0.66 |
| Semi-skimmed Milk x 4 | £4.00 |
| Greek-style Yoghurt | £1.54 |
| Creme Fraiche | £0.98 |
| Mozzarella Cheese | £1.49 |
| Nuts x 2 | £4.80 |
| Sunflower Oil | £1.36 |
| Simple Soap | £0.90 |
| Baby Powder | £0.94 |
| Toilet Rolls x 2 | £1.25 |
| | TOTAL | |
| | CASH | |
| | CHANGE | |

### Convenience Corner

| | |
|---|---|
| Jammie Dodgers x 3 | £3.63 |
| Family Assortments | £4.00 |
| Celebrations | £4.00 |
| Yorkie Bar | £0.56 |
| Pizza | £1.75 |
| Pies | £1.50 |
| | TOTAL | |
| | CASH | |
| | CHANGE | |

### Best For Less

| | |
|---|---|
| Swede and Carrot Mix | £0.72 |
| Pears | £1.69 |
| Carrots | £0.75 |
| Courgettes | £1.43 |
| Sweetcorn x 3 | £1.44 |
| Choc Fingers x 2 | £2.08 |
| Pickled Egg | £1.15 |
| White Kidney Beans | £1.13 |
| Wholemeal Flour | £1.52 |
| Fish Fingers | £1.47 |
| Clean Clothes Liquidtab | £7.00 |
| Thick Bleach | £0.55 |
| Sponge Scourers | £0.59 |
| Nivea Hand Cream | £2.17 |
| Cat Food x 6 | £2.94 |
| | TOTAL | |
| | CASH | |
| | CHANGE | |

# Digital times

✂

**7:43** ● a.m. ○ p.m.

**10:27** ● a.m. ○ p.m.

**3:38** ● a.m. ○ p.m.

**5:09** ● a.m. ○ p.m.

**2:56** ● a.m. ○ p.m.

**9:12** ● a.m. ○ p.m.

**8:22** ○ a.m. ● p.m.

**6:36** ○ a.m. ● p.m.

**4:15** ○ a.m. ● p.m.

**1:49** ○ a.m. ● p.m.

**11:03** ○ a.m. ● p.m.

**12:59** ○ a.m. ● p.m.

**07:24**

**14:43**

**03:18**

**05:35**

**16:21**

**21:48**

**01:30**

**18:12**

**23:06**

**10:57**

**08:09**

**19:54**

BUSY ANT MATHS Assessment Guide 4

© HarperCollins*Publishers* Ltd. 2015

# Blank digital clocks

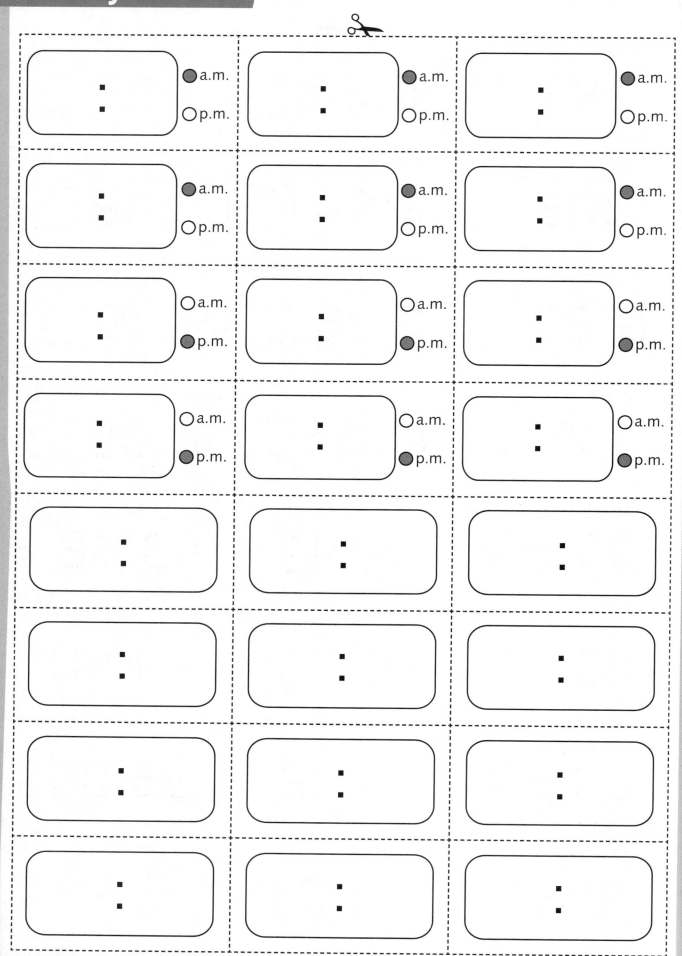

BUSY ANT MATHS Assessment Guide 4

© HarperCollinsPublishers Ltd. 2015

# Problems involving time

**1.** When Justin went to visit friends in Australia he travelled for 3 hours 25 minutes by train, 55 minutes by underground, 23 hours by plane and a further 4 hours and 45 minutes by car. How long was Justin's journey in days, hours and minutes?

**2.** Children attend school for 195 days per year. If there are three terms in a school year and each term is the same number of days, how many days are there in a term?

**3.** 6 times a week Stacey spends 45 minutes practising the piano. How many hours and minutes does Stacey spend practising the piano each week?

**4.** There is a half-hour episode of 'Bubble and Squeak' on TV each day, 5 days a week. For how many hours and minutes each week is 'Bubble and Squeak' on TV?

**5.** It takes Yves 20 minutes to walk from his home to school. How many hours and minutes does Yves spend walking to and from school in a week?

**6.** Felix can do 12 cartwheels in 1 minute. Each cartwheel takes the same time. How many seconds does each cartwheel take?

**7.** Faith works out how she spends her time. During the week, she spends $\frac{1}{3}$ of her day working, $\frac{1}{3}$ of her day asleep and $\frac{1}{3}$ of her day doing other things. How long does Faith spend working each day?

**8.** Oscar works very hard. He wasn't working for just $\frac{1}{5}$ of the days in November. For how many days was Oscar not working in November?

**9.** Jake's dad said that he has been alive for 500 months. How old is Jake's dad? Give your answer in years and months.

**10.** To make a perfect soft-boiled, medium-sized egg, you need to cook it for three and a half minutes. How many seconds is this?

**11.** Daniel's personal record for the 1000 m race is 3 minutes and 42 seconds. How many seconds is this?

**12.** A train journey takes 5 hours 45 minutes. It ends at 2 p.m. At what time does the train journey start?

**13.** Ruby is baking a cake. She puts the cake in the oven at 11:50 a.m. It comes out at 12:15 p.m. How long is the cake in the oven for?

**14.** Rob is always travelling abroad for work. Last year he was away for 161 days. How many weeks is this?

**15.** Harry got the DVD box set of 'Tales of the Knights'. He noticed on the back of the box that the total playing time is 720 minutes. How many hours is this?

**16.** How many days are there altogether in the last four months of the year?

**17.** It took Luke 480 seconds to run to the end of the school playground and back again. How many minutes is this?

**18.** Lisa's grandma is 60 years old today. Lisa made her gran a birthday card, but instead of writing 60 she wrote the number of months old her grandma is. What number did Lisa write on the card?

**19.** Simon and his family are going on holiday. Simon has counted that it is exactly 6 weeks before they leave. In how many days' time is this?

**20.** The flight time between Singapore and Sydney is 7 hours 55 minutes. How many minutes is this altogether?

# 3-D shapes

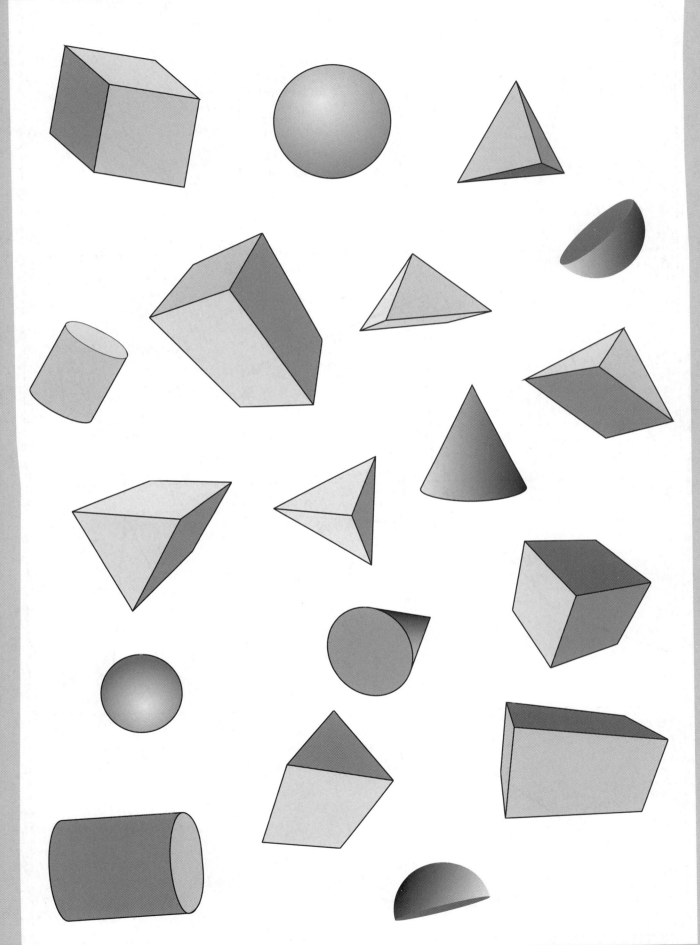

# Angle cards

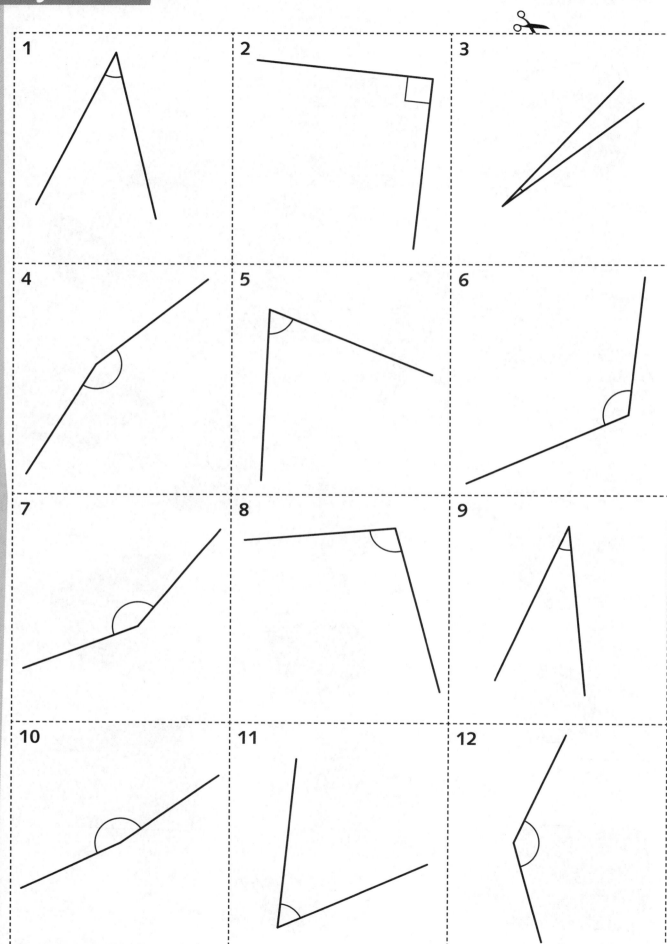

# Lines of symmetry

# Reflections (1)

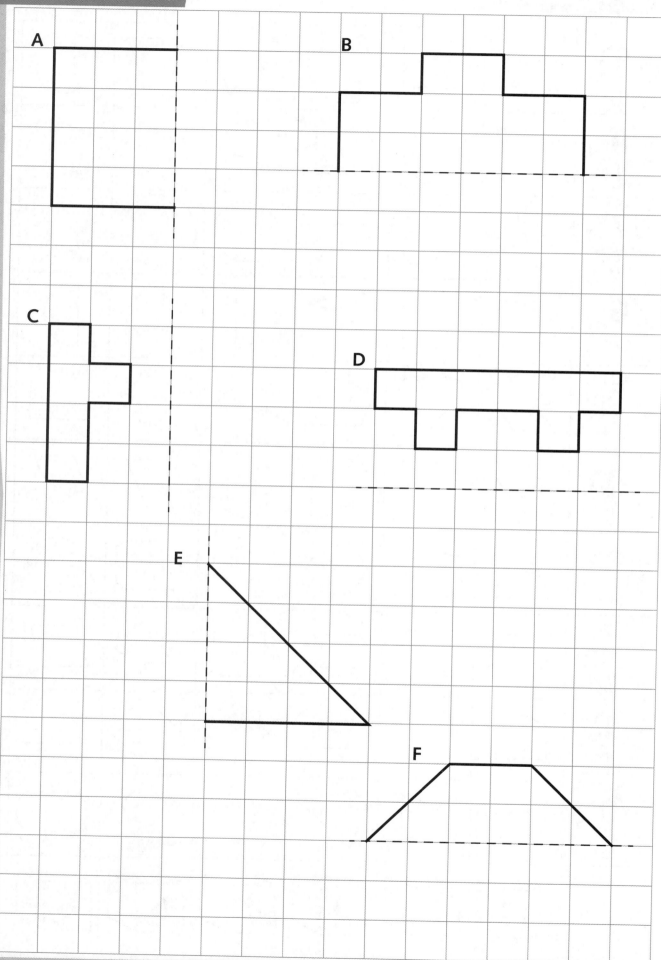

# Reflections (2)

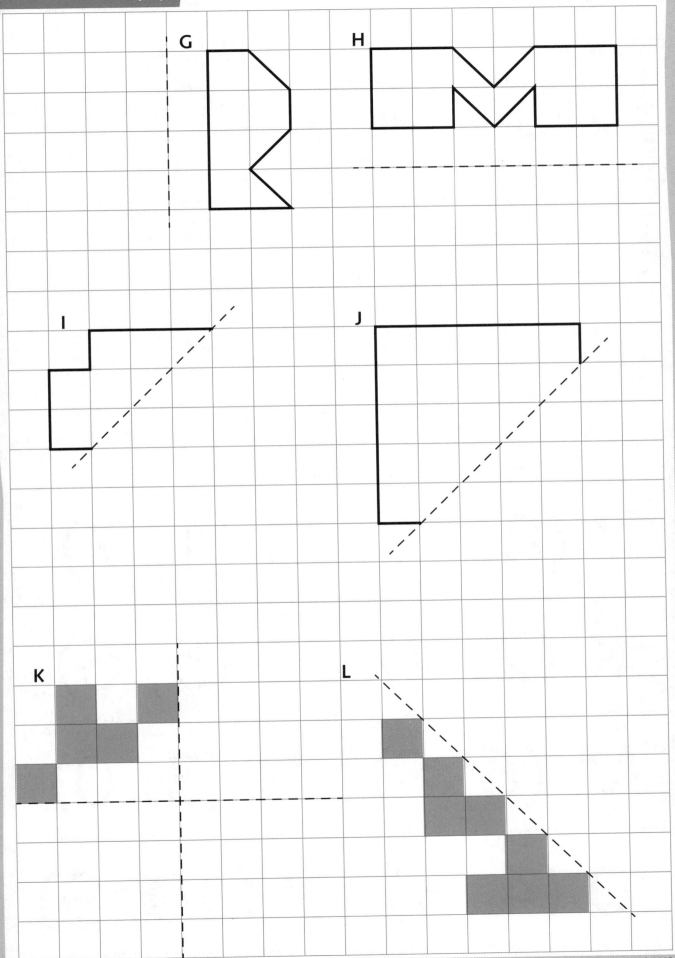

# Coordinates

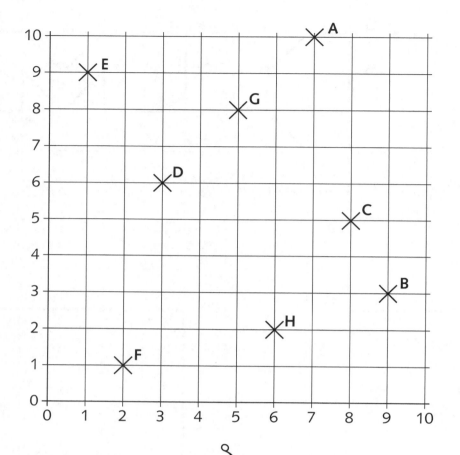

I (8, 1)

J (1, 7)

K (2, 4)

L (5, 6)

M (6, 8)

N (3, 0)

0 (4, 3)

P (10, 9)

# Translations (1)

A

A$^I$

B$^I$

C

B

C$^I$

D$^I$

E$^I$

E

D

F

H

G

I

J

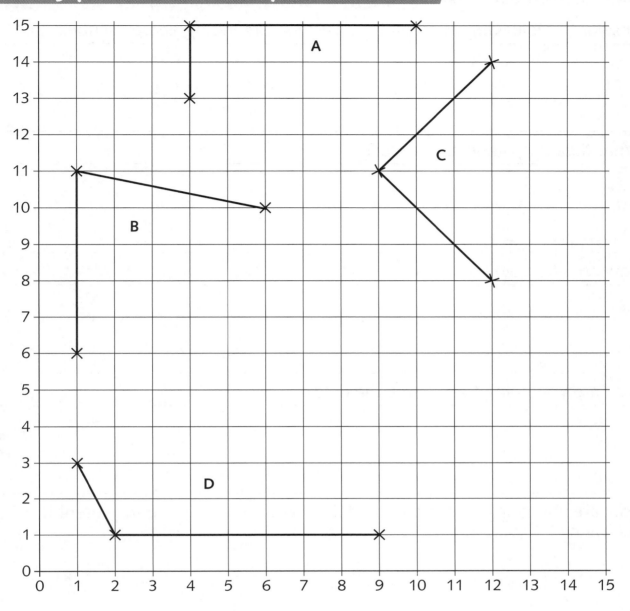

Shape A:

Shape B:

Shape C:

Shape D:

# Collecting, organising and presenting data

Answer the following question by collecting, organising and presenting data.

What data do you need to collect?

How are you going to collect the data?

How are you going to organise the data?

How are you going to present the data? Why are you going to present it this way?

**Now do it!**

What have you found out?

If you had to answer this question again, what would you do differently? What things would you keep the same?

# Statistics

### Travelling to school

| Transport | Most days | Occasionally |
|-----------|-----------|--------------|
| bus | 5 | 9 |
| car | 14 | 23 |
| cycle | 8 | 14 |
| walk | 27 | 11 |
| other | 0 | 2 |

### Travelling to work

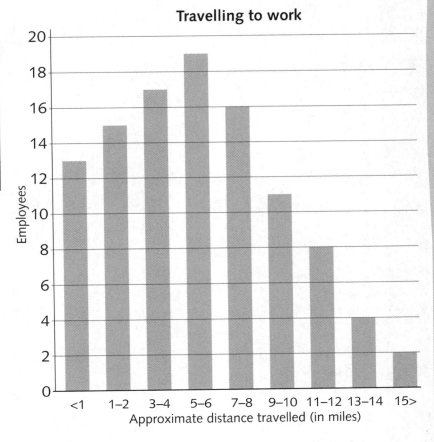

### Travelling to work

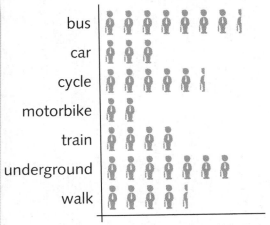

Number of employees

 = [ ] employees

### Tom's cycling trip

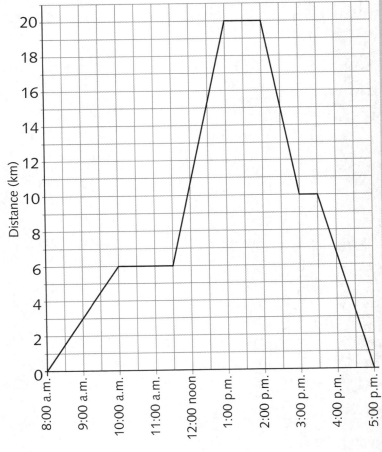

# Tracking back and forward through the Mathematics National Curriculum attainment targets – Year 4

If a pupil has Not yet achieved (NYA) mastery or has Achieved and exceeded (A&E) mastery, refer to the 'Tracking back and forward through the Mathematics National Curriculum attainment targets' charts below and on pages 311–320 to determine at what year group they are currently working. Related Assessment Tasks and Assessment Exercises can be found in the corresponding Busy Ant Maths Assessment Guide.

## Number – Number and place value

| Year 1 | Year 2 | Year 3 | Year 4 | Year 5 | Year 6 |
|---|---|---|---|---|---|
| count to and across 100, forwards and backwards, beginning with 0 or 1, or from any given number  count, read and write numbers to 100 in numerals; count in multiples of twos, fives and tens | count in steps of 2, 3, and 5 from 0, and in tens from any number, forward and backward | count from 0 in multiples of 4, 8, 50 and 100; find 10 or 100 more or less than a given number | count in multiples of 6, 7, 9, 25 and 1000 | count forwards or backwards in steps of powers of 10 for any given number up to 1 000 000 | |
| given a number, identify one more and one less | | count from 0 in multiples of 4, 8, 50 and 100; find 10 or 100 more or less than a given number | find 1000 more or less than a given number | | |
| | | | count backwards through zero to include negative numbers | interpret negative numbers in context, count forwards and backwards with positive and negative whole numbers, including through zero | use negative numbers in context, and calculate intervals across zero |
| read and write numbers from 1 to 20 in numerals and words | recognise the place value of each digit in a two-digit number (tens, ones)  read and write numbers to at least 100 in numerals and in words | recognise the place value of each digit in a three-digit number (hundreds, tens, ones)  read and write numbers up to 1000 in numerals and in words | recognise the place value of each digit in a four-digit number (thousands, hundreds, tens and ones) | read, write, order and compare numbers to at least 1 000 000 and determine the value of each digit | read, write, order and compare numbers up to 10 000 000 and determine the value of each digit |
| | compare and order numbers from 0 up to 100; use <, > and = signs | compare and order numbers up to 1000 | order and compare numbers beyond 1000 | | |
| identify and represent numbers using objects and pictorial representations including the number line, and use the language of: equal to, more than, less than (fewer), most, least | identify, represent and estimate numbers using different representations, including the number line | identify, represent and estimate numbers using different representations | identify, represent and estimate numbers using different representations | | |
| identify and represent numbers using objects and pictorial representations including the number line, and use the language of: equal to, more than, less than (fewer), most, least | | | | | |

# Tracking back and forward through the Mathematics National Curriculum attainment targets – Year 4

If a pupil has Not yet achieved (NYA) mastery or has Achieved and exceeded (A&E) mastery, refer to the 'Tracking back and forward through the Mathematics National Curriculum attainment targets' charts below and on pages 310 and 312–320 to determine at what year group they are currently working. Related Assessment Tasks and Assessment Exercises can be found in the corresponding Busy Ant Maths Assessment Guide.

## Number – Number and place value – continued

| Year 1 | Year 2 | Year 3 | Year 4 | Year 5 | Year 6 |
|---|---|---|---|---|---|
| | | | round any number to the nearest 10, 100 or 1000 | round any number up to 1 000 000 to the nearest 10, 100, 1000, 10000 and 100000 | round any whole number to a required degree of accuracy |
| | use place value and number facts to solve problems | solve number problems and practical problems involving these ideas | solve number and practical problems that involve all of the above and with increasingly large positive numbers | solve number problems and practical problems that involve all of the above | solve number and practical problems that involve all of the above |
| | | | read Roman numerals to 100 (I to C) and know that over time, the numeral system changed to include the concept of zero and place value | read Roman numerals to 1000 (M) and recognise years written in Roman numerals | |

## Number – Addition and subtraction

| Year 1 | Year 2 | Year 3 | Year 4 | Year 5 | Year 6 |
|---|---|---|---|---|---|
| | | add and subtract numbers with up to three digits, using formal written methods of columnar addition and subtraction | add and subtract numbers with up to 4 digits using the formal written methods of columnar addition and subtraction where appropriate | add and subtract whole numbers with more than 4 digits, including using formal written methods (columnar addition and subtraction) | |
| | recognise and use the inverse relationship between addition and subtraction and use this to check calculations and solve missing number problems | estimate the answer to a calculation and use inverse operations to check answers | estimate and use inverse operations to check answers to a calculation | use rounding to check answers to calculations and determine, in the context of a problem, levels of accuracy | use estimation to check answers to calculations and determine, in the context of a problem, an appropriate degree of accuracy |
| solve one-step problems that involve addition and subtraction, using concrete objects and pictorial representations, and missing number problems such as 7 = □ – 9 | solve problems with addition and subtraction: – using concrete objects and pictorial representations, including those involving numbers, quantities and measures – applying their increasing knowledge of mental and written methods | solve problems, including missing number problems, using number facts, place value, and more complex addition and subtraction | solve addition and subtraction two-step problems in contexts, deciding which operations and methods to use and why | solve addition and subtraction multi-step problems in contexts, deciding which operations and methods to use and why | solve addition and subtraction multi-step problems in contexts, deciding which operations and methods to use and why; solve problems involving addition, subtraction, multiplication and division |

# Tracking back and forward through the Mathematics National Curriculum attainment targets – Year 4

If a pupil has Not yet achieved (NYA) mastery or has Achieved and exceeded (A&E) mastery, refer to the 'Tracking back and forward through the Mathematics National Curriculum attainment targets' charts below and on pages 310–311 and 313–320 to determine at what year group they are currently working. Related Assessment Tasks and Assessment Exercises can be found in the corresponding Busy Ant Maths Assessment Guide.

## Number – Multiplication and division

| Year 1 | Year 2 | Year 3 | Year 4 | Year 5 | Year 6 |
|---|---|---|---|---|---|
| count, read and write numbers to 100 in numerals; count in multiples of twos, fives and tens [Domain: Number – Number and place value] | recall and use multiplication and division facts for the 2, 5 and 10 multiplication tables, including recognising odd and even numbers | recall and use multiplication and division facts for the 3, 4 and 8 multiplication tables | recall multiplication and division facts for multiplication tables up to 12 × 12 | | |
| | | | use place value, known and derived facts to multiply and divide mentally, including: multiplying by 0 and 1; dividing by 1; multiplying together three numbers | multiply and divide numbers mentally drawing upon known facts | perform mental calculations, including with mixed operations and large numbers |
| | | | | | use their knowledge of the order of operations to carry out calculations involving the four operations |
| | show that multiplication of two numbers can be done in any order (commutative) and division of one number by another cannot | | recognise and use factor pairs and commutativity in mental calculations | identify multiples and factors, including finding all factor pairs of a number, and common factors of two numbers | identify common factors, common multiples and prime numbers |
| | calculate mathematical statements for multiplication and division within the multiplication tables and write them using the multiplication (×), division (÷) and equals (=) signs | write and calculate mathematical statements for multiplication and division using the multiplication tables that they know, including for two-digit numbers times one-digit numbers, using mental and progressing to formal written methods | multiply two-digit and three-digit numbers by a one-digit number using formal written layout | multiply numbers up to 4 digits by a one- or two-digit number using a formal written method, including long multiplication for two-digit numbers | multiply multi-digit numbers up to 4 digits by a two-digit whole number using the formal written method of long multiplication |
| | | | | | multiply one-digit numbers with up to two decimal places by whole numbers [Domain: Number – Fractions (including decimals and percentages)] |

# Tracking back and forward through the Mathematics National Curriculum attainment targets – Year 4

If a pupil has Not yet achieved (NYA) mastery or has Achieved and exceeded (A&E) mastery, refer to the 'Tracking back and forward through the Mathematics National Curriculum attainment targets' charts below and on pages 310–312 and 314–320 to determine at what year group they are currently working. Related Assessment Tasks and Assessment Exercises can be found in the corresponding Busy Ant Maths Assessment Guide.

## Number – Multiplication and division – continued

| Year 1 | Year 2 | Year 3 | Year 4 | Year 5 | Year 6 |
|---|---|---|---|---|---|
| solve one-step problems involving multiplication and division, by calculating the answer using concrete objects, pictorial representations and arrays with the support of the teacher | solve problems involving multiplication and division, using materials, arrays, repeated addition, mental methods, and multiplication and division facts, including problems in contexts | solve problems, including missing number problems, involving multiplication and division, including positive integer scaling problems and correspondence problems in which n objects are connected to m objects | solve problems involving multiplying and adding, including using the distributive law to multiply two digit numbers by one digit, integer scaling problems and harder correspondence problems such as n objects are connected to m objects | solve problems involving multiplication and division including using their knowledge of factors and multiples, squares and cubes  solve problems involving addition, subtraction, multiplication and division and a combination of these, including understanding the meaning of the equals sign  solve problems involving multiplication and division, including scaling by simple fractions and problems involving simple rates | solve problems involving addition, subtraction, multiplication and division |

# Tracking back and forward through the Mathematics National Curriculum attainment targets – Year 4

If a pupil has Not yet achieved (NYA) mastery or has Achieved and exceeded (A&E) mastery, refer to the 'Tracking back and forward through the Mathematics National Curriculum attainment targets' charts below and on pages 310–313 and 315–320 to determine at what year group they are currently working. Related Assessment Tasks and Assessment Exercises can be found in the corresponding Busy Ant Maths Assessment Guide.

## Number – Fractions (including decimals)

| Year 1 | Year 2 | Year 3 | Year 4 | Year 5 | Year 6 |
|---|---|---|---|---|---|
| | write simple fractions, for example, $\frac{1}{2}$ of 6 = 3 and recognise the equivalence of $\frac{2}{4}$ and $\frac{1}{2}$ | recognise and show, using diagrams, equivalent fractions with small denominators | recognise and show, using diagrams, families of common equivalent fractions | identify, name and write equivalent fractions of a given fraction, represented visually, including tenths and hundredths | use common factors to simplify fractions; use common multiples to express fractions in the same denomination |
| | | count up and down in tenths; recognise that tenths arise from dividing an object into 10 equal parts and in dividing one-digit numbers or quantities by 10 | count up and down in hundredths; recognise that hundredths arise when dividing an object by one hundred and dividing tenths by ten | recognise and use thousandths and relate them to tenths, hundredths and decimal equivalents | |
| recognise, find and name a half as one of two equal parts of an object, shape or quantity | recognise, find, name and write fractions $\frac{1}{3}$, $\frac{1}{4}$, $\frac{2}{4}$ and $\frac{3}{4}$ of a length, shape, set of objects or quantity | recognise, find and write fractions of a discrete set of objects: unit fractions and non-unit fractions with small denominators | solve problems involving increasingly harder fractions to calculate quantities, and fractions to divide quantities, including non-unit fractions where the answer is a whole number | | |
| recognise, find and name a quarter as one of four equal parts of an object, shape or quantity | write simple fractions, for example, $\frac{1}{2}$ of 6 = 3 and recognise the equivalence of $\frac{2}{4}$ and $\frac{1}{2}$ | recognise and use fractions as numbers: unit fractions and non-unit fractions with small denominators | solve simple measure and money problems involving fractions and decimals to two decimal places | | |
| | | add and subtract fractions with the same denominator within one whole [for example, $\frac{5}{7} + \frac{1}{7} = \frac{6}{7}$] | add and subtract fractions with the same denominator | add and subtract fractions with the same denominator and denominators that are multiples of the same number | add and subtract fractions with different denominators and mixed numbers, using the concept of equivalent fractions |
| | | | | recognise mixed numbers and improper fractions and convert from one form to the other and write mathematical statements > 1 as a mixed number [for example, $\frac{2}{5} + \frac{4}{5} = \frac{6}{5} = 1\frac{1}{5}$] | |

# Tracking back and forward through the Mathematics National Curriculum attainment targets – Year 4

If a pupil has Not yet achieved (NYA) mastery or has Achieved and exceeded (A&E) mastery, refer to the 'Tracking back and forward through the Mathematics National Curriculum attainment targets' charts below and on pages 310–314 and 316–320 to determine at what year group they are currently working. Related Assessment Tasks and Assessment Exercises can be found in the corresponding Busy Ant Maths Assessment Guide.

## Number – Fractions (including decimals) – continued

| Year 1 | Year 2 | Year 3 | Year 4 | Year 5 | Year 6 |
|---|---|---|---|---|---|
| | | | recognise and write decimal equivalents of any number of tenths or hundredths | recognise and use thousandths and relate them to tenths, hundredths and decimal equivalents | identify the value of each digit in numbers given to three decimal places and multiply and divide numbers by 10, 100 and 1000 giving the answers up to three decimal places |
| | | | recognise and write decimal equivalents to $\frac{1}{4}$, $\frac{1}{2}$, $\frac{3}{4}$ | read and write decimal numbers as fractions [for example, $0.71 = \frac{71}{100}$] | associate a fraction with division and calculate decimal fraction equivalents [for example, 0.375] for a simple fraction [for example, $\frac{3}{8}$] |
| | | | find the effect of dividing a one- or two-digit number by 10 and 100, identifying the value of the digits in the answer as ones, tenths and hundredths | multiply and divide whole numbers and those involving decimals by 10, 100 and 1000 [Domain: Number – Multiplication and division] | identify the value of each digit in numbers given to three decimal places and multiply and divide numbers by 10, 100 and 1000 giving the answers up to three decimal places |
| | | | round decimals with one decimal place to the nearest whole number | round decimals with two decimal places to the nearest whole number and to one decimal place | solve problems which require answers to be rounded to specified degrees of accuracy |
| | | | compare numbers with the same number of decimal places up to two decimal places | read, write, order and compare numbers with up to three decimal places | |
| | | solve problems that involve all of the above | solve simple measure and money problems involving fractions and decimals to two decimal places | solve problems involving number up to three decimal places | solve problems which require answers to be rounded to specified degrees of accuracy |

# Tracking back and forward through the Mathematics National Curriculum attainment targets – Year 4

If a pupil has Not yet achieved (NYA) mastery or has Achieved and exceeded (A&E) mastery, refer to the 'Tracking back and forward through the Mathematics National Curriculum attainment targets' charts below and on pages 310–315 and 317–320 to determine at what year group they are currently working. Related Assessment Tasks and Assessment Exercises can be found in the corresponding Busy Ant Maths Assessment Guide.

## Measurement

| Year 1 | Year 2 | Year 3 | Year 4 | Year 5 | Year 6 |
|---|---|---|---|---|---|
| | | | convert between different units of measure [for example, kilometre to metre; hour to minute] | convert between different units of metric measure (for example, kilometre and metre; centimetre and metre; centimetre and millimetre; gram and kilogram; litre and millilitre) | solve problems involving the calculation and conversion of units of measure, using decimal notation up to three decimal places where appropriate |
| | | | | | use, read, write and convert between standard units, converting measurements of length, mass, volume and time from a smaller unit of measure to a larger unit, and vice versa, using decimal notation up to three decimal places |
| | | measure the perimeter of simple 2-D shapes | measure and calculate the perimeter of a rectilinear figure (including squares) in centimetres and metres | measure and calculate the perimeter of composite rectilinear shapes in centimetres and metres | recognise that shapes with the same areas can have different perimeters and vice versa |
| | | | find the area of rectilinear shapes by counting squares | calculate and compare the area of rectangles (including squares), and including using standard units, square centimetres (cm²) and square metres (m²) and estimate the area of irregular shapes | calculate the area of parallelograms and triangles |
| | | | | | recognise when it is possible to use formulae for area and volume of shapes |
| | | | | | recognise that shapes with the same areas can have different perimeters and vice versa |

# Tracking back and forward through the Mathematics National Curriculum attainment targets – Year 4

If a pupil has Not yet achieved (NYA) mastery or has Achieved and exceeded (A&E) mastery, refer to the 'Tracking back and forward through the Mathematics National Curriculum attainment targets' charts below and on pages 310–316 and 318–320 to determine at what year group they are currently working. Related Assessment Tasks and Assessment Exercises can be found in the corresponding Busy Ant Maths Assessment Guide.

## Measurement – continued

| Year 1 | Year 2 | Year 3 | Year 4 | Year 5 | Year 6 |
|---|---|---|---|---|---|
| compare, describe and solve practical problems for: <br>– lengths and heights [for example, long/short, longer/shorter, tall/short, double/half] <br>– mass/weight [for example, heavy/light, heavier than, lighter than] <br>– capacity and volume [for example, full/empty, more than, less than, half, half full, quarter] <br><br>measure and begin to record the following: <br>– lengths and heights <br>– mass/weight <br>– capacity and volume | compare and order lengths, mass, volume/capacity and record the results using >, < and = <br><br>choose and use appropriate standard units to estimate and measure length/height in any direction (m/cm); mass (kg/g); temperature (°C); capacity (litres/ml) to the nearest appropriate unit, using rulers, scales, thermometers and measuring vessels | measure, compare, add and subtract: lengths (m/cm/mm); mass (kg/g); volume/capacity (l/ml) | estimate, compare and calculate different measures, including money in pounds and pence | use all four operations to solve problems involving measure [for example, length, mass, volume, money] using decimal notation, including scaling | solve problems involving the calculation and conversion of units of measure, using decimal notation up to three decimal places where appropriate <br><br>use, read, write and convert between standard units, converting measurements of length, mass, volume and time from a smaller unit of measure to a larger unit, and vice versa, using decimal notation up to three decimal places |
| recognise and know the value of different denominations of coins and notes | recognise and use symbols for pounds (£) and pence (p); combine amounts to make a particular value <br><br>find different combinations of coins that equal the same amounts of money <br><br>solve simple problems in a practical context involving addition and subtraction of money of the same unit, including giving change | add and subtract amounts of money to give change, using both £ and p in practical contexts | estimate, compare and calculate different measures, including money in pounds and pence | use all four operations to solve problems involving measure [for example, length, mass, volume, money] using decimal notation, including scaling | solve problems involving the calculation and conversion of units of measure, using decimal notation up to three decimal places where appropriate |

# Tracking back and forward through the Mathematics National Curriculum attainment targets – Year 4

If a pupil has Not yet achieved (NYA) mastery or has Achieved and exceeded (A&E) mastery, refer to the 'Tracking back and forward through the Mathematics National Curriculum attainment targets' charts below and on pages 310–317 and 319–320 to determine at what year group they are currently working. Related Assessment Tasks and Assessment Exercises can be found in the corresponding Busy Ant Maths Assessment Guide.

## Measurement – continued

| Year 1 | Year 2 | Year 3 | Year 4 | Year 5 | Year 6 |
|--------|--------|--------|--------|--------|--------|
| tell the time to the hour and half past the hour and draw the hands on a clock face to show these times | tell and write the time to five minutes, including quarter past/to the hour and draw the hands on a clock face to show these times | tell and write the time from an analogue clock, including using Roman numerals from I to XII, and 12-hour and 24-hour clocks | read, write and convert time between analogue and digital 12- and 24-hour clocks | | use, read, write and convert between standard units, converting measurements of length, mass, volume and time from a smaller unit of measure to a larger unit, and vice versa, using decimal notation up to three decimal places |
| compare, describe and solve practical problems for:<br>– time [for example, quicker, slower, earlier, later]<br>measure and begin to record the following:<br>– time (hours, minutes, seconds)<br>recognise and use language relating to dates, including days of the week, weeks, months and years | know the number of minutes in an hour and the number of hours in a day | know the number of seconds in a minute and the number of days in each month, year and leap year<br><br>estimate and read time with increasing accuracy to the nearest minute; record and compare time in terms of seconds, minutes and hours; use vocabulary such as o'clock, a.m./p.m., morning, afternoon, noon and midnight | convert between different units of measure [for example, kilometre to metre; hour to minute]<br><br>solve problems involving converting from hours to minutes; minutes to seconds; years to months; weeks to days | solve problems involving converting between units of time | |

# Tracking back and forward through the Mathematics National Curriculum attainment targets – Year 4

If a pupil has Not yet achieved (NYA) mastery or has Achieved and exceeded (A&E) mastery, refer to the 'Tracking back and forward through the Mathematics National Curriculum attainment targets' charts below and on pages 310–318 and 320 to determine at what year group they are currently working. Related Assessment Tasks and Assessment Exercises can be found in the corresponding Busy Ant Maths Assessment Guide.

## Geometry – Properties of shapes

| Year 1 | Year 2 | Year 3 | Year 4 | Year 5 | Year 6 |
|---|---|---|---|---|---|
| recognise and name common 2-D and 3-D shapes, including: <br>– 2-D shapes [for example, rectangles (including squares), circles and triangles] | compare and sort common 2-D and 3-D shapes and everyday objects <br><br> identify and describe the properties of 2-D shapes, including the number of sides and line symmetry in a vertical line | draw 2-D shapes and make 3-D shapes using modelling materials; recognise 3-D shapes in different orientations and describe them | compare and classify geometric shapes, including quadrilaterals and triangles, based on their properties and sizes <br><br> identify lines of symmetry in 2-D shapes presented in different orientations | use the properties of rectangles to deduce related facts and find missing lengths and angles <br><br> distinguish between regular and irregular polygons based on reasoning about equal sides and angles | draw 2-D shapes using given dimensions and angles <br><br> compare and classify geometric shapes based on their properties and sizes and find unknown angles in any triangles, quadrilaterals, and regular polygons <br><br> illustrate and name parts of circles, including radius, diameter and circumference and know that the diameter is twice the radius |
| | | recognise angles as a property of shape or a description of a turn <br><br> identify right angles, recognise that two right angles make a half-turn, three make three quarters of a turn and four a complete turn; identify whether angles are greater than or less than a right angle | identify acute and obtuse angles and compare and order angles up to two right angles by size | know angles are measured in degrees: estimate and compare acute, obtuse and reflex angles <br><br> draw given angles, and measure them in degrees (°) <br><br> identify: <br> – angles at a point and one whole turn (total 360°) <br> – angles at a point on a straight line and $\frac{1}{2}$ a turn (total 180°) <br> – other multiples of 90° | recognise angles where they meet at a point, are on a straight line, or are vertically opposite, and find missing angles |
| | | | complete a simple symmetric figure with respect to a specific line of symmetry | identify, describe and represent the position of a shape following a reflection or translation, using the appropriate language, and know that the shape has not changed [Domain: Geometry – Position and direction] | draw and translate simple shapes on the coordinate plane, and reflect them in the axes [Domain: Geometry – Position and direction] |

# Tracking back and forth through the Mathematics National Curriculum attainment targets – Year 4

If a pupil has Not yet achieved (NYA) mastery or has Achieved and exceeded (A&E) mastery, refer to the 'Tracking back and forth through the Mathematics National Curriculum attainment targets' charts below and on pages 310–319 to determine at what year group they are currently working. Related Assessment Tasks and Assessment Exercises can be found in the corresponding Busy Ant Maths Assessment Guide.

## Geometry – Position and direction

| Year 1 | Year 2 | Year 3 | Year 4 | Year 5 | Year 6 |
|---|---|---|---|---|---|
| | | | describe positions on a 2-D grid as coordinates in the first quadrant | | describe positions on the full coordinate grid (all four quadrants) |
| | | | describe movements between positions as translations of a given unit to the left/right and up/down | identify, describe and represent the position of a shape following a reflection or translation, using the appropriate language, and know that the shape has not changed | draw and translate simple shapes on the coordinate plane, and reflect them in the axes |
| | | | plot specified points and draw sides to complete a given polygon | | |

## Statistics

| Year 1 | Year 2 | Year 3 | Year 4 | Year 5 | Year 6 |
|---|---|---|---|---|---|
| | interpret and construct simple pictograms, tally charts, block diagrams and simple tables | interpret and present data using bar charts, pictograms and tables | interpret and present discrete and continuous data using appropriate graphical methods, including bar charts and time graphs | complete, read and interpret information in tables, including timetables | interpret and construct pie charts and line graphs and use these to solve problems |
| | ask and answer simple questions by counting the number of objects in each category and sorting the categories by quantity | solve one-step and two-step questions [for example, 'How many more?' and 'How many fewer?'] using information presented in scaled bar charts and pictograms and tables | solve comparison, sum and difference problems using information presented in bar charts, pictograms, tables and other graphs | solve comparison, sum and difference problems using information presented in a line graph | |
| | ask and answer questions about totalling and comparing categorical data | | | | |